Strategic Leadership in the Public Services

In turbulent times, strategic leadership of public services becomes ever more important. Strategic leaders are steering their organizations into a new relationship with the public, often in conditions of intensified competition between public services providers, and thus the quality of leadership they offer is critical.

Providing insights into useful approaches and techniques for strategic leaders, *Strategic Leadership in the Public Services* covers topics such as the nature of leaders and how leaders lead. It probes strategic thinking and thoroughly explores strategic processes of implementation, monitoring and evaluation. It provides advice on being strategic and encourages the reader to appreciate the challenges of strategic leadership in practice. In the end, the book argues that leadership and strategy have become hegemonic ideas for reinventing the state.

Replete with real world practical case studies and examples, drawn from a range of countries, the book provides students with a truly international outlook on the subject and offers a clear understanding of the emerging significance of leadership, strategic management, and public services reform. Essential reading for postgraduate students taking leadership and management courses for the public services, the book will also be a useful resource for individuals currently pursuing executive management careers in the public services, or who hope to do so in the future.

Paul Joyce is a Professor and Director of Liverpool Business School at Liverpool John Moore's University. He is an author of books on strategic management, change management, and leadership. He has worked on education, research and management consultancy assignments in the UK and elsewhere.

ROUTLEDGE MASTERS IN PUBLIC MANAGEMENT

Edited by Stephen P. Osborne, Owen Hughes and Walter Kickert

Routledge Masters in Public Management series is an integrated set of texts. It is intended to form the backbone for the holistic study of the theory and practice of public management as part of:

- a taught Masters, MBA or MPA course at a university or college;
- a work-based, in-service, programme of education and training; or
- a programme of self-guided study.

Each volume stands alone in its treatment of its topic, whether it be strategic management, marketing or procurement and is co-authored by leading specialists in their field. However, all volumes in the series share both a common pedagogy and a common approach to the structure of the text. Key features of all volumes in the series include:

- a critical approach to combining theory with practice which educates its reader, rather than solely teaching him/her a set of skills;
- clear learning objectives for each chapter;
- the use of figures, tables and boxes to highlight key ideas, concepts and skills;
- an annotated bibliography, guiding students in their further reading; and
- a dedicated case study in the topic of each volume, to serve as a focus for discussion and learning.

Managing Change and Innovation in Public Service Organizations
Stephen P. Osborne and Kerry Brown

Risk and Crisis Management in the Public Sector
Lynn T. Drennan and Allan McConnell

Contracting for Public Services
Carsten Greve

Performance Management in the Public Sector
Wouter van Dooren, Geert Bouckaert and John Halligan

Financial Management and Accounting in the Public Sector
Gary Bandy

Strategic Leadership in the Public Services
Paul Joyce

Strategic Leadership in the Public Services

Paul Joyce

Routledge
Taylor & Francis Group

LONDON AND NEW YORK

First published 2012
by Routledge
2 Park Square, Milton Park, Abingdon, Oxon OX14 4RN

Simultaneously published in the USA and Canada
by Routledge
711 Third Avenue, New York, NY 10017

Routledge is an imprint of the Taylor & Francis Group, an informa business

British Library Cataloguing in Publication Data
A catalogue record for this book is available from the British Library

Library of Congress Cataloging-in-Publication Data
Joyce, Paul, 1952–
    Strategic leadership in the public services/Paul Joyce.
        p. cm. – (Routledge masters in public management)
    Includes bibliographical references and index.
    1. Leadership. 2. Strategic planning. 3. Public administration.
    I. Title.
JF1525.L4J69 2011
352.23'6–dc22   2011016449

ISBN: 978-0-415-61649-2 (hbk)
ISBN: 978-0-415-61650-8 (pbk)
ISBN: 978-0-203-60893-7 (ebk)

Typeset in Perpetua by Sunrise Setting Ltd

MIX
Paper from
responsible sources
FSC® C004839

Printed and bound in Great Britain by the MPG Books Group

Contents

List of figures, tables and boxes

FIGURES

TABLES

BOXES

Concept Boxes

Research Boxes

Preface

This book outlines some of what is known about leadership in public services. It presents the methods and techniques of strategic planning for the public services, and it explores developments that we often refer to as reform and modernization. It assumes the strategic leader is a positive agent of change in the public services, but that change is hard to accomplish successfully. It assumes, moreover, that leaders can approach strategic thinking in a variety of ways. It does not assume that there is a single preferred process of putting a strategic plan together; nor does the book suggest a single approach to implementation. It assumes that there has been a massive amount of experimentation with reform and modernization in the UK and elsewhere in the world, much of which has still to be properly evaluated. We have not been drawing as many lessons from the reform and modernizing experiences in various countries as we should. It has also to be admitted that there are limits to what we know about leading change in the public services successfully. In consequence, it is an aspiration of this book that the reader 'gets' that strategic leadership is a skilled, practical accomplishment informed as much by the results of trial and error and persistence as it is by ideas that are verified and put on display in academic books.

It is written primarily for postgraduate students on management courses, including those who are studying post-experientially. It helps the postgraduate student explore the concepts and theories of leadership, strategic planning and management, and also public services reform and modernization. These three things have been interrelated in practice even though academics have struggled to reflect this fact in the theories of public management. By the end of this book, hopefully, the reader will be convinced that the three are interwoven in practice even if the academic world has too often kept them in different intellectual silos.

One key idea that has inspired the approach to writing this book is the desire to present concepts, techniques, theories, models, research, and so on, as simply and clearly as possible. The reality in contrast is very complex, and evolving. The upshot of this is that the ideas and information contained in this book cannot be seen as just a snapshot of reality that portrays in words what the nature of the world of public services is about. This book, in other words, is not a written 'photocopy' of that complex and evolving world. The ideas here will, I hope, be seen as tools to make sense of that reality. And hopefully, maybe, the book will prompt the reader to ask new questions about leadership and strategy in the changing and modernizing world of public services.

As will become apparent from reading this book, I am indebted to a number of people who have generously contributed very significantly to it – they have written about their experiences, their judgements, and their research. These people include practitioners: Adrienne Roberts, Roger Latham, and Nahit Bingöl. They also include academic colleagues: Robert Fouchet, Emil Turc, Anne Drumaux, and Francesco Longo. My thanks to Ed Parker for the idea about how to get managers to think about a performance trajectory when planning implementation. And, as always, my thanks to my family: Theresa, Thomas, Caitlin, and Patrick; and to my parents, Rita and Albert.

Paul Joyce
August 2011

List of abbreviations

ADP	automatic data processing
BHA	Boston Housing Authority
CSR	Comprehensive Spending Review
DARD	Department of Agriculture and Rural Development
DBG	Delivering Better Government
DEFRA	Department for Environment, Food, and Rural Affairs
DETR	Department of the Environment, Transport, and the Regions
DfES	Department for Education and Skills
DGB and SMI	two Irish government reform programmes
GAO	General Accounting Office
GDP	gross domestic product
GPRA	Government Performance and Results Act
GRPP	General Review of Public Policies
HPD	Houston Police Department
HR	human resources
HRM	human resources management
ICI	Imperial Chemical Industries
IS	information systems
KRA	key results area
LOLF	*Loi Organique relative aux Lois de Finances* (Constitutional Bylaw on Budget Acts)
LSP	Local Strategic Partnership
MRSA	Methicillin-resistant Staphylococcus aureus
NFI	non-financial indicators
NHS	National Health Service
NPM	New Public Management
NTU	Nottingham Trent University
OECD	Organisation for Economic Co-operation and Development
OMB	Office of Management and Budget
OPEC	Organization of Petroleum Exporting Countries
PART	Programme Assessment Rating Tool

PCSU	Public and Commercial Services Union
PEST	political, economic, social, and technological
PMSU	Prime Minister's Strategy Unit
PPB	programming, planning, and budgeting
PR	public relations
PSA	public service agreement
PSG	Professional Skills for Government
PUCO	Public Utilities Commission of Ohio
SMG	Strategic Management Group
SMI	Strategic Management Initiative
SPS	senior public service
SRA	strategic results areas
SWOT	strengths, weaknesses, opportunities, and threats

Chapter 1

Leaders in the public services

LEARNING OBJECTIVES

■ To consider the key characteristics of a public services leader

■ To review both landmark ideas about leadership and some relevant research findings

■ To take a first look at how being strategic fits into public services leadership

INTRODUCTION

This book is about leadership of public services through the use of strategic planning and management. An OECD (Organization for Economic Co-operation and Development) report on modernizing government connected leadership not only to being strategic, but also to the delivery of changes in public services. This report, published in 2005, noted that many countries were emphasizing the development of leaders, defined as people who would be in a position to change their organization, and it said that:

> the leadership profile includes focusing on delivery of results, challenging assumptions, being open to learning from the outside, understanding the environment and its impact, thinking and acting strategically, building new patterns and ways of working, and developing and communicating a personal vision of change.
>
> (OECD 2005: 178)

Leaders expect themselves to be strategic. 'As evidence that strategic planning is viewed by agency leaders as an act of leadership, 65 per cent of National Survey respondents said that they believed initiating strategic planning was an important "symbol of their personal leadership"' (Berry 2000: 324). Attempts to clarify the nature of leadership sooner or later suggest being strategic is involved, and clarifications of effective strategic management sooner or later say good leadership is needed (see Research Box 1.1).

RESEARCH BOX 1.1   RESEARCH IN THE UNITED STATES IN THE 1990s

This research was carried out by Jo Brosnahan, Chief Executive Officer of Auckland Regional Council, as a Harkness Fellow in 1995–96. Brosnahan interviewed top level leaders and reported that the leadership role required the following (OECD 2000: 218–9): A leader must

- be forever challenging the reality
- have a commitment to mission
- have the ability to strategize (determine the path to the vision)
- lead by example
- be the keeper of the values of the organization
- be prepared to accept personal responsibility for whatever happens and encourage a similar responsibility among staff.

Nowadays others often expect public services leaders to be strategic (Charlesworth *et al.* 2003). What does being strategic mean? In part it can mean we expect them to be looking ahead and planning ahead when making decisions. In part it can mean we expect them to make use of strategic thinking, planning and management techniques to support their decision making and action planning. Strategic management, of course, could be said to offer obvious advantages to a leader in terms of handling both issues of knowledge and issues of leading people. Justification for this claim should be apparent at various points in this book.

CONCEPT BOX 1.1   STRATEGIC LEADERSHIP

'We define leadership as a process of guidance carried out to make something happen . . . Strategic leadership makes the motive or purpose explicit. The strategic leader wants to enrol others in transforming the organization by changing it in some significant way . . . Thus, strategic leadership can be thought of as a process of guidance that sets a new strategy in place.' (Nutt and Backoff 1993: 324)

There is now widespread acceptance of the concept of leadership in the public services, and thus for the need for individuals who can be effective leaders in public services. There is also widespread acceptance of the importance of public services leadership being strategic in nature (see Research Box 1.2 for an outline of strategic leadership in the Italian public sector). At the same time, there appears to be a corresponding shift in attitudes towards the functions of the state and of government organizations. We seem to be increasingly looking to the state to provide societal leadership in the solving of problems rather than seeing the state as always the self-sufficient provider of solutions. Moreover, it has been argued that changes and reforms are needed to make the state more strategic in its functions (OECD 2000). In the UK, policy specialists coined the phrase the 'strategic, enabling' state (PMSU 2006) to describe the impact of modernization on public services. On this basis, the turn to leadership and strategy is not something that is only applicable to the individual executive in public services; it is also potentially applicable when describing an evolutionary process to a post-bureaucratic state (Osborne and Gaebler 1992).

RESEARCH BOX 1.2   STRATEGIC LEADERSHIP IN THE ITALIAN PUBLIC SECTOR

By Francesco Longo, Bocconi University, Milan, Italy

Who are the strategic leaders in the different public sector settings?

Over the last two decades, the Italian public sector's organizations underwent major reforms to implement the global managerial wave. Municipalities became very autonomous and each of them established a number of new agencies and companies. To effect these reforms, municipalities were able to appoint a director general. The director general is the head of the administration. All companies and agencies owned by municipalities have a governance structure such as share companies with a director general on top. Public health organizations have been reduced from 630 to 240 and they are directed by a director general appointed by the regional government, on a three to five year contract, without any board above him/her. He/she is both the institutional and legal representative of the public health care organization and its administrative chief. Even at regional and central state government, departments have been dramatically merged into much bigger ones (central government's ministerial administrations were reduced from over 20 to 13). To effect this change, the government has had the facility to appoint top managers, with medium term contracts, related to their political mandate.

Formally, there has been a deep shift in strategic power from the political level to top bureaucrats. Even in the presence of national laws, substantial differences in governance structures at the local level have significantly increased, according to the local institutional cultures and competences. In the best cases, there has been a real and honest search for the best available public managers by politicians; they may enjoy wide autonomy in their mandate while government members focus more on politics and policy design. In the worst cases nothing has changed; politicians still act de facto as heads of both administrative and managerial structures, and the appointed public managers are either politicians (maybe someone who was not elected) or very weak technical figures. Of course there are also many mixed and balanced situations, where everyone is fighting to find his/her right role. In this power game, boards' members, where they exist, are also often involved. At the change of every political majority the power game is again open, and strong public managers can be substituted by the return of politicians, and vice versa.

Generally speaking, in the 1990s, the cultural movement for managerialism was stronger, and increasing strategic room was given to top bureaucrats. In the last ten years, there has been a shift to the politicians' strategic role instead, which has been enacted without a managerial perspective.

Still, big differences can be noticed between distinct public sectors. For example, in public utilities, owned by local or central government, and in health care organizations the managerial strategic room has been deeply established. However, in municipalities and central government, there has been less managerial development.

Summed up, Italy is an interesting natural experiment where, even if the rules are the same everywhere, we find different situations about who controls the stake for strategic management. This example clearly shows the relevance of local cultures, emergent political personalities and the availability of a group of competent public managers.

What kind of strategic orientation?

Italy is in the middle of relevant institutional and economic changes. The state has become a federal state with power and resources transferred to regions and local governments. The state has to tackle the challenge of the public debt reduction (foreseen, by the end of 2012, as close to 120 per cent of GDP), which affects the entire public sector. The economy has suffered less financial shortfall because of the global economic crisis compared with other countries because, in Italy, the private debts' level is low. However, there is still a great repositioning process going on for the economy, that has to progressively shift towards high added value products and services to deal with the global competition. In this scenario it is relevant to ask which kind of strategic orientation public administrations have to assume. The major changes occurring in the country, and in the world, need a long-term vision. Historically this was guaranteed by lifelong appointed public bureaucrats and by the stability of the Italian system dominated by political parties. Paradoxically, the New Public Management (NPM) reform has created a stronger link between the managerial mandate and the political one, through the introduction of a strong spoil system. It focused both managerial and political mandates on the short-term. Central governments have never been so long and stable in Italy as in the last 15 years, but the party system has never been so unstable – because of the continuous repositioning around and against Berlusconi. So, even politics have reduced the already short timeframe for decisions. At regional and local level, however, governments are very stable for 20 years, often over many mandates. Thus, for local government it is easier to develop strategies than for the central government; it represents another paradox in front of the classical central-local control chain.

The biggest difference we can notice between different public administrations is between an internal and an external orientation for strategies. The first are committed especially to organizational development and to the increase of both efficiency and productivity; and the second try to work within networks, involving both public and private partners. Their indicators are more process-related, since network building is considered as a good indicator in itself.

Which strategic tools are in place?

The tendency is to have many different strategic planning tools. There are at least mandate programmes of the politicians in chief, investments and budgeting planning for three to five years, many comprehensive plans for different sectors, human resources and organizations' development projects, and often also a formal strategic plan. The different tools do not necessarily have a clear hierarchy, since they derive from different organizational processes and they are not perfectly coherent one to the other. There is a sort of strategic formal overproduction in place, which gives place to intended and not formalized or emergent strategies.

Some strategic plans concern the organization itself, and others concern the social environment: are they steering the city or its administration? Some ambiguities are often related to this issue. In any case, plans and announced actions are often broad and far-reaching. Implementation rates register mixed results. The control key focus is always strictly focused: cost cutting and service standards increases. Even if the strategy concerns how we can foster the socio-economic development of the community, control processes tend to focus on service costs and productivity.

> Does it matter?
> Our suggestion is that it clearly matters. For example, you can easily see the differences between administrations where there are clear vision and actions over time, together with involvement of the local networks and others (think about the great success of Torino 2006 winter Olympic games which left a renewed city with a new economic orientation), and administrations where there is no room for management, for strategic thinking or action (think about the waste problem in Naples).
>
> It matters and there is a lot of room for strategic management.

There are three themes in this book. First, the book is concerned with leadership through strategic management. This is the primary theme. Second, the book also addresses the role of leadership and strategic decision making in public management reforms. And third, it considers the significance of leadership and strategic functions in the emergence of post-bureaucratic states.

In this first chapter we will be exploring some of the elements of being a leader in the public services. Arguably, these are things that a leader in public services has to learn; or, maybe, you could say that they are aspects of the identity of being a leader that develop over time. While there may not be a single really compelling or convincing empirical study that could be the basis of a comprehensive model of the leader in public services, there are a number of studies, stretching over many years, that can be used to piece together a provisional picture of the make-up of a leader in the public services.

SOME KEY CHARACTERISTICS OF THE PUBLIC SERVICE LEADER

A review of studies taking place over many years can be used to suggest the key characteristics of a public services leader. The list below is not presented as a definitive or final list; also it is possible to argue that the characteristics identified are not completely separate from each other. However, it is a plausible list based on empirical studies. It is argued here that effective public service leaders have these characteristics as personal capabilities or qualities and that all of them can be developed by leaders (see Figure 1.1). The eight key characteristics, in no particular order, are:

1 Knowing the situation (including foresight)
2 Knowing how to lead people
3 Good at learning and personal development
4 Challenging people to change
5 Understanding and managing stakeholders

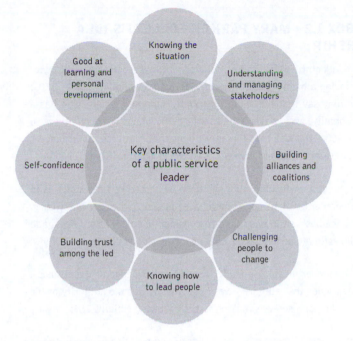

Figure 1.1 *Characteristics of a public service leader*

6   Building trust among the led
7   Self-confidence
8   Building alliances and coalitions.

We will look at each of them in turn to clarify their meaning and point to some evidence to underpin the claim for their importance.

Knowing the situation

Why does anyone listen to a leader and carry out their decisions? The early landmark contributions to the theory of leadership, which date from the early part of the twentieth century, challenged the idea that leaders should expect that they could make decisions – give orders – that would be obediently followed without question. These early contributions were, in effect, saying that the responsibility of the leader was not simply to make decisions. There was more to being a leader than simply making decisions.

The first of these early landmark contributions was by Mary Parker Follett, who essentially argued for decision making by leaders based on the necessity of the situation, and she thus saw leadership as being exercised by those with knowledge of the situation, insight and foresight. Echoes of her thinking can be heard in leading management ideas from the post-war period and her thinking even has a resonance today.

7

CONCEPT BOX 1.2   MARY PARKER FOLLETT'S IDEA OF LEADERSHIP

Back in 1928, in a lecture, Mary Parker Follett identified the accepted theory of leadership as placing a big emphasis on personal qualities (Follett 1941: 270): 'In general, we may say that the leader is usually supposed be one who has a compelling personality, who wields a personal power, who constrains others to his will.' She rejected the idea that the only things that mattered about leaders were ascendancy traits or aggressiveness traits. She suggested (ibid.: 272):

> I am merely suggesting further study of those possessed of such qualities in order to see whether these men or women have not also had an unusually large knowledge of the business in hand, and to consider whether history has made a wholly valid estimate of the balance between knowledge and 'personality'.

At issue was the manner in which a leader used this knowledge of the business. Follett famously argued that authority was best when it was the authority of the situation. This is the point she was making in the following (ibid.: 275):

> Perhaps the greatest difference between theory and practice in regard to the orders is that the old theory envisaged the leader as one who could get orders obeyed – any order – while in the best modern practice the leader is the man who can show that the order is integral to the situation. An order of this kind carries weight because it is the demand of the situation.

There were optimistic elements in the arguments of Follett. Crucially, she argued that people wanted to do things in the right way. This created the viability of leading on the basis of the requirements of a situation. The leader's task was to show what was right in the situation. Follett rejected the idea of imposed order. By submitting to the authority of a situation, Follett believed, individuals gained their freedom.

Following this line of argument, she anticipated ideas that would surface several decades later in attempts to make sense of more innovative organizations that had adopted non-bureaucratic structures (Burns and Stalker 1961). She argued that different situations required different types of knowledge, and that leadership should be assumed on a temporary basis by whomever had the knowledge required by a specific situation. The drift of her argument was that leadership based on personality was becoming less important; those with knowledge to control the situation increasingly mattered to organizational success. She said leadership went to people who could think and see how facts were related. It went to people who had foresight (ibid: 279–80):

> And the most successful leader of all is one who sees another picture not yet actualized. He sees the things which belong in his present picture but which are not yet there. Indeed, the kind of insight which is also foresight is essential to leadership...no leader of however small a group can forget, without disastrous consequences, that the activities of each group have to be fitted into a whole which is constantly changing.

With this last argument, Follett anticipated the radical rethinking of strategic planning undertaken by Hamel and Prahalad (1994) about 60 years later. A fundamental point made by them was that leadership had to be based on foresight, and that this was not the same as prediction. Hamel and Prahalad argued that having developed foresight, leaders had to then develop the necessary organizational capabilities and finally deliver foresight through successful marketing of new products or new services.

Follett did not rule out the possibility that leadership could still be a function of personality, or position in the management hierarchy, or ability to operate within the political system of the organization. She contended that this new type of leadership, in line with the requirements of the situation, based on knowledge, insight, and foresight, was to be found in progressively managed organizations.

A contemporary expression of the recognition of the importance of knowing a situation is to be found in the idea of conducting a strategic analysis. If we take this as our clue for what might need to be included within the scope of knowing a public services situation, we could list:

1 the policies of elected politicians and the pressures for change from the political system;
2 the degree of feelings of satisfaction (or otherwise) of existing consumers (or clients or customers) and their needs (met and unmet);
3 the external environment of an organization (trends, events, and discontinuities, all potentially offering the alert leader to opportunities as well as threats);
4 the performance of the organization (judged as a trend over recent years as well as against goals);
5 the reputational threats and vulnerabilities of the organization;

9

6 the values, culture, and capabilities of the organization; and

7 the activities, strengths and weaknesses, and plans and missions of other organizations (partners as well as rival organizations).

This is just a preliminary idea of the matters that might be covered in a strategic analysis and is not meant as a complete listing.

Is there any evidence showing that knowing a situation helps a leader in the public services be more effective? Actually there is some evidence from a study by Boyatzis (1982) which he conducted using a sample of private and public sector managers in his search for job competencies; which he defined as the cause of effective or superior performance in a job. The public sector managers were working in four federal departments or agencies within the United States government. Data on effectiveness and ineffectiveness was collected using critical incident interviewing, and was analysed by coding the data and then relating the competencies identified through coding to job performance data. His data analysis included a comparison of public sector managers in poor and superior performance groups. This is shown in Table 1.1. At the present time, we are only concerned with one of the competencies – 'diagnostic use of concepts' – but we will return to these findings a couple more times in this chapter.

According to Boyatzis, diagnostic use of concepts means that an individual applies a concept to a situation to interpret it. He also claims that when such people encounter a situation and lack a concept they can apply, then they will search quickly for one they can use. This skill in applying concepts may, he suggests, be helpful in sorting out what is relevant and what is not relevant. As Table 1.1 shows, Boyatzis identified that superior performing public sector managers had a higher skill level in diagnostic use of concepts than did their poor performing counterparts. His comment on this was: 'The observation that effective managers in the public sector utilize this competency more than do their less effective peers suggests that diagnostic use of concepts may be an important competency in effectively applying the standardized concepts that public sector managers are required to use' (Boyatzis 1982: 85). Alternatively, a

Table 1.1 Boyatzis' Study: Mean Skill Level for the Public Sector Sample

Competencies	Poor performance group ($N = 63$)	Superior performance group ($N = 39$)	Significance level of T-Tests
Self-confidence	0.111	0.436	0.0001
Use of socialized power	0.286	0.846	0.002
Use of oral presentations	0.048	0.256	0.004
Diagnostic use of concepts	0.476	0.923	0.004
Proactivity	0.905	1.41	0.0053
Managing group process	0.302	0.513	0.037

Source: Table A-3 on page 270, Boyatzis (1982)

simpler explanation to that of Boyatzis might be that superior managers were better at reading situations, better at understanding them, and better at developing insights and foresights because they applied concepts to them.

A more recent recommendation for the importance of knowledge and understanding comes from the work of Borins on public sector turnarounds. His evidence was drawn from case studies, and his conclusions about the turnaround process were tested against the experience of New York City Department of Juvenile Justice. We are interested specifically in his remarks on leaders. Borins provides the following summary of his conclusions about leaders of turnarounds in the public sector (Borins 1998: 157):

> They are energetic, dynamic, and often relatively young for the post. They either know the business well, or they are well acquainted with one or more of the major stakeholders. Knowing the business is important because immediate action is necessary . . . Knowing key stakeholders is also important because gaining their support is often the critical first step in the reform process.
>
> The leaders in my sample were not all charismatic leaders. They did, however, display an unusual ability to create vision and inspire others, certainly to a greater extent than their predecessors . . . Their expertise in the business or their knowledge of the stakeholders appears to have been the critical factor . . .

We will return briefly to the point about stakeholder knowledge later, but here we are concerned with Borins' point that leaders knew their business well. Knowledge, he argues, was more important than visionary and inspirational abilities. Obviously, knowing your business and how it works is an important part of knowing the situation.

Finally, we suggest that, as Mary Parker Follett believed, knowledge of the situation does include foresight. One of the justifications for using strategic analysis and planning techniques is to arrive at strategic foresight. We can offer some modest (and oblique) support for the value of strategic analysis from an investigation of chief executives in local government in the United States. Later we will be looking into this study in more detail, but here we note that the use of advanced strategic planning techniques was not only associated with a better record of adapting the organization to its environment, and a better record on the overall effectiveness of the organization, it was also associated with effective leadership behaviour by the chief executive (see Gabris et al. 2000). The presumption here is that the advanced strategic planning techniques were analytical techniques and in part helped to analyse the situation of the local government organization.

Knowing how to lead people

Another landmark contribution to the development of leadership theory was that by Elton Mayo, who is often identified as the main figure in the human relations school of

11 ◼

management. Mayo rejected the idea that the best form of management relied on motivating individuals through economic rewards. He is often credited with the discovery of social needs at work, and he certainly championed the idea that managers should consciously promote co-operative work groups. It seems that the realization that work groups existed and mattered emerged unexpectedly from a study based on interviewing individuals. Through these interviews the researchers started to realize not only that groups existed within the workplace, but also that the norms of the groups were a major factor in explaining individual worker behaviour. Mayo advocated a more sensitive style of management, believing that technical progress had outstripped social skills. He applied this same judgement to society as a whole – believing that social skills were lagging behind technical changes – and even suggested that this had created international conflicts as well as problems in industry.

Mayo presented his conclusions as based on evidence from studies carried out before the Second World War. Perhaps the most immediately relevant study was the one looking at absenteeism in three companies. One of them – Company 'C' – had the best record on absenteeism. Mayo drew attention to the training given to the foremen in this company. He reported that they had been trained to handle human relationships on the job and to communicate on the basis of being patient, listening, and avoiding emotional upsets. He believed that this meant that leaders with social skills of these kinds were superior to leaders who were aloof and simply gave orders.

CONCEPT BOX 1.3   THE WORK OF ELTON MAYO (1949)

Mayo provided a summary of a number of studies carried out before the Second World War, which he combined with his own assessment of problems in a modern society (which he called an adaptive society). While the studies themselves may have seemed very specific in nature, in his book he drew out some very general conclusions about leadership. He was very critical of the political, industrial, and scientific leadership characterizing society before the Second World War, and regarded this as a factor in the fall of France during that war (Mayo 1949: 107):

> France is perhaps an object lesson. A society divided into hostile camps, its leaders venal and contemptuous of humanity, mutual hatred rather than co-operation the mainspring of action, personal reputations dependent on material possession rather than any human quality – what wonder that such a society fell apart instantly at the advent of an aggressor and went down in defeat. Across the English Channel, most fortunately for civilisation, the first touch of the adversity had the opposite effect. Senseless opposition was abandoned, the exponents of imbecile hatreds were suppressed.

Mayo moved in his analysis between shop floor and the whole of a society, and even international relations. He defined the top problems of administration at all levels as being the satisfaction of needs and the maintenance of spontaneous co-operation. The trouble was that technical skills were developing fast and social skills were not keeping up. He even blamed this failure to develop social skills for the Second World War.

We are concerned here, however, with his analysis of business. Quoting Chester Barnard, he argued that the efficiency of an organization depended upon individuals accepting the orders of those in authority within the business. He said (1949: 45):

Authority therefore in actual exercise demands a capacity for vision and wise guidance that must be re-achieved daily: since the co-operation of others is a vital element in it, social understanding and social skill are involved equally with technical knowledge and capacity. Under the influence of economic theory, we have a system of education that trains young men in technical understanding and technical skill; we do nothing whatever to develop social insight or to impart social skill . . . . And the general public, business leaders, and politicians are left with the implication that mankind is an unorganised rabble upon which order must be imposed.

Elton Mayo and the human relations school of management are famous for discovering the group at work and believing in the importance of management communications. These same points emerge from Mayo's book, published just after the Second World War. He described how a programme of interviewing individuals had discovered that groups existed, and he emphasized his rejection of a theory of management based on financial incentives for individuals. He argued that management should focus on organizing team work and developing and sustaining co-operation. The aim, he described, being to achieve the workers' double loyalty to their workgroup and to the larger organization.

In summary, Mayo was clearly not keen on leadership by the imposition of orders. He was essentially optimistic as well. He thought that ordinary people had a desire for a co-operative society and he believed that this could be achieved within business by intelligent and straightforward management to handle the human relationships within organizations. Above all, he continually argued that training and education for technical skills alone were not enough in a modern society. Do we still make this mistake today when leadership courses predominantly teach the analytical skills needed for leadership roles?

Rensis Likert's ideas of leadership were recognizably descended from the human relations theory of Elton Mayo. Likert defined what he called a System 4 leader as being someone with behaviour that is supportive; someone who is approachable; and someone who shows they are interested in the well-being of subordinates (Likert 1981: 674). Like Mayo, Likert was a supporter of co-operative groups. In consequence, he defined System 4 leaders as working to develop co-operative teams and as opposed to creating competitive relationships between subordinates. He also stressed the linkages between teams at different levels of the organization, which he argued required overlapping memberships. Logically, this last argument extends the idea of the desirability of co-operative group working to all levels of the organization, and not just something for those directly involved in production activities.

System 4 leaders, according to Likert, created System 4 organizations and these were 'a particularly effective form of participative management' (ibid.: 674). Obviously, this type of leadership would enable participation in the sense that leaders who use supportive and approachable behaviour will be open to being influenced by their subordinates. This should not be taken as implying an indulgent leadership approach, because his prescriptions for leadership behaviour included the following: making sure that subordinates had the necessary resources to do the job, keeping everyone informed of overall plans, and having high performance expectations (of self and others).

He was of the view that System 4 could be applied to government organizations to improve their performance, reduce costs, and increase service quality. His evidence in support of this view is reported in Research Box 1.3.

RESEARCH BOX 1.3   LIKERT AND SYSTEM 4

Rensis Likert quoted several studies to support his view that System 4 approaches produced good results in government organizations. The first was a Masters thesis that compared high-producing and low-producing automatic data processing (ADP) units in a federal agency. The high-producing units were closer to System 4 than the low-producing units. The second study was hardly a rigorous or major study, but it did yield findings that were suggestive of his view of the benefits of System 4. A group of city managers at a meeting of the Michigan Municipal League were asked to complete a questionnaire on a high-producing unit and a low-producing unit that they had known well. Likert summarized the findings of this questionnare data as showing that the low-producing units were characterized as benevolent but authoritarian systems, whereas the high-producing units were in between a consultative group type (System 3) and the participative group type (System 4).

A third study was an evaluation of a year long organizational development programme carried out in two parts of the Hawaii State Department of Labor and Industrial Relations (Likert and Araki 1979). Likert and his colleagues used a survey-guided development cycle with measurements of organizational climate and leadership variables being conducted at two points in the cycle (1976 and 1977). The analysis of this data indicated to Likert that the organizational climate and leadership had definitely shifted towards System 4 between 1976 and 1977. Some of the more fine grained analysis suggested that there were marked improvements in two variables: (i) supervisors being open to ideas, and (ii) team building; both of which are obviously key aspects of System 4 leadership. Importantly, he also provided evidence of improved performance in the Employment Services Division comparing 1976 and 1977, but it seems performance was already improving if the couple of years immediately before the programme are considered.

Two UK researchers found what we might call a human relations type variable — 'genuine concern for others' — as the most important factor in leadership behaviour in the UK's public and private sectors. They did not want their findings to be interpreted as simply saying that leadership is about meeting staff needs, so they argued: 'it is also about creating a fertile, supportive environment for creative thinking and for challenging assumptions about how a service or business should be delivered' (Alimo-Metcalfe and Alban-Metcalfe 2002: 34). Of course, it should be remembered that this study obtained data from managers about their near leaders, and maybe it was this aspect of the research design that made 'genuine concern for others' such an important variable.

RESEARCH BOX 1.4   ALIMO-METCALFE AND ALBAN-METCALFE'S UK STUDIES OF LEADERSHIP

Their research study was designed to explore what they called nearby or close leadership in the public sector of the UK. In the first instance they planned to identify the constructs of leadership held by men and women at different levels in the public sector (local government and public health services), and then to use the constructs in a questionnaire survey of managers in local government in the UK. They sampled organizations in local government on a random basis and arranged for questionnaires to be distributed to a random sample of managers within each one. Each manager surveyed was asked to rate a manager (boss). This could be someone they worked with currently or someone they had worked with previously for at least six months. They achieved a national sample of nearly 1,500 local government managers (and a credible 46 per cent response rate).

Their quantitative analysis of the data from the questionnaires led them to propose nine factors:

1 Genuine concern for others
2 Political sensitivity and skills
3 Decisiveness, determination, self-confidence
4 Integrity, trustworthy, honest and open
5 Empowers, develops potential
6 Inspirational networker and promoter
7 Accessible, approachable
8 Clarifies boundaries, involves others in positions
9 Encourages critical and strategic thinking.

Finally, they calculated correlation coefficients between the nine factors and five criterion variables. The five criterion variables were (Alban-Metcalfe and Alimo-Metcalfe 2000):

1 Enables me to achieve more than I expected
2 Behaves in ways which increase my job satisfaction
3 Increases my motivation to achieve
4 Leads in a way that I find satisfying
5 Leads in a way which reduces my job-related stress.

Judged in terms of high correlation coefficients with the criterion variables, 'genuine concern for others' appeared to be the most important of the nine factors (with correlation coefficients ranging from 0.75 to 0.85). The next most important factors appeared to be 'integrity, trustworthy, honest and open' and 'encourages critical strategic thinking'.

They reflected on their findings and raised the issue of national context (Alimo-Metcalfe and Alban-Metcalfe 2001: 18–9):

The emphasis in the UK understanding of transformational leadership appears to be on what the leader does for the individual, such as empowering, valuing, supporting, and developing. In contrast, the US model is primarily about the leader acting as a role model and inspiring the 'follower'...the leader envisioning a valued future, articulating how to reach it, and setting him/herself as an example with which followers can identify, and which they can emulate

They comment that the UK approach to leadership seems to be consistent with the notion of 'leader as servant'. In the end they decide to keep an open mind about this contrast, allowing that the difference might be due to cultural, organizational or gender influences that suggests organizations should be wary of relying on approaches which dominate the literature of leadership (i.e. the approach associated with Bass, whose ideas will be considered later). In a subsequent paper, now drawing on evidence from the health service and the private sector as well, they were still highlighting the same factors they had found in the local government study (Alimo-Metcalfe and Alban-Metcalfe 2002: 32):

Leadership is not about being a wonder-man or wonder-woman. It is about being someone who values the individuality of their staff, who encourages individuals to challenge the status quo and who has integrity and humility.

Finally, there was some indication in the Boyatzis study (see above) that managers with a superior performance were more likely to possess higher skill levels in 'managing group process' than were those in the poor performance group. His elaborations of this skill do convey a human relations type approach (Boyatzis 1982: 129): 'People with this characteristic use personal contact and friendliness as instrumental behavior in building the group members' commitment to the team and their task effort.' He said such people also emphasize the need for collaboration and co-operation.

Learning and personal development

Maybe there is some truth in the idea of the natural leader who is born with exceptional personal qualities that gives them the power to lead others. But it is also true that a classic study of leadership in the 1980s discovered that the personal quality that was most evident in leaders in the private and public sectors was an orientation to learning. It seems that leaders are perpetual learners, that learning is 'the essential fuel for the leader, the source of high octane energy that keeps up the momentum by continually sparking new understanding, new ideas, and new challenges', and 'those who do not learn do not long survive as leaders' (Bennis and Nanus 1985: 188). Someone who becomes a leader has to learn new attitudes, new ways of thinking, and new ways of behaving. But the leader has not done with learning when they have ceased to be a novice. Leaders keep on learning.

Bennis and Nanus suggested (1985: 59): 'It's the capacity to develop and improve their skills that distinguished leaders from followers.' Furthermore, the leaders were very aware of their strengths and weaknesses, which is probably a very important attribute of most people that are good at self-development.

17

Challenging people to change

Many researchers into leadership have been influenced by the work of Bass and his colleagues on the existence of transformational and transactional leadership. It should be noted that it is sometimes suggested that that this work was heavily focused on the North America situation.

Bass and Avolio (1994) define two key concepts to capture a variety of leadership approaches. In essence, transformational leaders are those that produce organizational change through emphasis on new values and a vision of the future. They say such leaders inspire followers to put aside self-interest for common purpose (idealized influence). They are intellectually stimulating, they also inspire action and belief in the cause (inspirational motivation) as well as treating individuals with care and concern (individualized consideration). What about transactional leaders? Bass and Avolio say that transactional leaders operate on the basis that followers are rewarded for accomplishing agreed-on objectives; and they extend this notion of transactional leadership to include laissez-faire management and management by exception when the followers are left to get on with things unless there are mistakes. The key thing we are highlighting here is that, in the case of transformational leadership, the leader challenges followers to put aside self-interest and to think about things differently because the leader stimulates them to think about new solutions to problems (intellectual stimulation).

This theory has been tested with at least one public sector sample. This is the questionnaire-based study by Gellis (2001) of 187 hospital social workers' views of their social work managers. It is reported that the social work managers that scored highly on the transformational dimensions did appear to have better results (as measured by extra effort, rating of leadership effectiveness, and satisfaction with the leader). Statistical analysis of the questionnaire data suggested, first, that transformational dimensions as a set of factors help to explain the scores on outcome variables significantly better than the transactional ones by themselves. Second, analysis showed that the 'idealized influence attributed' and 'individual consideration' were the key factors in explaining the social workers' satisfaction with their managers. And in the case of the perceptions of leader effectiveness, the key factors were 'idealized influence attributed', 'individual consideration', and 'contingent reward'. Gellis also found that contingent reward was correlated with all five of the transformational dimensions. So, to underline the conclusion, the study by Gellis also indicated that contingent reward mattered – a factor associated with transactional leadership. The overall summary might be stated as: transformational variables plus contingent rewards explain positive leadership outcomes. This is represented in Figure 1.2.

Gellis commented (2001: 24): 'This article provides some evidence that transformational leaders can be found in social work practice fields.... Therefore, encouraging staff to reflect on new goals and to champion new ideas were essential components of transformational leadership, according to the study participants.'

18

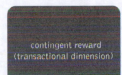

Idealized influence attributed; idealized influence behaviours; individual consideration; intellectual stimulation; inspirational motivation (transformational dimensions)

contingent reward (transactional dimension)

Followers' extra effort, leadership effectiveness, and satisfaction with the leader

Figure 1.2 *Gellis (2001) Social workers*

Understanding and managing stakeholders

As we have seen, Borins (1998) described knowledge of stakeholders as critical to public sector leaders engaged in a turnaround process. This is another area where formal strategic planning techniques could prove useful to public services leaders. According to leading texts on strategic management for public sector leaders (e.g. Nutt and Backoff 1992; Bryson 1995), stakeholder analysis is a useful component of a strategic planning process. This encourages leaders to initiate surveys and other studies of stakeholders (e.g. focus groups) to get to know their stakeholders better. The formality of a stakeholder analysis as part of a strategic planning process can prompt a more comprehensive stock-take of all the key stakeholders. And if stakeholders' priorities and interests are better understood by leaders of public services they stand, logically speaking, more of a chance of creating a vision for the future or goals that serve those priorities and interests and gets public support (Thomas and Poister 2009).

Building trust among the led

Back in the 1980s Kouzes and Posner (2007) began researching what people look for and admire in a leader whose direction they would follow willingly. They initially began by surveying business and government executives, and have now surveyed the views of 75,000 people around the world. It seems that the same four characteristics tend to head the list of twenty qualities (see Table 1.2). They conclude that we look for leaders who are honest, forward-looking, inspiring and competent (Kouzes and Posner 2007: 29).

19

Table 1.2 *Kouzes and Posner's surveys of admired leaders (2007)*

Characteristic	%
Honest	89
Forward looking	71
Inspiring	69
Competent	68
Intelligent	48
Fair minded	39
Straightforward	36
Broad minded	35
Supportive	35
Dependable	34
Co-operative	25
Courageous	25
Determined	25
Caring	22
Imaginative	17
Mature	15
Ambitious	16
Loyal	18
Self-controlled	10
Independent	4

Base: respondents from Africa, North America, South America, Asia,
Europe, and Australia. Respondents from United States are in the majority.
Source: Table 2.1, page 30, Kouzes and Posner (2007).

They comment on the significance of the leader having been perceived as honest
(Kouzes and Posner 2007: 32):

> It's clear that if people anywhere are to willingly follow someone – whether it's
> into battle or into the boardroom, the front office or the frontlines – they first
> want to assure themselves that the person is worthy of their trust. They want to
> know that the person is truthful, ethical, and principled . . . We want to be told
> the truth. We want a leader who knows right from wrong.

They state that, in respect of being forward-looking, leaders must have a point of
view about the future and they have to be able to imagine or discover a desired future
towards which the organization should head. One of the key points they make, in
respect of leaders being inspiring, is that leaders need to be enthusiastic, positive and
upbeat. They connect this with the requirements of those being led to be hopeful about
the future. The competence of the leader is interpreted as founded on experience and
sound judgement.

They put a very interesting construction on these findings about leadership characteristics. They suggest that three of them – honest, competent, and inspiring – together form the basis of credibility. And then, if this is combined with being forward-looking, this is the essence of leadership. To paraphrase, leaders are people who are credible and forward-looking.

Having defined credibility as the basis of leadership, they provide examples of phrases used to describe credibility in a leader. Three examples are (Kouzes and Posner 2007):

- 'They do what they say they will do'
- 'They practice what they preach'
- 'They follow through on their promises'.

Remarkably similar findings were obtained in a survey of public sector managers in the UK. This was a survey of 1,890 public sector managers (Charlesworth *et al.* 2003). In this case it was discovered that the five top attributes that public sector leaders should possess were:

- Clarity of vision 66 per cent
- Integrity 52 per cent
- Sound judgement 50 per cent
- Commitment to people development 49 per cent
- Strategic 46 per cent.

If we assume that 'integrity' can be mapped to honest, 'clarity of vision' can be mapped to inspiring, 'sound judgement' can be mapped to competent, and 'strategic' can be mapped to forward-looking, then we might conclude that this sample of British public sector managers wanted as their leaders people who were credible and strategic.

In summary the argument is as follows: credible leaders are leaders who know how to build trust in their leadership and do this on the basis of their honesty, their competence, and their ability to inspire. We trust such leaders with this set of characteristics. Could leaders be credible if they were perceived as dishonest? Could they be credible if they were incompetent? Could they be credible leaders if they could not build hope in the future direction they wanted their followers to take?

There is evidence from research in American local government that credible leadership – trustworthy leadership – works. Gabris *et al.* (2000) operationalized the definition of credible leaders and applied it to chief executives.

Credible leaders:

1 Communicate purpose and rationale for change
2 Actively work to communicate the vision and mission to employees
3 Work to get shared vision and set of core values
4 Hold employees trust
5 Delegate power and authority

21

6 Practice what is preached
7 Keep promises made
8 Seek to reward, praise, and recognize high performance.

The study found statistical correlations between leaders who had such behavioural attributes and better organizational performance. Both the effectiveness of the organization and how well the organization adapted to its external environment were correlated with the extent of leadership credibility as defined by the eight characteristics listed above. So we can think of these credible leaders as having a strategic vision and being active in communicating with employees what the vision is. But they also acted in a way that conveyed their personal integrity, they delegated, and they recognized and rewarded those who performed well.

Their analysis suggested that the strategic nature of credible leadership was not dependent solely on communicating and sharing strategic visions. As noted already, they found a statistical correlation between leadership credibility and the organization's use of advanced strategic planning techniques (see Figure 1.3). The use of advanced strategic planning techniques was also associated with the overall effectiveness of the organization and how well the organization adapted to its environment. This suggests that credible leaders sponsor, or possibly directly use, strategic planning processes to achieve their organization's better performance. One possible interpretation of this statistical pattern is that leaders realize visions through strategic decisions made in formal planning processes (Bennis and Nanus 1985). While we see some evidence in this study that the best leaders were to be found in organizations that used advanced strategic planning techniques, we cannot quite conclude that the best leaders were themselves great strategic planners. But the evidence does suggest that leadership makes a difference to the performance of a public service organization, that this leadership involves communicating a vision, that in some way or other this leadership is associated with the use of strategic planning techniques, and that the use of such

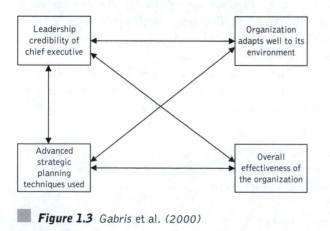

Figure 1.3 *Gabris* et al. *(2000)*

22

techniques also makes a difference. Arguably this evidence also echoes the point made by Kouzes and Posner that leaders are not only people with credibility, they are also people who are perceived as forward-looking (that is, strategic).

Before we leave the issue of trust, we should note the existence of concerns that public trust in government and in elected politicians is low. For example, the report of an OECD symposium about government in the future claimed that trust in government was declining because it was seen as out of touch with public needs, and recommended that it rebuild trust though offering the public more choice, democracy and transparency (OECD 2000). There is some evidence for the lack of trust in politicians from opinion polling. A YouGov Survey for the *Daily Telegraph* (February/March 2003) found that estate agents and 'red top' journalists (i.e. journalists writing for mass circulation newspapers) were the least trusted people in Britain, but almost as distrusted were leading Conservative politicians and current Labour government ministers. At the other end of the continuum in terms of trust were family doctors, school teachers and local police officers, who were mostly trusted a great deal or a fair amount by the public. Negative public attitudes towards local politicians were sympathetically reported by one UK local authority chief executive:

> One of the things I find really worrying at the moment is that the trend in public opinion about their respect for local politicians is just continuously downward, and it's now at an incredibly low level, I mean something like less than 20% of citizens polled believe that Councillors are doing a good job, or doing a job that's not about their self-interest. And I think that's dangerous for local democracy because I know, being a Chief Executive, that by and large, there are always bad eggs and rotten apples, but by and large Councillors do a good job. They work hard. They get bugger all out of it in terms of status and recognition. And they are always these days on the butt end of local newspapers for any little thing that the press think they've done wrong or that goes wrong.
>
> (Interview with author)

This low trust situation is a complex topic and will not really be addressed in this book. We can only offer here more questions. Is this lack of trust a symptom or cause of cynicism about politics? Is this a negative factor in election turnouts and other forms of political participation by citizens? Has the media caused or contributed to the lack of trust in politicians? What effect does the lack of trust in political leaders have on public services and its leaders?

Self-confidence

Leaders may appear self-confident. Sometimes they confess that contrary to external appearances they are often not at all self-confident. Nevertheless, the research by

Boyatzis (1982) suggests that self-confidence was much higher in the case of superior performance managers in the public sector than in the case of their poor performance counterparts. Boyatzis makes several points to amplify the meaning of self-confidence. He suggests, for example, that this is often called decisiveness or presence. Perhaps this is the same as the concept of 'ascendancy' which was referred to by Mary Parker Follett. Leaders who have self-confidence convey to others that they know what they are doing. They are good at self-presentation. They have a belief in the outcome of their endeavours being successful.

We could link this back to the discussion of credible leadership. Leaders who have credibility inspire others with hope. Arguably, some of this hope is generated by the self-confidence of the leader who believes that they are doing the right thing and will be successful.

Building alliances and coalitions

The skill which is used to build alliances and coalitions, as well as networks and teams, is called socialized power by Boyatzis. He also found this substantially higher for superior performance groups than for poor performance groups in the public sector. Boyatzis suggested that such a skill was important in all sectors, private as well as public.

It also seems logical to suggest that building alliances and coalitions would be a useful skill for someone who was good at understanding stakeholders, and that it overlaps with skill in managing stakeholders. Throughout the book by Nutt and Backoff (1992) on strategic management in the public and third sectors you will find not only a recognition of the importance of stakeholder analysis and management in terms of making judgements about feasibility and planning implementation of strategic action, you will also find many references to the building of coalitions to bring about strategic change against the resistance of coalitions formed to protect the status quo.

DEVELOPING LEADERS

The UK has had a range of bodies involved in leadership development, including public sector institutions, universities, and private providers. The public sector organizations address different parts of the public services. For example, the National School of Government which was a non-ministerial government department (until 2011) provided programmes for the civil service; the Improvement and Development Agency is for local government; the NHS Institute for Innovation and Improvement is for health services; the National College for School Leadership is for state schools; and the Defence Academy develops leaders for the armed forces.

Leadership development in the US was the responsibility of the Office of Personnel Management. Training was designed to deliver Executive Core Qualifications and addressed creative thinking, negotiating ability, staff relations, business acumen, information technology, and talent identification.

Strategies for leadership development were also developed by ministries and government departments in Germany. 'The German public administration of today also favours generalists, and increasingly needs leaders with international skills and competence in European matters' (OECD 2005: 179).

Developing Public Services Leaders in The Netherlands (circa 2004)

A few years back the Dutch Ministry of the Interior and Kingdom Relations developed a Senior Public Service (SPS) Candidates Programme for civil servants with four or more years of executive experience who might, within a couple of years, move into a director's job. One of the central ideas of the programme was to get participants to address paradoxes that they experienced in their everyday work as dilemmas. There were six such paradoxes:

1 Free steering
2 Autonomous collaboration
3 Constructive deconstruction
4 Unity in diversity
5 Risky security
6 Leadership in service.

The candidates were expected to engage with the paradoxes and also their personal competencies. The programme was intended to be self-development, and to focus on and uncover the person's values, talents, qualities, etc. It was very concerned with the inner development of the civil servant.

Even based on this very sketchy introduction it can be seen that the development programme wanted to foster the inner development of executives in a way that addressed the paradoxical quality of external challenges. This seemed a long way removed from the common competency-based approach to training that was more focused on helping public services managers learn the behaviours needed to carry out their function. The Dutch SPS Programme points the way to a new type of training and development for leaders. This new training fosters talent, not just competence. It fosters leaders who can innovate, not merely people who are a 'functionary'. It

25

fosters capacity for handling paradoxes, not just standardized behaviour. It fosters people who have passion for the public service, not people who are just conscientious. Leadership development for the new public services has to be more focused on the values and talents of the individual – especially talents for problem solving (paradoxes) and communication.

SUMMARY

There is a lot more to successful strategic leadership than being an inspiring communicator of a strategic vision. For a start, leaders need to be good at understanding situations and good at developing insights into a situation. They need good knowledge of the details of how their organization works and good understanding of key stakeholders. Vision without knowledge and insight to back it up is unlikely to stand the test of time. Leaders need to show they are trustworthy, display honesty and integrity, show competency in decision making, thus giving hope to others about the future. They not only need to provide intellectual stimulation, they also need to recognize and reward good performance. Effective leaders are strategic leaders and act with foresight. They are associated with the use of strategic management techniques to bring about adaptation and success for organizations.

Work-based assignment: critical incidents analysis

The work-based assignments in this book are for civil servants and other public services staff who have four or more years of management experience.

Write in-depth accounts of three recent events in which you felt effective or ineffective when acting as a leader. At least one incident should be an effective one and at least one should be an ineffective one. Try to identify in the accounts you have produced some evidence of you displaying the leadership characteristics highlighted in this chapter. Assess in each case whether the characteristic had contributed or not to effectiveness or ineffectiveness. Reflect on your analysis to identify areas that you think might be priorities in terms of your self-development.

Work-based assignment: self-assessment

Do you have the personal qualities in Table 1.3? Which of the qualities in the table do you consider to be very important qualities for an effective leader? Which qualities would you like to develop yourself? Identify the top three.

Table 1.3 *Self-assessment*

Personal quality	Self-assessment (Yes/a little/No)	Very important? (Yes/No)	Top three for self-development (tick top 3)
1 I have a genuine interest in staff as individuals			
2 I demonstrate trust in the abilities of my staff and delegate and empower			
3 I am good at reading situations			
4 I am approachable			
5 I am self-confident			
6 I encourage staff to question traditional approaches and think strategically			
7 I am honest			
8 I am very resilient			
9 I know and understand the interests and priorities of key stakeholders			
10 I have integrity			
11 I know how to lead my staff			
12 I am decisive in decision making			
13 I have charisma and can inspire others			
14 I am always learning and developing myself			
15 I can build alliances and coalitions for change			
16 I am good at analytical thinking and at creative thinking			
17 I am good at communicating my organization's strategic vision to people in other organizations and in external networks			
18 I am good at clarifying objectives for my staff and at defining the boundaries of their work and responsibility			
19 I have a clear strategic vision and a clear view of the strategic direction we should take			
20 I know my own strengths and weaknesses			

DISCUSSION QUESTIONS

1   Are leaders born and not made?
2   Why do people follow leaders?
3   Has the human relations school of Elton Mayo got any relevance to our understanding of effective leaders in the twenty-first century?
4   Does a leader need to be strategic? Why?

FURTHER READING

Bichard, M. (2000) 'Creativity, Leadership and Change', *Public Money & Management*, April–June, pp. 41–6.

Dunoon, D. (2002) Rethinking leadership for the public sector, *Australian Journal of Public Administration*, 61, 3, pp. 3–18.

Chapter 2

The leadership process

INTRODUCTION

Leadership in the public services seems to become more important when governments engage with a public service reform agenda requiring transformational change. Indeed, in such circumstances good management may be seen as not enough (Bichard 2000). Furthermore, where the public services reform agenda is defined as public services becoming less bureaucratic and more responsive, leaders are needed to refocus the public services organizations to the needs of the public.

If this is true, that leadership is needed for transformational change, and management (even good management) is not enough, what is the difference between leadership and management?

A MODEL OF THE LEADERSHIP PROCESS: STRATEGIC AND INSPIRING

A very striking differentiation of leadership and management is to be found in an article written by John Kotter, which appeared in the *Harvard Business Review* in 1990.

Kotter summed it all up in the following proposition: management controls complexity and produces order, while leadership copes with change and produces useful change (see Figure 2.1). While he argued that they complemented each other, and

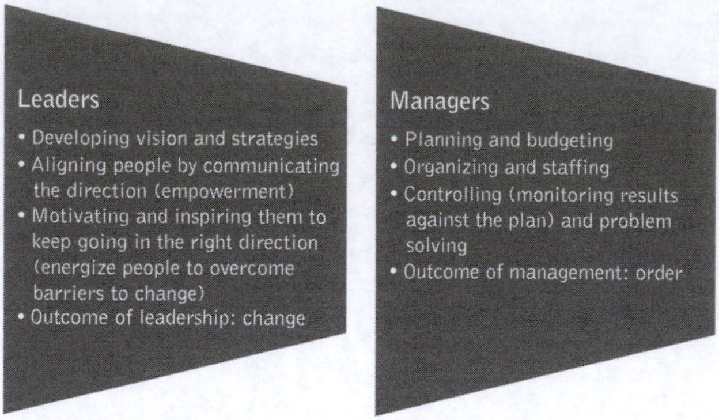

Leaders
- Developing vision and strategies
- Aligning people by communicating the direction (empowerment)
- Motivating and inspiring them to keep going in the right direction (energize people to overcome barriers to change)
- Outcome of leadership: change

Managers
- Planning and budgeting
- Organizing and staffing
- Controlling (monitoring results against the plan) and problem solving
- Outcome of management: order

Figure 2.1 *John Kotter (1990)*

were both required, he did claim that US companies were over managed and under led. He also claimed that people could be developed to both lead and manage at the same time.

Leaders start by setting a direction, which Kotter describes in terms of developing a vision and strategies. He denies that this first step in the leadership process is any way magic (Kotter 1990: 105): 'People who articulate such visions aren't magicians but broad based strategic thinkers who are willing to take risks.' Having come up with a vision and strategies, leaders then need to communicate them and motivate people to keep heading in the right direction. Alignment rather than control is significant – leaders empower while aligning people. They involve people in deciding how to deliver the vision and they reward success. He echoes a point that has been made by others, he states (Kotter 1990: 107): 'Another big challenge in leadership efforts is credibility – getting people to believe the message.' Motivating and inspiring has to engage needs, values, and emotions and energize people so they persevere and overcome barriers to change.

Based on these kinds of ideas, we can suggest that the process of leadership, as seen by Kotter, is shown in Figure 2.2.

A POSTMODERN LEADERSHIP MODEL

Peters and Waterman (1982) wrote at a time when there was much concern about the international competitiveness of US companies. They introduced their study as interested in how organizations could be responsive to change in their environment, specifically how they could be innovative. The key features of their model were that successful businesses were innovative because of leadership that encouraged entrepreneurship and experimentation, created a framework of values to engage their

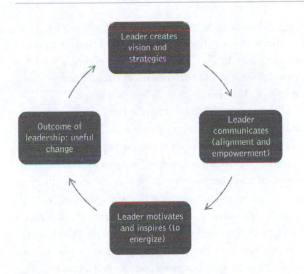

Figure 2.2 *Leadership process (based on Kotter 1990)*

employees, and did not rely on analytical thinking and strategic planning to set the direction of the organization. It should be emphasized that, according to their arguments, strategic plans came at the end of the process of leadership rather than the beginning. This was because leaders labelled successful actions emerging from informal activities and orchestrated them so that they became major strategic commitments through an incremental process.

They were blunt about the fact that, in their opinion, the structures and systems of many American companies inhibited action. So, what was the nature of the innovative companies that were held up as the way forward by Peters and Waterman? Peters and Waterman criticized centralized control by central staffs, detailed specifications of organization structure, and long job descriptions. The innovative companies they described were values based, informal, and experimental. They claimed that the innovative organizations 'allowed some chaos in return for quick action and regular experimentation' (Peters and Waterman 1982: 13). These innovative organizations were said to be administratively fluid. They saw central staffs as using power to suffocate local discretion and action (ibid 1982: 31): 'The central staff plays it safe by taking a negative view; and as it gains power, its stamps all verve, life, and initiative out of the company.'

Essentially, they thought that innovation could not be ordered up rationally according to a strategic blueprint. The origins of the successful innovations, for them, did not come from rational decision making processes, but from creativity and trial and error. In terms of innovation, action came first and this was then made sense of through leadership behaviour that gave it meaning.

They condemned what they termed the 'rational model' and they criticized analytical thinking and 'analysis-first' thinking. (Actually, they did remark at one point

31

that they accepted the need for good analysis, but they thought that analysis had been overdone.) One aspect of their attack of the rational model was to claim that people were not rational (Peters and Waterman 1982: 55): 'The central problem with the rationalist view of organizing people is that people are not very rational.' Indeed, they state (ibid 1982: 86), 'we have argued that man is quite strikingly irrational'.

So, for them, the right style of leadership created and instilled sets of values and fostered rich and informal communication and temporary structures. They believed the good leaders encouraged a 'bias for action', with leaders supporting experiments as a way of trying things (ibid 1982). The experiments could be 'bootleg' activities – outside of the mainstream of the organization using money and people formerly allocated for other purposes. They quoted one respondent as saying that surreptitious bootlegging was a measure of a company's innovative health. The champions of innovations were described as working at odds with the usual ways of management. (The impression is almost that innovation is subversive to the usual authority structures and not simply clandestine or surreptitious.) Leaders orchestrated and labelled successes. This is quite different from a strategic planning model in which there is a plan first, and then it is implemented. On this specific point, they were very different from John Kotter who saw leaders as communicating the vision and strategies, and then motivating and inspiring others to deliver them.

One of the clearest statements of their ideas about leadership follows on from a remark by them about the importance of incrementally acting into major commitment (ibid 1982: 74–5):

> . . . only if you get people acting, even in small ways, the way you want them to, will they come to believe in what they're doing. Moreover, the process of investment is enhanced by explicit management of the after-the-act labelling process – in other words, publicly and ceaselessly lauding the small wins along the way. 'Doing things' (lots of experiments, tries) leads to rapid and effective learning, adaptation, diffusion, and commitment; it is the hallmark of the well-run company.
>
> Moreover, our excellent companies appear to do their way into strategies, not vice versa. A leading researcher of the strategic process, James Brian Quinn, talks about the role of leadership in strategy building. It doesn't sound much like a by-the-numbers, analysis-first process . . . The role of the leader, then, is one of orchestrator and labeller: taking what can be gotten in the way of action and shaping it – generally after-the-fact – into lasting commitment to a new strategic direction. In short, he makes meanings.

The making of meaning is on the back of action (see Figure 2.3) and is, of course, the reverse of coming up with a strategic vision and plan that offers meanings to steer action.

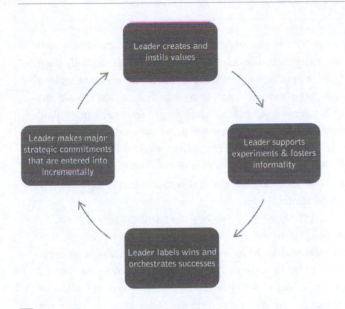

Figure 2.3 *Peters and Waterman's model of leadership process*

CONCEPT BOX 2.1   POSTMODERNIST LEADERSHIP?

It is possible to make an argument that several motifs in the Peters and Waterman model of leadership are also to be found in the postmodernist analyses of philosophers Lyotard (1984) and Baudrillard (1975, 1981). So, for example, whereas Peters and Waterman condemned the impact of central staffs because they stifled and constrained line managers, Lyotard was concerned with the effects of the top decision makers in a social system that imposed control over the interactions (language games) of participants at the local level (Lyotard 1984: xxiv):

> The decision-makers [the ruling class in society], however, attempt to manage these clouds of sociality according to input/output matrices . . . They allocate our lives for the growth of power. In matters of social justice and of scientific truth alike, legitimation of that power is based on its optimizing the system's performance – efficiency. The application of this criterion to all of our games necessarily entails a certain level of terror, whether soft or hard: be operational (that is, commensurable) or disappear.

If Peters and Waterman were looking for ways to create innovation, Lyotard, at one point in his obscure terminology, asserted that 'moves' that were simply reactions were not good moves. He argued for 'unexpected' moves.

This unexpected move idea is equivalent to the Peter and Waterman's support for action and experimentation as a response to change. Indeed, given their rejection of the rational model, Peters and Waterman were not looking for changes based on prior analysis – and so we can assume that the actions towards innovation are in some sense 'surprising' since there was no prior plan. Then again, Lyotard is concerned with meanings being created at the local level against the top-down rationality of the decision makers in society, which arguably parallels Peters and Waterman's idea of the creation of meaning by leaders in individual businesses as against the stifling and suppressing analysis and controls of central staffs.

Baudrillard (1975, 1981), using equally obscure terminology, was preoccupied with the late capitalist system ('neo-capitalism'). He did not believe that the system would be transformed by a revolutionary working class as an organized movement with a plan for changing society. He saw the working class as integrated into the functioning of the system. The capitalist system had developed so that consumption was now defined 'strategically as a mechanism of power' (Baudrillard 1981: 85). The system, which at one point he described as a totalitarian economy, mobilized needs so that people were integrated, participating, and consuming. He stated (ibid 1981: 200): 'Thanks to consumption, the system not only succeeds in exploiting people by force, but in making them participate in its multiplied survival.' For Baudrillard, this integration through needs and consumption works for the system and not for the individual (ibid 1981: 86):

'The system can only produce and reproduce individuals as elements of the system. It cannot tolerate exceptions.'

If change would not come from the rational and purposive planning and action of the working class, where would it come from? He pointed to the existence of new marginal social groups – 'de facto dropouts'. He claimed that they were challenging the system on the basis of their 'irresponsibility'; being subversive by refusing to play the game of the system. He included in these new social groups black people, women, and youth. So hope for Baudrillard came not from the formal system or from planning, but from groups that did not properly participate in the formal system and did not act as revolutionaries who planned to transform the system. The challenge to the system came from people who were, in a sense, excluded from production relations and whose irresponsibility was, therefore, not a political response to exploitation.

So, Peters and Waterman saw the redemption of US business as coming through leaders who helped innovative strategic moves to emerge from people operating in informal and bootlegging ways to make experiments, often working in clandestine and almost invisible ways. (We might say the innovations came from people at the margins of the mainstream organization.) This was not innovation by consciously following a strategic plan to innovate – it was action first. Similarly, Baudrillard had given up on the left's traditional champion of societal change (the working class) and looked instead for irresponsible action by marginal social groups that called into question the system's functioning. In both cases, innovation/change was coming from outside of what had been defined as the mainstream system and from people who were not acting rationally on an analytical basis or according to a plan.

One final comment on the Peters and Waterman model may help to place it in relation to the model of Kotter. In the Peters and Waterman model the leader supports informality and the champions of innovation who are at odds in their ways of working with the management systems. This seems to provide a contrast with Kotter's view that the management and leadership functions are both needed and complementary. However, his suggestion that organizations may be over managed and under led then creates some movement towards theoretical convergence with the Peters and Waterman model.

POLITICAL LEADERSHIP

Even if Kotter's or Peters and Waterman's models of leadership stand up as largely valid in the public services, at least one modification seems likely to be essential – the recognition of the role of politicians in the policy making and direction of public services. Change very often originates with politicians, and very often in the context of the competition between political parties to win elections. Some political parties will stress that they stand for traditional values and continuity, more than they stress their interest in change. Some political parties will stress their interest in a progressive project for the government of a country that entails radical change. Nonetheless, all political parties, as part of electoral politics, promise voters that they will bring about change, even if that change consists of restoring things to the way they were before. Therefore, a managerial leader of a public service organization may find they are working to implement the strategic plans of politicians (e.g. a government minister), or find they are launching strategic change because elected politicians have made a new policy or changed an existing policy. The politicians are a major influence on developments in public services. It was because of politicians, for example, that there was a major transfer of concepts, models, and people from the private sector into the National Health Service (NHS) of the UK in the 1980s (Pettigrew *et al.* 1992: 5).

35

We can view the political leadership as being part of the strategic leadership of the public services. Sometimes this is definitely correct, as in cases where strategic planning is managed as well as owned by politicians. In contrast, political leaders may be seen as part of the external environment of a public services organization. This was the view taken by Heymann (1987) in his study of strategic planning in the US. Moore's later (1995) study of strategic management in government supported Heymann's proposition that the external support of elected politicians was a crucial part of strategic planning by a government agency. Moore stated (1995: 292): 'Without close contact and active support from their political environments, managers can neither know what is worth producing nor achieve it.' His analysis of a set of case studies led to a set of conclusions about leadership inside a government organization. One of these conclusions was that the organizational leaders needed to establish the 'terms of accountability' with the politicians who had oversight of the organization.

The political leader operating in a democratic government has their own set of political processes to consider when making policy changes and directing developments in public services. Here we can only make a number of general points about the political world out of which emerges such policy changes, and changes in the direction of public services.

First, political leaders have to focus on several sets of relations: their relationship with the party or government of which they are a member; the relationship between the party or government and the public; and their own relationship with the public. The states of these relationships are affected by, and reflected in, votes in the legislature, elections, the media and public opinion. The political leader may be trying to manage – bring into some sort of balance – their party's prospects at the next election, party support for their leadership, and their popularity and credibility with the electorate. One leadership challenge may be to get the party to give up some if its policies and replace them with new ones to make re-election more likely without losing too much support in the party, or to seek popularity in the party by supporting traditional policies with the risk of electoral failure. In government, the political leader may decide to risk some disaffection in the party, but will have to work to minimize a revolt when it comes to voting in the legislature. There are many other challenges for the political leader in handling the two key constituencies – their party and the public.

Second, political leaders may work over time to get their supporters into key positions within the party and in ministerial roles. They may be looking for supporters who share their vision and will work on the agenda they are pursuing. If they succeed in this respect, the political leader has created a powerful grouping to get things moving in the direction they want.

Third, political parties have internal debates on policy, which are partly debates about what is right (i.e. what would bring about improvement and progress), but also reflect factionalism and power struggles within the party. A government leader, for example, proposing public services reforms may find they have a battle inside their party with a faction that has itself designs on the leadership role. If in government, the faction may have effective control of one or more government departments and then the power struggle appears to be on departmental issues rather than reform as such. Resistance to leadership policies may be dressed up in departmental terms and have the appearance of being legitimate departmental concerns (e.g. a finance ministry may object to a reform on grounds of affordability when in fact it is a factional manoeuvre to block the leader's new policy initiative). Struggles between the leader's supporters and rival factions may flare up at some times, and, at other times, there may be truces or even agreements to work more co-operatively.

Fourth, as well as factional difficulties, political leaders have to be sensitive to, and contend with, the individual career ambitions of rising politicians. If the political leader has to make decisions about filling ministerial roles, and there are more politicians aspiring to promotion than there are places, the result is likely to be individuals who feel resentful towards the leader at not being promoted or not promoted to a position they wanted. Over a period of time, a political leader may find they have accumulated a significant number of people they have disappointed.

Fifth, political leaders have to decide what to do about policies they believe to be right in the national interest, but will be very unpopular with the public. Putting green taxes up to discourage people using their cars, and thereby easing road congestion, might be the right thing to do from a certain perspective, but it is likely to be very unpopular. So, should the political leader press on with such a policy and hope that opposition to the policy and the unpopularity of the government will give way to public acceptance?

Finally, political leaders have to think about the timing and manner of their own departure from the leadership role. The UK provides many examples of this departure being an uncomfortable one for the prime minister; the examples are Prime Ministers Callaghan, Thatcher, Major, Blair, and Brown. The power struggles, factionalism, individual resentments, as well as media attacks, scandals, and political crises of one sort or another, may sap the resilience of a political leader and be a factor in their decision to stand down. Alternatively, events over a period may drain away their credibility and be part of the explanation for their party's electoral failure, leading to their subsequent replacement.

This rather general set of assertions about political leaders and political leadership processes mainly serves to emphasize the need to recognize the part played by the political world and political pressures in the story of strategic leadership in the public services. This matters whether the political leaders directly involve themselves in strategic planning or are crucial in making themselves accountable for the strategic direction of the public services. Existing leadership theories drawn from the management literature cannot help us with understanding this aspect of the public services context.

POLITICAL LEADERS AND MANAGERIAL LEADERS

Managerial leaders require support from elected politicians in order to be successful (Heymann 1987), but this does not mean that everything that politicians want is simply implemented by managerial leaders. For example, in the 1980s, Metcalfe and Richards (1990) drew attention to belief systems in the UK civil service that were barriers to politically imposed change. How can senior civil servants or managerial leaders justify opposing or lacking enthusiasm for pressure for change from politicians? One justification that could be used by officials is that politicians are very short-term in their thinking and are looking for political advantage rather than genuine improvements in public services (Mulgan 2009: 94). Policies may be attributed to the personal agenda of a government minister rather than a manifesto commitment, or a change may be put down to a politician's desire for some good public relations rather than a genuinely needed change in the public interest. However, it is unlikely that the politicians or the public's pressures for change can be frustrated permanently. If change is stalled over a length of time, the public services may then need to catch up with changes in society and reconnect to the public only through a period of painful change (Crozier 1964).

Case study research by Wechsler and Backoff (1986) suggests that it is important to understand the process by which the political leadership's wishes are understood and then responded to by the managerial leaders. This makes the relationship between the politicians, who are responsible for the policy agenda, and the appointed managers, who administer the implementation of the policies, a crucial element of the leadership process. (The role of the board does not feature in mainstream theories of leadership. Why? Is it because many boards in private sector businesses simply 'rubber stamp' both the strategic plans and the strategic changes presented by the executives (Davies *et al.* 2002)?) Arguably the role of the political leader in the public services could be seen as equivalent to the role of the board in the private sector – both are formally superior to the managerial leadership.

The role of elected politicians in strategic leadership deserves attention in its own right, but here we focus on the interaction between politicians and appointed managers, and, specifically, how the latter respond to pressure from politicians for change. Wechsler and Backoff's case studies showed that a range of responses was possible. In the first case, the managerial leaders were more concerned to protect the organization and its staff from the change than they were to implement the change in the way the politicians' desired. Under a protective response such as this they could, for example, seek to persuade elected politicians that change is not needed or that the change would be harmful. A developmental response is defined as one wherein managerial leadership combines an appearance of responsiveness to the politicians with an avoidance of fundamental changes in the roles of people, processes, and organizational systems. So, there might be considerable effort expended on communication strategies and training programmes, but there is no appreciable change in the activities of the organization and the service users' experience of them. A political response might be understood as one of the managers not taking responsibility for the consequences of the change, and thus they are not concerned with maximizing the public value of the impact of the change. The final response, labelled by Wechsler and Backoff as transformational, is where managerial leaders seek to make use of creativity to produce innovative changes, and thereby achieve a highly successful result in terms of outcomes for the public.

These case studies suggest a very interesting way of looking at the leadership of change in the public services. They suggest, first, that leaders can see themselves as enablers of changes that begin as pressures from the political system. If leaders act in this way, and if the politicians are democratically elected and are acting on promises made to the public, then leadership in the public services is a part of the democratic process. Second, if leaders are enabling changes that begin as pressures from politicians, they can choose to act 'politically' (using Wechsler and Backoff's term), which involves delivering the change as required, or they can seek to turn the change into an innovation, which produces more public value. Both of these options involve enabling change, but in the latter case, the leader takes responsibility for the success of the change in better meeting the needs of the stakeholders of public services. This would seem to be a very important modification in the concept of the leadership process to make it suitable for a public services context.

Before we leave this topic, it should be noted that there have been deliberate attempts to foster a more cohesive strategic leadership involving politicians and senior civil servants. These were described by Mulgan who had led the Prime Minister's Strategy Unit (PMSU) when it was set up in 2002 (House of Commons Public Administration Select Committee 2007: Ev7):

> In the last two or three years there were some interesting changes . . . in particular trying to get Cabinet ministers and permanent secretaries spending more time in away-days, in discussions, in evening sessions, mixing up different departments, looking at future challenges and looking at what was happening in other countries, trying to get any more common cross-governmental view of what really did need to be done to be ready for the next five, ten or fifteen years.

CONVENTIONAL STRATEGIC DECISION MAKING VERSUS 'MAGPIE DECISION MAKING'

Some years ago, when studying cases of innovation in local government, my colleagues and I kept looking for evidence that the innovations were the result of decisions made in strategic plans, and had thus been the result of attempts at strategic foresight. We concluded, based on the case studies, that strategic documents might be used to justify an innovation, but that this was not the same as saying it resulted directly from the implementation of a strategic plan. We also tried to collect evidence to show that the

39

innovations had been a success, and normally discovered that there was no system for monitoring its impact or for evaluating its success. Sometimes, the response elicited was that it was self-evidently a success since the innovation had taken place – in other words, success was an existential innovation. If the innovation had taken place and now existed, it was therefore a successful innovation. It did not seem immediately obvious to those we questioned that the success of the innovation was to be measured by its positive impact; that is, measured in terms of a desired outcome. For example, a new service (the innovation) should increase the quality of life (a desired outcome) of a client group as against the old service it replaced. The mere fact that the new service existed was not evidence that the innovation was successful.

The official report to the Economic and Social Research Council on the research (Joyce 1999a) included the following remark:

> The prevailing culture in many local authorities appears to be one which values and rewards innovation and which appreciates managers who can make things happen. It appears not to be a culture which puts so much value on outcomes, securing innovations, and learning from them.

We subsequently coined the phrase 'ineffectual conservatism' to make sense of this situation, by which we meant an environment in which there was a lack of appetite for change, but innovations kept on being launched (see Research Box 2.1).

RESEARCH BOX 2.1   STUDY OF USER-LED INNOVATION IN LOCAL GOVERNMENT (CORRIGAN *ET AL.* 1999)

Extract from a conference paper, which explores lack of focus on outcomes by managers in local government in middle 1990s:

> This judgement is shared by at least one manager in local government, an assistant director, who played an important role in a successful service innovation studied by us:
>
> 'And I think where traditionally local authorities are not good, they're getting a lot better at monitoring, they're not as good at evaluation and learning from what you've done. And very often, I think, people will look at where things have gone wrong but don't often enough look at when we've done well and understood why we've done well.'
>
> These conditions allow the vested interests in the status quo to create 'ineffectual conservatism'. This we see as being a tendency to resist modernization

but an inability by the vested interests to prevent the application of innovation. The downside of 'ineffectual conservatism' is to bring about one of the major problems of user led innovation in local government – the tendency to starting but not finishing innovations. To quote one of our interviewees, a senior local government manager:

'It's quite slow to change things here. Things are very embedded. And there's a history of initiatives happening and not being seen through.'

This particular problem may create the opportunity for radically different local government reputations to exist inside and outside local government. To many people, especially senior managers and policy and strategy specialists in local government, local government is constantly reorganizing and making changes, whereas to outsiders who know little about local government there is an image of local government as a stagnant and unchanging sector. In fact, local government managers are continuously involved in making changes happen, and public and community consultation initiatives are being instigated widely. Yet, few local authorities appear to have the data capacity to generate systematic evidence and monitoring of innovations. In this sense, local government managers are not outcome oriented. The evidence of management actions to stabilise changes, see them through to completion, and to learn from them is also thin.

Perhaps a related phenomenon is what might be termed 'magpie decision making'. The essence of this phenomenon is that there are individual public service managers who are attracted by new ideas in the same way that a magpie is attracted by shiny objects. Such a magpie decision maker may acquire good ideas and champion their application. The key point about such decisions is that they do not start with a clear sense of strategic priorities or a goal, and they do not get evaluated as one of a number of possible options that have to show, not only their instrumentality for the strategic direction being pursued, but also their feasibility. They are ideas led innovations and not strategic.

Magpie decision making does not compare well with strategic decision making in terms of the percentage of the decisions being implemented. The evidence for this comes from studies by Paul Nutt (1999, 2008). In Nutt's studies, he called one decision making process 'idea imposition', which is where ideas offer what appear to be ready made solutions that will be appealing to decision makers and it is the ideas that prompt action. This might be equated with magpie decision making. The second main decision making process is termed by him a 'discovery' process. This involves gathering intelligence, consideration of needs and desired results, the evaluation of

41

options, and the implementation of the most beneficial options. This could be seen as consistent with a strategic decision making process in which strategic goals are based on assessment of public needs, and success is measured in terms of desired outcomes. His more recent study found again that discovery was superior to idea imposition (Nutt 2008). This superiority was judged in terms of whether the decision was sustained (two years later), the extent of the decision adopted, and the speed with which it was completed.

Based on the findings of Nutt, it is possible to argue that the usual approach pre-scribed for strategic decision making (researching needs of intended beneficiaries, deciding on measures of strategic effectiveness, identifying options and selecting the best options and ones that are feasible) is more likely to be successful for leaders in public services (and in other sectors) than is a magpie approach where the latest good idea is seized upon as a ready made solution. Leaders need to give attention not only to setting the vision and direction, but also working hard on feasibility, implementation, and sustaining a decision.

Can leaders afford to be complacent about their choice of decision making process? Just a small number of sound decisions may take a business to a position of dominance in its industry (Slywotzky 1996). Could this also be true in the public services sector, that key decisions can make the difference between success and failure? The case stud-ies by Moore (1995) provide a set of illustrations of public sector leaders making big decisions, with very varied results.

LEADERS AND CONFLICTS

Speaking about his experiences of private sector management, John Harvey-Jones (1988: 73), ex-chairman of ICI (Imperial Chemical Industries), expressed the view that internal politics are normal: 'It would be foolish to believe that any group of peo-ple can interact without a political undercurrent.' Internal politics are also to be found in public services, and may be seen as causing change (Pettigrew *et al.* 1992: 8):

> . . . changes are also a product of processes which recognise historical and contin-uing struggles for power and status as motive forces, and one needs to consider the 'cui bono' question: how do interest groups and individuals gain or lose as proposed changes surface, receive attention, are consolidated and implemented or fall from grace before they ever get off the ground?

Looking at strategic leadership using a pluralistic frame of reference (see Concept Box 2.2) introduces a whole new dimension to the strategic leadership process: how to manage and even mobilize interest groups so that their separate (but related) interests can be reconciled sufficiently for public services to be changed for the better. It has been argued that consensus is important in government because a 'government has more stakeholders than a business' and to 'change anything important, many of those stakeholders must agree' (Osborne and Gaebler 1992: 233). A pluralistic frame of reference does not extol consensus, but rather the search for compromise so that an agreement for the time being can be found. Compromise and agreement are seen as provisional and temporary rather than a permanent state of affairs.

CONCEPT BOX 2.2 PLURALISTIC FRAME OF REFERENCE

A pluralistic frame of reference suggests that society and organizations are both composed of interest groups with separate and related interests. For example, Kerr *et al.* said (1973: 271) that any pluralistic society faces the internal problem of 'conflict among the various power elements'. One example they gave of this conflict is that between managers and managed within enterprises. They pointed to occupational and professional groups as a locus of power within the state, as well as enterprises, and they outlined all the forms conflict might take in pluralistic society (ibid 1973: 273):

> Conflict will take place in a system of pluralistic industrialism . . . Groups will jockey for position over the placement of individuals, the setting of jurisdictions, the location of authority to make decisions, the forming of alliances, the establishment of formulas, the half-evident withdrawal of support and of effort, the use of precedents and arguments and statistics. Persuasion, pressure, and manipulation will take the place of the face-to-face combat of an earlier age. The battles will be in corridors instead of the streets, and memos will flow instead of blood.

The pluralist thinkers of the 1960s drew attention to the creation of institutions (i.e. rules) for settling conflicts – electoral systems in politics and collective bargaining in enterprises and industries. These approved institutions enabled conflict to be expressed, and then a basis for decisions and actions to be found. For example, election campaigns allowed different perspectives and interests to be voiced and argued about, but then the votes were counted and a government elected with a mandate to rule for a given period. In the case of collective bargaining, there could be industrial action and threats of industrial action, but eventually an agreement would be negotiated on pay or other matters to allow industries and organizations to resume normal activity for the duration of the collective agreement.

One of the recent models of leadership that approaches a pluralistic perspective is that of Heifetz. Heifetz's key concept was the 'adaptive work' of leadership (Heifetz 1994: 22):

> Adaptive work consists of the learning required to address conflicts in the values people hold, or to diminish the gaps between the values people stand for and the reality they face. Adaptive work requires a change in values, beliefs or behaviour.

For Heifetz there are not only conflicts of values between people, but also conflicts between values and reality. In Heifetz's thinking of the leadership experience, strategy is not only a matter of organizing and using knowledge of trends and situations, it is also about knowing how to lead people through change. At one point, Heifetz suggests that strategy begins with a question about adjustments to be made by stakeholders to enable problem solving to occur.

While Heifetz (1994) did not explicitly embrace the language of interest groups and power struggles, he did understand that leadership was dangerous. He said (ibid 1994: 235), 'Leaders are always failing somebody'. He got close to a pluralistic perspective when he discussed the loss people incur because of what he called the adaptive work of leaders (ibid 1994: 236):

> Often, however, the loss is real and sustained; adaptation for some people means accepting the loss . . . Only a little less stark were the losses of Asarco Copper plant workers in Tacoma. They lost their jobs; they had to pick up and find new work. For some, that meant uprooting their homes and families . . . Leaders and authority figures get attacked, dismissed, silenced, and sometime assassinated because they come to represent loss, real or perceived, to those members of the community who feel that they have gotten, or might get, the bad end of the bargain.

Like Mary Parker Follett, Heifetz places some importance on leaders understanding their situation and testing that understanding (ibid 1994: 24):

> There are several advantages to viewing leadership in terms of adaptive work . . . Conceptions of leadership that do not value reality testing encourage people to realize their vision, however faulty their sight . . . To produce adaptive work, a vision must track the contours of reality; it has to have accuracy, and not simply imagination and appeal.

Unlike leadership gurus who dwell on the visionary and inspirational powers of leaders, Heifetz was highly aware of the disruption caused by change and the consequences and impacts of change on others in terms of their distress. Moreover, he developed an

44

understanding of the resistance to change through what he termed 'work avoidance mechanisms' (ibid 1994: 37):

> . . . people fail to adapt because of the distress provoked by the problem and the changes it demands. They resist the pain, anxiety, or conflict that accompanies a sustained interaction with the situation. Holding onto past assumptions, blaming authority, scape-goating, externalizing the enemy, denying the problem, jumping to conclusions, or finding a distracting issue may restore stability and feel less stressful than facing and taking responsibility for a complex challenge. These patterns of response to disequilibrium are called *work avoidance mechanisms* in this study, and they are similar to the defensive routines that operate in individuals, small groups, and organizations.

We can understand the meaning of the adaptive work of leaders better by considering the idea that there are two basic types of problems: technical problems and adaptive challenges (Heifetz and Linsky 2002). The first type, a technical problem, requires authoritative expertize, and, if authoritative expertize is available, it is relatively easy to solve. The second type of problem, an adaptive challenge, is the type Heifetz associated with danger for leaders. Because adaptive solutions are not immediately obvious, people and organizations have to learn and the learning is not painless. There are losses and learning to adapt involves people moving away from their existing norms of behaviour, moving away from their existing values. So, according to Heifetz and Linsky (2002: 20) leaders carry out adaptive work, and that creates risk, creates conflict, and creates disturbance. The leader, however, is not someone who simply disturbs people. The skilful leader disturbs people at a rate that they can cope with, creating a level of disturbance that they can absorb.

So, how does a leader manage this situation of danger? How do they, in Heifetz's terms, 'stay alive'? Heifetz and Linsky (2002: 100) claim: 'Relating to people is central to leading and staying alive.' It is suggested that the leader develops people who share their vision into allies by keeping them informed and building trust. The leader has to work at keeping close to opponents so that they understand what they are thinking and feeling. The leader relates to those who are currently uncommitted to the change through different methods (see Figure 2.4). These include the leader taking some of the responsibility for the situation in which adaptive change has become necessary, admitting that there will be risks and losses as a result of the proposed change, and modelling the new behaviour required. Heifetz and Linsky also argue that leaders have to be prepared to sacrifice those who will not adapt in order to ensure that successful change occurs. They illustrate this using an anecdote in which a chief executive asked senior managers to endorse a new plan and accepted the resignation of the third most senior manager in the organization who was not prepared to commit to the change.

45

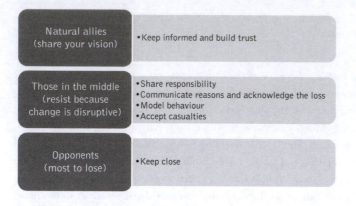

Figure 2.4 *Leaders' relations with allies, people in the middle, and opponents (based on Heifetz and Linsky 2002)*

Heifetz and Linsky (2002) also provide the following guidance to leaders on how to handle their adaptive work:

1 Do not always engage opposition – sometimes retreat or outflank
2 Work as closely with opposition as with supporters
3 Pace the change – do not do too much too soon
4 Explain 'why' change is needed
5 Think constantly about giving back the work of adaptation to the people who need to take responsibility
6 Listen to people but do not take what they say at face value
7 Avoid embodying issues – get others to ripen them.

THINK POINT

What do leaders do to quicken the pace of change? What do leaders do to slow the pace of change? Please give examples from practice.

This approach to leadership fits fairly easily with ideas of strategic issue management and stakeholder analysis and management. First, in terms of strategic issue management, it can be argued that strategic issues can often be recognized by looking for conflicts and then probing to see how the conflict is occurring between different stakeholders. With the use of stakeholder analysis and stakeholder management leaders can identify, or try to identify, measures to build alliances and coalitions for change (Nutt and Backoff 1992). The following advice to leaders links up ideas of issues, stakeholders, and alliance building (Heifetz *et al.* 2009a: 115):

If people see the issues as systemic rather than personal, they will begin to look for the leverage points in the system (such as a tradition protecting underperformers or centralized control) as targets of attention to effect change. By making systemic interpretations, you can help them think politically and map the issue's stakeholders, spot opportunities to build unusual alliances, and determine what is at risk for each stakeholder group.

RESEARCH BOX 2.2   CHANGE AND EXTERNAL STAKEHOLDERS

Perrott's case (1996) of New South Wales State Railway Authority in Australia illustrates the importance of understanding the different interests of stakeholders among the public. The services had not kept up with population changes in the Sydney region. Perrott (1996: 341) commented: 'As a result, the established suburbs were overserviced and the growing suburbs were underserviced.' The Authority could switch resources to ensure all were serviced equally. If this occurred, the established suburbs would be losers and the growing suburbs would be winners. Not all changes have this effect. For example, if an organization has new overall priorities, but can access new resources to create new services with new sets of service users, there would appear to be no losers, only winners.

Wechsler and Backoff's (1986) case study of the Public Utilities Commission of Ohio (PUCO) is also a useful illustration of the importance of external stakeholders. After 1973, PUCO came under pressure to change the way it regulated utility companies. In effect, the pressure meant its overall priority changed from regulating the utilities in a way that balanced producer and consumer interests to one that put the consumers first. External events – including the world oil crisis, inflation, nuclear industry issues, and changes in public policy – had served to disturb PUCO's relationships with utility companies and consumers. Wechsler and Backoff (1986: 325) say:

Following from its mandate to ensure service at the lowest possible rates while allowing the utility companies a fair rate of return, the Commission employed a regulatory strategy aimed at balancing the competing interests of producers and consumers. As negative reactions to this approach increased, PUCO decisions retained a rhetorical commitment to the concept of balancing competing interests but produced results more favourable to consumers.

If you have examined what is at risk for each stakeholder group, what then? One well known way of building support is for the leader to reframe a strategy to make it more acceptable to more interest groups (Nutt and Backoff 1993). Another way is to co-create strategy through an inclusive process that allows some participation in deciding strategies to achieve priorities. Such participation allows those important in implementation to select or create options for action that are in their interests. It may not always be possible or easy, but participation can sometimes mean greater likelihood of public managers choosing actions that are effective in both delivering strategic priorities and getting support within the organization. In management jargon, participation can produce win-win outcomes.

Essentially, we have been exploring the idea of leadership as a political process, and not a purely technical or analytical one. In this political world of leadership, how does a leader know that their strategy is succeeding? Moore (1995: 93–4) may provide some clues in this following description of successful strategy:

> If the new strategy attracts political support, if it attracts publicity, if it attracts volunteers, if budgets begin to increase, if new legislative sponsors appear, if old political opponents back off a little, then the strategy begins to have some political bite. If the manager seems committed because he or she keeps saying the same things, and his or her substantive and administrative actions have some interpretable relationship to the articulated mission, then the strategy begins to exercise some administrative torque on the organization's operations. If the manager's personal stock seems to increase as he or she pursues the strategy, then the strategy will gather momentum inside the organization as subordinates figure either that now is their chance to do what they always wanted to do or that they are going to have to adjust to the manager's terms. It is not easy to change what people take for granted, but in the end, that is what a successful strategy does: it moves politicians and midlevel managers in an organization to a different set of expectations about the purposes and capabilities of a given public enterprise.

CASE STUDY

The Finwin Change Programme in Finland

The Finnish Government created a change programme called Finwin, which began in 2007 and was aimed at improving understanding of future challenges and their management. This appears to have been done to support two change projects. One change project was a regionalization initiative, which involved asking civil servants to move to new service centres in the regions. This was aimed at moving ten per cent of all government functions out of Finland's capital. The second change project was a productivity programme to anticipate the impact of demographic changes on the availability of skilled people.

The Finwin programme comprised seminars, workshops, and learning cafes for senior civil servants and representatives of employees. The essence of the seminars was discussion of various topics. It was managed by the Ministry of Finance with the help of private consultants. A steering group and a working group were also set up to co-ordinate the Finwin programme. According to Melchor (2008: 42), 'Finwin intends to facilitate the implementation of change through the dissemination of information and the exchange of positive and negative lessons on reform programmes in different areas and levels of government'.

Case questions:

1 What is the underlying logic of the Finwin Change Programme approach?
2 Does it match any of the strategies in Thurley and Wirdenius's (1989) typology of strategies for change? (See Table 2.1 for summary.)

Table 2.1 *Typology of strategies*

Type	Name	Definition	Relies on . . .
1	Power-based strategy	Those in top positions order the change to occur	Obedience to hierarchical decisions
2	Method-based strategy	Experts are brought in to design a change programme	Trust in experts
3	Empirical/rational strategy	A process of research, fact finding, analysis and solution finding is carried out	Perception of objectivity in research and analysis
4	Problem-solution strategy	Those who will be affected by change, or will have to implement change, are involved in problem solving	Engaging the self-interest of those affected by change and widening the sense of ownership and responsibility for change

Source: Thurley and Wirdenius (1989)

CASE STUDY

The reforms of the Italian public service

The Italian public services began reforms in the early 1990s and these have been consolidated in the last decade. The reforms faced resistance at a variety of levels by a range of stakeholders:

Politicians and representatives of trade unions have perceived their interests to be affected by the increasing mobility or distribution of civil servants in different sectors and/or levels of government and have therefore opposed the reforms. Cultural resistance has been manifested through the idea that public administration has a social role in the distribution of economic resources. Moreover, the idea of changing long-standing habits and practices has produced behavioural resistance from managers, civil servants and trade union leaders.

(Melchor 2008: 53)

So, how did the Italian government respond to this resistance to change? Apparently, the government response was to use dialogue and information sharing in an effort to explain to stakeholders what the changes were, and what the reasons for the changes were. It has also been claimed that the media was used as a channel for communication by the government to get its explanations for the reforms across (Melchor 2008).

Case question:

1 What are the other options for managing resistance in such a situation and how does a leader choose between them?

SUMMARY

Leading successful strategic change is a major accomplishment in public services – not easily achieved. We could see leadership processes as a sequence of steps. For example, leaders should begin by creating a vision and strategy, then communicate them, and finally inspire and motivate people to deliver the strategic change. However, we have tried to enrich the understanding of leadership processes in at least three ways.

First, we have highlighted the role of both politicians and appointed managers in leadership in the case of public services. Second, we have highlighted the challenges of decision making. We noted the problems of change occurring, for example, when there is 'ineffectual conservatism'. We also noted the research evidence that suggested that decisions that begin with an idea are the least effectively implemented, and this was associated with 'magpie decision making'. Third, this chapter has explored a pluralistic frame of reference and its implications for leadership. One implication is that conflict is regarded as a normal aspect of strategic change. In effect, we have been discussing leadership as political process. Leaders have to handle conflict and seek to create, as much as possible, compromise and, maybe ideally, consensus. We noted that conflict is found in strategic issues. A range of different interest groups will take up positions around a strategic issue. Some will be external stakeholders, maybe different sections of the public. Some will resist change. Some will support it. Strategic leaders have to pay attention to the political dimension of making strategic changes and building coalitions of interest to bring about change.

Work-based assignment: disturbance

The work-based assignments in this book are for civil servants and other public services staff who have four or more years of management experience.

Reflect on some of the changes you know could or should make in your own part of the organization. Think about the ones that would make the biggest difference in terms of being responsive to citizens or service users. Especially think about changes that could be seen as your responsibility. Why have you not made these changes yet? What is holding you back from making them? What risks have held you back? To what extent have you held back because you think it would disturb things and cause conflict?

Work-based assignment: decision making

Think about any important leadership or management decision you made at least a year ago. Did you implement it? Has it been fully implemented? How was the decision made? Was it an example of 'magpie decision making' – it looked like a good idea that offered a readymade solution? Or was it made in a more strategic way (did you identify needs, desired outcomes, did you generate options for action and then discard those that were not feasible, etc.)? How happy are you now with the decision and the way it was implemented?

DISCUSSION QUESTIONS

1   Should elected politicians be the strategic leaders or is this something they should leave to senior civil servants or appointed top executives?

2   How do the political leadership processes of ministers and prime ministers affect their ability and performance as strategic leaders?

3   Are leaders in the civil service and public services best as labellers and orchestrators of emergent strategies or should they be proactive in strategic leadership?

4   How important is the insight that conflict is a normal phenomenon within strategic planning and management processes?

51

5   What would you do if you were a senior manager in a public service organization and managers reporting to you resisted the performance measurement system you are trying to set up to check on delivery of your strategic priorities?

FURTHER READING

Gabris, G.T., Golembiewski, R.T. and Ihrke, D.M. (2000) 'Leadership credibility, board relations, and administrative innovation at the local government level', *Journal of Public Administration Research and Theory*, 11, 1: 89–108.

Heifetz, R. A. and Linsky, M. (2002) *Leadership on the Line*. Boston. Massachusetts: Harvard Business School Press.

Kotter, J. P. (1990) 'What Leaders Really Do', *Harvard Business Review*, May–June: 103–11.

Milner, E. and Joyce, P. (2005) *Lessons in Leadership: Meeting the Challenges of Public Services Management*. London: Routledge.

Chapter 3

Leaders and change situations

LEARNING OBJECTIVES

- To explore the different situations in which a public services leader brings about change
- To consider if different leadership approaches are needed for different change situations
- To identify key concepts that help leaders to make sense of these situations

INTRODUCTION

The old concept of the civil service was of a steady, reliable, honest, and impartial administrative machine. Added to this concept in recent years has been the requirement of the civil service to be business-like in its efficiency, effectiveness, and adaptability, and with enhanced capabilities for delivery and innovation. Some of this is captured in Boyle's (1995a) remarks about the Irish civil service, when he diagnosed the need for a change in the culture towards innovation, and underlined civil service responsibilities for making sure new policies were effective in practice. In fact, he prescribed a civil service role as change agent in response to the developments that had been occurring. This change agent role entailed, in his opinion, taking government priorities and plans and developing a vision of a proposed change, planning the resources required for change, planning to overcome resistance to change, and leading the process of adapting to what was required by change.

Why is there this change in what we expect of the civil service? The usual answer is that society is changing. It is often reckoned that the pace of change has been accelerating in the last 30 or 40 years. This requires more decisions. It requires more changes of organizational strategy. It leads to more changes in public policy on public services reform.

While the rate of change may be accelerating both inside and outside the public services, the nature and causes of the change situations are very complex and diverse. Sometimes the change has been triggered by a specific political decision, for example, to create a new government agency. In other cases, governments create pressures on public services affecting many more than one public services organization. There are times when governments cut budgets in an attempt to bring down public spending. There are times when governments create performance management regimes that subject public services generally to pressures for improved performance and which may also involve special measures being applied to the poorest performers. In many countries, public services have been changing as a result of programmes for public services reforms.

One consequence of all this is that change is often seen as something forced on the public services organization by the external world. In the face of pressure for change leaders in public service organizations have to work out what change is needed in response, and how to make it. In addition, since change has been forced on the organization, leaders may find themselves trying to deal with interest groups who wish to keep things as they are and may even deny the legitimacy of proposed changes. There are then a whole set of associated phenomena; such as organizations responding to pressures compliantly, but not necessarily creating better services for the public; organizations in which there are frequent complaints of change fatigue accompanied by slowness to make changes; and organizations which make the least possible change, and hope to outlast the external pressures. In short, public services are not always experienced by their leaders as receptive contexts for change (Pettigrew *et al.* 1992).

Change programmes are probably poorly done in all sectors and in all sizes of organizations. There is some evidence that change programmes often fail in the private sector (see Research Box 3.1). Things appear to be no better in the public sector. A survey of senior civil servants in the UK found only a third thought their departments were good at managing change (Capability Reviews Team 2007: 31).

RESEARCH BOX 3.1   CHANGE PROGRAMMES IN THE PRIVATE SECTOR

If the findings of a survey by the consultancy firm A T Kearney are true, we should be quite pessimistic about change programmes in organizations. A T Kearney surveyed 294 senior executives in medium and large European companies during 1999. It appears that nearly two-thirds reported a temporary improvement as a result of their change programme, but said that change had failed in terms of sustained improvement. Only one in five change programmes were considered successful (*The Economist* July 15th 2000, p. 87). Would it be any different in the public services?

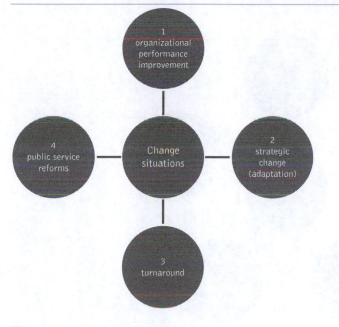

Figure 3.1 *Change situations*

In this chapter we consider four different change situations and will address the challenges for leaders in each of them. The first situation is where a public service organization is not an especially bad performing organization, but is under the same pressure as other organizations to make improvements. This may arise as a result of performance management regimes. The second situation is where a public service organization reacts strategically to its environment and undertakes strategic analysis and strategic implementation. Third, there is the special situation of a poorly performing public services organization that goes through a turnaround process. And, fourth, we consider change situations in which organizations are changing as part of a programme of public services reform (see Figure 3.1).

ORGANIZATIONAL PERFORMANCE IMPROVEMENT

Ostroff (2006) approached the issue of change management in the government sector by assuming that high performing government agencies are like well run private businesses. He proposed a set of five principles of change management for public sector organizations, one of which concerns leadership behaviour. These principles were to formulate a vision for the change; to develop stakeholder support; to identify the steps required to bring about the change; to design an integrated system of leadership, organization structure, processes, infrastructure, people, and performance management; and to provide leadership of change (see Figure 3.2).

Figure 3.2 *Ostroff (2006)*

What does his model mean for the work of leaders in relation to organizational change? First, he discusses the importance of leaders paying attention to the danger of the organization drifting off course, which means the leader should ensure that its mission and performance metrics are right. If an agency has lost sight of its purpose, then leaders work to help the organization rediscover its mission, and then define the goal of change as being to improve performance in line with the mission.

Second, leaders have to win the support of internal and external stakeholders. This involves understanding their issues and concerns. It also involves understanding the values of stakeholders. This point emerges when Ostroff offers the following assessment based on his own consultancy work (2006: 144):

> In my experience, at any given agency, about a quarter of employees are initially receptive to a change initiative (sometimes out of frustration with how things have been handled in the past), a quarter are resistant, and the remaining half are on the fence. The continuing receptivity of the first group cannot be taken for granted. To keep those employees on board, the goals of the change effort must be consonant with the values – the reasons they came to the agency in the first place.

Third, some people may resist change because they have doubts about their skills in the new organization. Ostroff thinks training might help with this problem of resistance. Leaders can increase receptivity to change by asking employees for their knowledge of operational matters, thereby gaining knowledge they need for designing the change and also gaining employee support. Leaders may also cultivate more willingness to change among managers and employees by creating 'diagonal slice' teams to diagnose performance problems, and by organizing visits to other high performing organizations. The agency leader may set up a change team to work on the steps to be followed in making changes. The team may, for example, identify the goals for performance improvement; hold workshops to find ideas for action; evaluate proposed ideas for impact and difficulty; and plan and implement changes. Leaders may retain oversight of the steps in making changes through steering committees to which change teams report and are accountable.

Fourth, Ostroff argues that leaders of change have to understand the complexity of change and avoid only addressing one element of the organization. It is important that all the key elements are integrated and aligned (e.g. leadership, structure, processes, people, performance management, etc.), and even that activities are aligned, where necessary, across organizational boundaries. This insistence on a comprehensive approach to change management, when underpinned by a requirement to integrate and align, makes leaders responsible for the overall coherence of change (see also Pettigrew *et al.* 1992). Finally, Ostroff argues that leaders have to find ways around bureaucratic barriers to change and convince stakeholders of their sincerity and commitment to improving performance against mission.

While Ostroff does refer to finding out employees' knowledge about operational matters as a basis for designing change, arguably his focus, in terms of leading change, is more on conflict and resistance. This is because one of the five principles concerns stakeholder support, and because his notion of leadership of change involves both overcoming bureaucratic barriers and also convincing people that the leader is committed to change.

ORGANIZATIONAL STRATEGIC CHANGE

A practical and simple view of making changes at organizational level is to be found in the conceptual framework offered by Thurley and Wirdenius (1989). While these authors are not concerned with change in the public services, it does not require much imagination to see that the framework of Thurley and Wirdenius could be adapted for use in the public services. They suggest an approach to change that begins with 'searching'. This involves market research, and concentrates on customer needs and future social trends, and ends with an evaluation stage in which there is evaluation, discussion, and reviews of problems and mistakes. Clearly, they envisage change as best carried through in a pragmatic way, and informed by an understanding of the situation and by learning. In this sense, they are more concerned with knowing what changes to make and how to make them than they are with handling conflicting interests – at least in this aspect of their modelling of how changes could be brought about (see Figure 3.3).

57

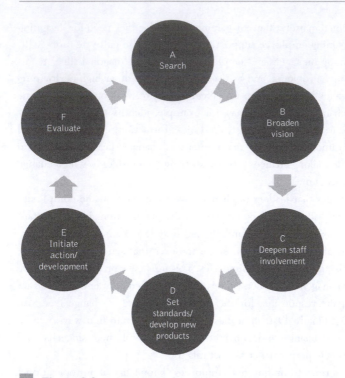

 Figure 3.3 *Organization level strategy for innovation (Thurley and Wirdenius 1989)*

Pettigrew and his colleagues have carried out one of the few detailed empirical studies of strategic change processes in the public services. This was in the UK's NHS. In the end they rejected the idea of a simple recipe to effect change. They did, however, provide conclusions that could help leaders with some insights to tackle change. Their key proposition from the study was that it was possible to see patterns in strategic change and that these could be summed up in a distinction between receptive and non-receptive contexts (Pettigrew *et al.* 1992: 268):

> A good focus for this analysis is the distinction between receptive and non-receptive contexts for change where we mean by the term 'receptive context' that there are features of context (and also management action) that seemed to be favourably associated with forward movement. On the other hand, there is in non-receptive contexts a configuration of features, which may be associated with blocks on change.

They suggest that the factors making up a context are 'a linked set of conditions which provide high energy around change' and that they 'represent a pattern of association rather than a simple line of causation . . .' (ibid: 295). The factors are listed in Table 3.1 below.

Table 3.1 *The eight factors in receptive contexts for change*

1   Quality and coherence of policy
2   Availability of key people leading change
3   Long-term environmental pressure
4   Supportive organizational culture
5   Effective managerial-clinical relations
6   Co-operative inter-organizational networks
7   Simplicity and clarity of goals and priorities
8   The fit between the district's change agenda and its locale

When discussing the quality and coherence of policy, Pettigrew *et al.* came down in favour of evidence and analysis as a basis for creating convincing policy. They cautioned against presentation of policy as blueprints and instead recommended the use of broad vision statements. In part they justified this by referring to interest groups, and this may be seen as integral to their pluralistic conception of the National Health Service (Pettigrew *et al.* 1992: 277):

> . . . a broader vision seemed more likely to generate movement than a blueprint. Such broad visions were found to have significant process and implementation benefits in terms of commitment-building and allowing interest groups to buy in to the change process, and allowing top-down pressure to be married with bottom-up concern as the field gets scripted in rather than scripted out.

Pettigrew *et al.* stated that strategic and policy ideas had to be coherent with functional strategies, with operational changes, and with financial decisions, and change had to be coherent over time in the sense of requiring persistent pursuit of long-term issues.

Their explanation of the next factor, the importance of the availability of key people leading change, includes the argument that continuity of leadership is helpful and, therefore, that losing key people leading the change may hurt the change process. A similar point was made at about the same time by Osborne and Gaebler (1992), who were looking for ways to reinvent public services (see below).

The third factor on the list is long-term environmental pressure. Pettigrew *et al.* seemed to argue that pressure from the environment is an opportunity that may be orchestrated by management and used within the change process. However, they believed that external pressure may become counterproductive if too excessive and, instead of producing successful change, may deflect energy or drain energy. In one of their case studies they suggested that excessive financial pressure created paralysis and a loss of managerial control. This idea that external pressure may be too much may be seen as reworked in the idea that people need to move out of their comfort

59

zones, but too much disruption creates dysfunctional distress (Heifetz and Linsky 2002: 108).

Pettigrew *et al.* argued that cultural change (fourth factor) is not easy to accomplish. On the other hand, they concluded that a supportive organizational culture may help with a high rate of change and they implied that an obstructive culture caused inertia. Their fifth factor was effective managerial-clinical relations, which might be seen as more generally a factor concerned with effective relationships between managers and professionals in the public services. The simple point made by Pettigrew *et al.* was that the clinicians were a powerful stakeholder group and could be a powerful block on change if they decided they were opposed to it. A sixth factor in defining receptive contexts was inter-organizational networks, which they said were most effective when they were informal networks. Pettigrew *et al.* (1992: 284) suggested that: 'at their best such networks provided opportunities for trading and education, for commitment and energy-raising and for marrying top-down and bottom-up concerns.' However, they also considered them to be fragile assets because they were vulnerable to changes of people.

The seventh factor was simplicity and clarity of goals and priorities. Pettigrew *et al.* argued that focus on a set of key priorities was necessary, as was ensuring persistence over a long period of time. We can link this point back to an earlier consideration of external pressures; changes in such pressures could lead to an accumulation of priorities and then the loss of focus that is needed for successful strategic change. Pettigrew *et al.* say (1992: 285): 'Skills in complexity and conflict reduction could also be important here, in trying to contain complex problems in simpler organisational frameworks.' The final factor was referred to as the fit between the district's change agenda and its locale. Pettigrew *et al.* acknowledged that some of the factors in their notion of locale may be difficult for managers to change. Factors identified by them included the number of major towns in the district, the existence of a teaching hospital, the local political culture, and local workforce.

While they listed eight factors in receptive and non-receptive contexts, their remarks indicated the special importance they attached to coherence (Pettigrew *et al.* 1992: 292): '... managing incoherence remains the most-wide ranging challenge in producing change in the NHS...'.

In drawing their study to a close they highlighted the need for leaders to address what they labelled as dualities and dilemmas (ibid 1992: 298). They identified a series of these, including combining top-down pressures and bottom-up concerns; managing both projects and longer term processes; combining continuity and change; managing through formal hierarchies and informal networks; sometimes developing matters into issues and at other times narrowing issues down; and directing from the centre while allowing local freedom to customize. One example of this, which has echoes in some ideas of Heifetz and Linsky (2002), is to be found in the following statement,

(Pettigrew *et al.* 1992: 298):

> But the crises which can help to mobilise change could be both opportunities and threats. Those crises can create a fragmented and defensive atmosphere which can inhibit change, as well as a purposive and coherent environment that can drive change. One of the great dilemmas of change management is how to create zones of disturbance, to energise a process of creative destruction, while also building a zone of comfort for new directions to be constructed and legitimacy and support built.

A different, but related, tension in leading change is identified by them in a series of crisp remarks (1992: 299):

> There is also the duality of simultaneously managing continuity and change. The development of a receptive context for change has to share its influence with the needs for continuity . . . To change the world one must live with it.

This duality of the need to both maintain and change organization has been noted by others, including Beckhard and Harris (1987, vii): 'In addition, the dilemma of achieving or managing change while maintaining enough stability to continue to do whatever the organization is supposed to do provides new challenges and new requirements for executive management.' It is also echoed in Kotter's (1990) differentiation of the functions of managers (order) and leaders (change).

To conclude, Pettigrew *et al.* drew their ideas about receptive contexts from case studies, and so their eight factors have the merit of being based on proper research. The eight factors also provide useful guidance to leaders on how they might begin to create receptive contexts. But Pettigrew and his colleagues do not favour the simple models found in some popular treatments of change management. This comes across clearly in their discussion of dualities and dilemmas, which makes the point quite powerfully that to lead change is a complex business. It also comes across in their characterization of strategic change. They stated that change is iterative, cumulative and informed by learning. They also warned that change could be reversed, 'with perhaps the single most significant cause of reversibility being the changing priorities and attention spans of the power figures who often champion the original idea for change' (Pettigrew *et al.* 1992: 297).

THINK POINT

How do leaders create zones of disturbance? How do they build a zone of comfort? What examples of these zones can you identify from practice?

ORGANIZATIONAL TURNAROUNDS

Turnarounds in the public sector have two defining features. First, change is under-taken against a background of politicians and the public having a perception that the organization is failing. Second, a turnaround is a change in which a new leader has been brought into the organization and has been asked to turn the organization from a failing one to a successful organization. While this may seem to be change undertaken under extreme conditions, Borins (1998: 303) quoted the view of Mark Moore that any public sector organization that has been in existence for a long time will probably have experienced a turnaround.

One of the case studies presented by Moore (1995) was based on Boston Hous-ing Authority (BHA), which had 17,000 housing units. In July 1979 a Superior Court Judge ordered BHA into receivership. Subsequently, the BHA board was suspended and Harry Spencer appointed by a judge to take any actions necessary to bring housing units into compliance with the state sanitary code and government regulations. The organization had a $5 million deficit, and it suffered from splits at the top and demor-alized staff. A second case study concerned Houston Police Department (HPD), which had a poor reputation for the way its officers treated citizens and for the high numbers of citizens being killed by police officers. Crime levels had increased. Lee Brown took over as chief of HPD in 1981 following the election of a new mayor who had promised political and administrative reforms.

Moore suggested that these organizations were improved by the following measures (Moore 1995: 273–90):

1   The leaders focused on political management and built political support by will-ing acceptance of accountability to the politicians, which built confidence and gained them support in terms of resources and authorization
2   The leaders brought in new subordinates to their team or gave existing people clear organizational assignments whose results could be checked
3   The leaders made structure serve strategic purposes (and signalled the strategi-cally important jobs to get done)
4   The leaders made internal standards of accountability more important
5   The leaders encouraged innovation
6   The leaders reengineered 'some of the basic operational procedures of their organizations'
7   The leaders decentralized their organizations to give citizens and clients the feeling 'that they have effective influence over the organization's operations and purposes'; this he believed would pay off in terms of continuing community responsiveness.

Given the initial state of both the BHA and HPD, this list of measures might be taken as a checklist for turnaround leaders in the public services.

Figure 3.4 *Borins' turnaround model*

Borins' analysis of eight public sector cases generated a model with four variables: visible problems; new leadership; organizational change; improved results (see Figure 3.4):

The four variables of the model appear to form the turnaround process. The start of the process is when the organization's problems of poor service are perceived as major ones because of the spotlight provided by the media, auditors, legislative committees, or electoral politics. Then the existing leader is dismissed or moved, and a new leader is appointed to take over. The new turnaround leaders, according to Borins, make changes in the organization. While he noted very many different types of changes that might be made (including decentralization), he put most stress on changes that reorganized the work at the front line of the organization. Finally, the efforts of the new leader and the organizational changes are said to improve performance in terms of outcomes, efficiency, etc.

The model was generated by Borins from an analysis of eight case studies. It was tested by him on a ninth case and by assessing its fit with accounts of another turnaround at the New York City Department of Juvenile Justice. Borins suggested that these two tests confirmed the robustness of the model.

PUBLIC SERVICES REFORM

A long-term trend in the public services has been the increased interest in the management of service delivery and projects. Politicians have wanted increased managerial capacity to cope with what appears to be an increasing rate of change in politics and policy. Reforms have involved marketization, and there has also been much emphasis on performance measurement and performance management. One of the pioneering countries of public service reform was New Zealand. Lonti and Gregory (2004: 23) reported:

> The state sector reforms in New Zealand during the 1980s and early 90s introduced a new budgeting and managerial regime strongly focused on the production of 'outputs' across the whole range of public service functions. An integral part of this new structure was the quest to more effectively measure performance. The aim was to render the delivery of public goods and services both more efficient and more accountable at the politico-bureaucratic nexus. During the past couple of years, however, the state sector in New Zealand has begun moving to a system which is more focused on 'managing outcomes', whereby the production

of outputs will be better aligned with desired policy outcomes, to overcome the inherent problem whereby output production tends to become an end in itself.

The phenomenally influential book by Osborne and Gaebler (1992) noted the emergence of modern budget systems, which were mission-driven and results-oriented in countries such as Great Britain, Australia, and New Zealand. It synthesized the lessons from other countries with success stories from the public services in the United States to produce a manifesto for reinventing government and putting an end to bureaucratic structures and practices. They summarized this in ten principles that they stated were found in entrepreneurial governments (Osborne and Gaebler 1992: 19–20):

> Most entrepreneurial governments promote competition between service providers. They empower citizens by pushing control out of the bureaucracy, into the community. They measure the performance of their agencies, focusing not on inputs but on outcomes. They are driven by their goals – their missions – not by their rules and regulations. They redefine their clients as customers and offer them choices – between schools, between training programs, between housing options. They prevent problems before they emerge, rather than simply offering services afterward. They put their energies into earning money, not simply spending it. They decentralize authority, embracing participatory management. They prefer market mechanisms to bureaucratic mechanisms. And they focus not simply on providing public services, but on catalysing all sectors – public, private, and voluntary – into action to solve their community's problems.

CONCEPT BOX 3.1   ENTREPRENEURIAL GOVERNMENT

According to Osborne and Gaebler (1992), entrepreneurial governments do the following:

- steer more than row
- empower communities
- encourage competition between public service providers
- focus on their missions
- fund outcomes (results-oriented)
- put customer needs first
- earn money rather than spend
- invest in prevention
- decentralize
- leverage change through the market.

One of the key points to note about the concept of entrepreneurial government is that it is about putting customers first. Many of the public service reform programmes in Great Britain and elsewhere have been similarly focused on putting the customers (or citizens or service users) first. This gives the reform situation something distinctive by definition. The reform situation is a change situation in which leaders have to get those who work for the organization to change so they can better serve the public. And if the public's needs have changed, and the organization has lagged behind the changed needs, then the leader's responsibility is to bring about organizational change so that the lag is removed. This seems to imply that the leader in a reform situation has to put the interests of the public before the interests of those who work in the public services. The chances are that as the leader makes the changes, or enables the changes required by the reform agenda, the opposition will be inside the organization they lead, while the beneficiaries will be relatively silent and passive service users! This is a new twist on the observation by Machiavelli that those who look likely to lose from change are more strident than those who hope to gain from the change.

The ideas of Osborne and Gaebler have been influential and several of them became central to the reform ideas of the Blair government in Great Britain. In particular, in the years between 2001 and 2007, the government introduced a service user choice of provider; competition between public service providers; funding of outcomes (for example, the payment by results regime introduced into the National Health Service); and commissioning. These formed the essence of the reforms in public service systems. The reform agenda was broad in scope and included: health, schools, universities, law and order, and welfare.

Huerta Melchor (2008) notes that the words change and reforms are used interchangeably, but managing change is important because it affects the success or failure of a reform initiative. He used the concept of receptivity to interrogate the experiences of public sector reform in six countries: Finland, France, Italy, Portugal, Spain, and Switzerland. While considering that receptivity is an underdeveloped concept, he proposed that receptivity can be understood in terms of four factors: ideological vision, leading change, institutional politics, and implementation capacity.

Melchor's discussion of the conceptualization of ideological vision makes reference to coherence and to cultural change, which echoes two of the eight factors identified by Pettigrew *et al.* He also makes the point that leadership may be by a group rather than by an individual. Why do leaders matter? He says that leaders are important for getting an acceptance of change. His discussion of the concept of institutional politics contains references to co-operative organizational networks (which of course may be compared to the Pettigrew *et al.* idea of interorgansiational networks) and to what he calls advocacy coalitions. Finally, implementation capacity is discussed with reference to learning and to the need for political support to bring about change, possibly recognizing that it is not just an issue of learning, but also one of conflict and resistance.

65

Isolating the effects of changes caused by public services reforms is far from easy. In the case of Great Britain, there is clear evidence of improved performance by the NHS in respect of waiting lists and waiting times. But what caused that? Was it the persuasive skills of political leaders? Was it the improved and modern budgetary system introduced by government in 1998? Was it the improved capabilities in central government, both in terms of performance management and long-term thinking? Or was it the implementation of the reforms designed to create a more entrepreneurial National Health Service?

Moreover, is a change situation created by public service reform fundamentally different from other kinds of change, including strategic change? And, therefore, is leadership a different process in the case of public service reform? Public services reform situations can involve the sorts of loss discussed by Heifetz and his colleagues – job losses being one example. Pressures for public services reform may also be unwelcome inside public service organizations leading to issues of resistance and receptivity as already discussed. However, as with other kinds of change, these are matters that call for effective leadership. Indeed, Osborne and Gaebler (1992) claimed that there was nothing more important than leadership for the reinvention of government on entrepreneurial lines. They specifically point to the importance of leaders sticking around, and argue that a high turnover of leaders is detrimental to reinvention. They also say that a leader has to get community leaders to buy into a vision of change. This, presumably, flows from the idea of entrepreneurial governments being catalysts.

CASE STUDY OF STRATEGIC CHANGE

Creating a new executive agency in the UK

Jobcentre Plus was created in 2002 by integrating two government services, one that had provided benefits to unemployed people and one that had assisted job seekers. The change was described by a Jobcentre Plus manager based in one of the regions as follows:

> ...about two or three years ago we had a network of Social Security Offices run by the Benefits Agency, and we had a network of Job Centres run through the Employment Service...September/October 2001 it would have been now, we had 56 Employment Jobcentre Plus offices. And that would have been the essence, the merging of both those services, so actually you [i.e. the public] had one office to go through, so you didn't go into one office to [look for] jobs, and another office to get your benefit. You actually merged the two together.
>
> (Interview with author in 2003)

The Prime Minister, who was Tony Blair, provided the political formulation of a vision in a statement to the House of Commons.

In a sense there was a vision, the Prime Minister in I think March 2000 set out the vision, the Government's vision, there was a statement in the House of Commons as to why the Government was doing this and what it wanted to achieve.

(Milner and Joyce 2005: 118)

Leigh Lewis had the responsibility of making the vision meaningful both within the civil service and also within and beyond the new organization:

... out of a whole set of discussions came gradually more detailed iterations of the Prime Minister's vision and they started to be drawn down to a lower level. I had a lot of influence in that process, but it was not my process to control in its entirety. I had to ensure that a lot of other stakeholders were alongside me, that Ministers were comfortable with the way we were articulating the Prime Minister's vision and so on. And there were a lot of people involved; first of all you have Government Departments with interests quite rightly to pursue and defend, so the interests of the Treasury is 'Is this going to cost a lot of money, what are we going to get from it, how are we going to know we are succeeding, what are the outcomes going to be, what are the targets going to be, were they stretching enough, were they tough enough?' You had the Secretaries of State most directly concerned wanting to be sure that the policy outcomes and objectives were the ones they wanted to achieve and not some group of objectives that belonged to somebody else, and it's not impossible of course in any Government system, that different departments have different competing priorities. And then you had a set of other stakeholders, stakeholders representing the staff, stakeholders representing the customers, stakeholders representing employers, etc., and again part of the challenge is to try and emerge with a vision and a way ahead and structures which command the confidence of the widest possible group of the people you are trying to work with, and it's not an easy process.

(Milner and Joyce 2005: 118–9)

A new office network of 1,000 merged offices was planned, and each of these was intended to offer an entirely new quality of service to the public who were to be treated like valued customers. Leigh Lewis, the first chief executive of Jobcentre Plus, commented on the offices of the past:

Former Social Security Offices that had not been lavished with investment were pretty grim places in many cases. They were not places you would want to stay in for any length of time. A single parent with a child would not have wanted to go into that environment.

(Interview with the author)

67

New offices were rolled out across the whole country, beginning with 56 in 2001–2. Resistance to the change began at the pilot stage. A strike was called by the Public and Commercial Services Union (PCSU) on the day the pilot offices opened, and the members called out were in the new offices. It was called because of what the union said was a safety issue – the absence of screens to protect their members from the public. Leigh Lewis saw the screens as an impediment to offering a high quality service to the clients of Jobcentre Plus. Putting up large screens in the new offices to keep the public separate from the staff working in the offices was not the kind of service environment that he wanted. He wanted it to be predominantly open plan and unscreened. In December 2001 there was a national strike on this issue with the union leader on record as saying that the new offices were unsafe. It lasted six months. However, the new agency, Jobcentre Plus, remained a largely unscreened environment.

When asked, Leigh Lewis said this about leadership:

> Leadership is about painting a picture. Leadership is about standing up at the front. Leadership is about saying we're here today, but we want to be there tomorrow. Leadership is about giving people the belief and confidence that they can get there. Leadership is saying I'm not going to ask you to do anything that I wouldn't do myself. Leadership is saying that I'll back you on the bad days as well as the good days if you are doing your best. Leadership is about saying I'm hugely demanding but I'm hugely supportive. I used to say that I was the organization's proudest champion and its fiercest critic, and in some ways that's what you've got to be in a leadership role, I think.
>
> (Interview with author in 2003)

A 2008 report by the UK Comptroller and Auditor General pronounced the introduction of a new office network in an executive agency of the Department of Work and Pensions as relatively well done, and said that it provided lessons to others. The development was described as a 'profound change in the way the largest government agency does business with its five million customers' (Comptroller and Auditor General 2008: 5). The Comptroller and Auditor's report concluded that the roll-out of the new offices had contributed to improvements in customer service while at the same time delivering savings against the agreed budget. The savings were estimated to be about £135 million per year by 2006–07.

The 2008 report on Jobcentre Plus identified six sets of lessons:

- **Communicating a vision of improvement**
  - ○ Senior management had provided leadership and communicated the vision and this resulted in staff buy in to the roll-out process.

- **Consistent leadership, strong governance and close monitoring by a central project management team**
  - o The experiences of the early stages of the change had led to an effective project management structure being set up (which included the formation of a stable core project management team and senior management assuming ownership and accountability for the change programme)
- **Planning in detail and developing a replicable process**
  - o Among other things, going for a single design for the new office allowed costs to be closely controlled
- **Change was managed well at sites that learnt from previous experience**
  - o Experienced implementation managers supported local managers in the set up of the new design offices
- **Using partnering to incentivize contractors to innovate and reduce costs**
  - o Target pricing and performance management was combined with a partnering approach in 2003 to create a positive relationship with contractors
- **Being prepared to learn as the roll-out progressed**
  - o The review of the initial phase of the roll-out led to the appointment of someone from the private sector as a works programme manager to make various adjustments to the change programme, including the adoption of a single design for the offices and changes to procurement arrangements.

Case questions:

1 Who was the strategic leader in this case and who created the vision for Jobcentre Plus?
2 What were the biggest leadership challenges in this change?
3 How did Leigh Lewis manage the key stakeholders?
4 Was the union being unreasonable? Could Jobcentre Plus have done something to avoid strike action?
5 Were the lessons of this case about handling technical problems or adaptive challenges?

CASE STUDY

Leading reform through strategic plans in the UK

The priorities set by the UK government in the period 2000–02 had some continuity with the five pledges made by the Labour Party in the 1997 General Election:

1 Health – cut waiting lists in the public health service

2　Education – cut class sizes for five to seven year olds

3　Crime – fast track punishment for persistent young offenders

4　Welfare – get under 25-year-olds off welfare and into work

5　Tax and Economy – no rise in income tax and keep inflation and interest rates low.

A government desire for a more integrated and joined up approach was made clear in the late 1990s, but it needed Number 10 Downing Street (the prime minister's organization), the Cabinet Office, the Treasury, and individual government departments to develop a sense of common purpose and to weave together their decision making processes. This weaving together involved, first, making use of the new system of Public Service Agreements (PSAs) created by the UK's Treasury. This was done by absorbing the 1998 PSA performance targets set by the Treasury into the formulation of the Prime Minister's government priorities. This meant that the subsequent attention given to ensuring the national priorities were delivered at the same time reinforced the PSA targets. Then, second, when the 2002 PSA performance targets were influenced by the performance targets set to track the delivery of the national priorities, this kept two key parts of the 'centre' working in unison. Barber (2007) outlined these and other steps in his account of the process of getting coherence between the Labour Party's political agenda, the Prime Minister's priorities, departmental strategies, and the new system of PSAs.

> ... we in the new Delivery Unit spent several long meetings with Treasury officials ... ensuring that the Prime Minister's new priorities and the PSA targets published in 2000 were brought into alignment. Indeed, the PSA targets became the basis of our work. ... The Treasury is always tough to negotiate with ... but we hammered out, for each of the departments the Delivery Unit was to work with, an agreed delivery contract, which set out both the prime ministerial priorities to which the department was committing and the measurable outcomes which would show whether or not they were on track to achieve them. These were then cleared by the Prime Minister ... and by the Chancellor, who accepted them once his justifiable concerns had been addressed ... In 2002, when refined PSA targets were negotiated as part of the spending review that year, the alignment achieved in 2001 was completed.
>
> (Barber 2007: 56–7)

One aspect of the process of developing a consensus between the various parts of the 'centre' was the care taken not to antagonize the Treasury by inadvertently encouraging government departments to think that a new channel was opening up for pressurizing the Treasury to increase budget allocations. This care, and other behind the scenes work, was successful in creating some cohesion between the Treasury and Number 10.

Trying to move to an integrated approach in the period 2000–02 was bound to look like the Prime Minister wanting a more centralized system, even if it was only that he wanted Number 10 to be able to steer and influence departments. If a more centralized approach did develop, it could lead to the government departments losing some sense of drive and initiative because they began to wait for leadership by Number 10 (see Campbell and Stott 2007: 566).

Getting a consensus on priorities is a significant achievement, but it has then to be turned into strategy and then action. In the summer of 2003, the then British Prime Minister, Tony Blair, challenged his cabinet ministers to think long-term.

> There are some policy solutions that neither party nor government want. But we have to do what we think is right for the long term. He [Blair] said 'There is no division in my mind between the need to reform and staying true to our values. It is not inconsistent. We are being true to our values in making the reforms needed to improve life for the people we represent.' He said he wanted people [i.e. ministers] to think over the summer about how that applied to their departments. Think long term.
>
> (Campbell and Stott 2007: 717–8)

In 2004 and 2005 a series of five-year plans were produced by UK government departments. For example, the Department for Education & Skills published a five-year strategy for children and learners. Michael Barber (2007) provided some insights into the Prime Minister's direct involvement in the creation of these strategies for the departments. Barber reports that in May 2004 the Prime Minister's focus was on:

> the culmination of a five-year strategy process ... he was now looking forward to irreversibly changing the public services so that, as he would put it, they could become self sustaining, self improving systems. One after another, ministers brought their plans before the Cabinet for debate, refinement and approval ... the five-year strategies that emerged ... of course involve contributions from many hands, but they were also a personal triumph for Blair. His constant cajoling, driving, persuading and urging pushed most of his ministers to be significantly more radical than they would otherwise have been, and dramatically more radical than the departments would have been if left to their own devices.
>
> (Barber 2007: 216)

It is important that strategy is developed and integrated with performance management and budgeting. In the UK case there was a need to link together two formally separate processes in 2003 and 2004 when there was both a strategy process and a spending review process. Barber (2007: 329), who had been the head of the Prime Minister's Delivery Unit (PMDU), has commented on the

71

2003–04 processes that they 'happened at the same time, but largely separately, which was utterly exhausting and, though the outcomes were miraculously, usually sensible, no one believed they had been maximized' (Barber 2007: 329). He also commented, 'there have been major positive strategic developments, but no one, least of all the participants, would argue that this has been the most efficient or elegant way to arrive at a strategy' (Barber 2007: 328). The process of producing departmental strategies in 2004–05 was summed up by him as 'draining and painstaking' (Barber 2007: 328).

Case questions:

1 How were politicians involved in strategic leadership in this case?
2 What were the key characteristics of the decision making process?
3 What conflicts occurred in this case and why did they occur?

SUMMARY

This chapter has been about the change situations faced by leaders in the public services. It has been concerned also with the barriers to change, including that barrier often referred to as resistance to change. The existing attempts to conceptualize and theorize change in different types of change situation create an additional issue: should models of leading change be understood as depending on whether the change situation is one of performance improvement, turnaround, strategic change, or public services reform? If those who have attempted to conceptualize and theorize leading change in these different situations have used different factors, or concluded that there are different factors at work, to what extent are they reflecting the different situations, or to what extent have they brought in prior assumptions about leadership of change?

Logically, the reform situation does seem to have something distinctive about it. This is that many reform programmes in different countries include the goal of putting the customer first. It follows, therefore, that leaders have to change their organizations to better suit the public, and this means disrupting those who work for the organization to put the public first. It is also likely that the public will be relatively silent beneficiaries (silent supporters) of reforms, whereas those who are disrupted or suffer loss will make clear to leaders that they are unhappy with the changes. Leaders in such a situation may find that they will have to endure opposition by employees to changes meant to provide a service until the new service becomes established – as happened in the case of Jobcentre Plus in 2002.

What has emerged from this chapter? Some of the points are as follows. First, leadership and leading change are generally seen as important factors in successful change. Second, some points have emerged as important in more than one model.

Take the importance of the outside. In the case of turnarounds, Borins identified the beginning of the process as the creation of a visible problem by interested groups outside the public organization – including the media, auditors, and electoral politics. In the study of strategic change by Pettigrew *et al.* the outside was important in terms of the environmental pressure for change. In this case, the researchers were keen to argue that the role of leadership is to take that external pressure and to turn it into change issues, or, at other times, to manage the pressure so that the change agenda does not become overloaded with too many priorities. In these ways, leaders take external attention and pressure and they orchestrate its influence within the organization to create strategic change and indeed, on occasion, innovative and transformational change. A key set of ideas from Pettigrew *et al.* concern the turning of external pressure into change through leaders working to ensure focus and persistence.

From Pettigrew and his colleagues we also get the idea that top-down change has to be combined with bottom-up concerns. From Pettigrew and his colleagues, and from Ostroff, we also have clear messages about the importance of ensuring the coherence and integration of change. Pettigrew *et al.* said, for example, that strategic changes need to align with operational and functional strategies. Ostroff also said that the approach to change should be a comprehensive one, which may be linked to the idea of designing an integrated system around change – and it may be speculated that this may be important for stabilizing the change.

If one concept has emerged as likely to prove of enduring interest, it is that of the receptive context (Pettigrew *et al.* 1992). A moment's thought will also suggest the possibility that this is in some way connected with a very familiar concept, that of resistance to change. Will the concept of entrepreneurial government also endure? It has an opposite concept in bureaucracy. Both of these concepts – receptive contexts and entrepreneurial governments – together provide parts of a new framework for viewing change and progress.

Work-based assignment: assessing readiness for change

The work-based assignments in this book are for civil servants and other public services staff who have four or more years of management experience.

■ This assignment is focused on assessing readiness for change. It is concerned with whether individuals, groups, and organizations are willing, supportive, or enthusiastic about a proposed change and, if so, to what extent they are willing, supportive, or enthusiastic. For example, there may be individuals who are supportive, but for whom the change is of marginal importance and so their readiness would be assessed as less than someone who is highly enthusiastic and keen to make the change a success

73

Table 3.2 *Importance and readiness chart*

Stakeholders	Importance of stakeholders (low, medium, high)	Readiness for change		
		Low	Medium	High
1				
2				
3				
4				
5				
6				

Table notes: Adapted from Beckhard and Harris (1987), page 63. An individual, group, or organization is rated as high in terms of state of readiness if it sees a specific change as a top priority for them and tends to welcome the change and support its implementation. Importance ratings of stakeholders may be based on an assessment of their power, influence, degree of need, etc., or combinations of things.

Table 3.3 *Commitment chart*

Individuals or groups or organizations	Commitment rating			
	No commitment	Let it happen	Help it happen	Make it happen
1		O		X
2		O	X	
3		O	X	
4	O		X	
5		O		
6	OX			

Notes: Adapted from Beckhard and Harris (1987). Current commitment might be shown by O and amount of commitment required by X.

■ Please prepare an importance and readiness chart (see Table 3.2) for a specific organization based on your understanding of how the stakeholders would react to a specific case of reinvention, modernization, or reform. Also, please outline the specific case of modernization or reform, and identify some implications of the assessments in the chart.

Work-based assignment: commitment

Please consider a current or recent change that you know well and prepare a commitment chart as a way of capturing your judgements about the amount of commitment that is needed (or was needed) from the stakeholders in order for the change to be a success (see Table 3.3). You may judge that some groups are unimportant and that no commitment is required from them. For other groups you may make the judgement that it is important that they are committed even if it is merely to the extent that they are prepared to let the change happen. From others you may want them to help it happen, or to take responsibility for making it happen. Such a commitment chart, when completed for all stakeholders, or for the most important stakeholders, demonstrates a meticulous approach to the assessment of the initial conditions for a change. This chart may be further developed by also showing the ratings of the current amounts of commitment for each of the stakeholders.

DISCUSSION QUESTIONS

1   Is change stemming from modernization of public services with the accent on putting customers or the public first different by definition from other change situations in public services? Are the principles of leadership of reform the same as for other types of change in the public services?

2   Is a turnaround just the same as any other strategic change in terms of the challenges faced by leadership?

3   Is the ideas of 'receptive contexts' an important concept for a leader to understand and, if so, what can a leader do to create them?

FURTHER READING

Ostroff, F. (2006) 'Change Management in Government', *Harvard Business Review*, 84, 5: 141–47.

Pettigrew, A., Ferlie, E., and McKee, L. (1992) *Shaping Strategic Change*. London: Sage.

Chapter 4

The political context

In local government, to quote the old maxim, 'to govern is to choose'; the issues behind strategic plans are invariably about the application of scarce resources to meet key priorities in the absence of compelling scientific evidence. Roger Latham, former chief executive of an English county council and currently Visiting Fellow of Nottingham Trent University (NTU) Business School

INTRODUCTION

The system of government and the political context are bound to be important in determining the circumstances of strategic leadership in the public services. Strategic leaders in the public services may themselves be politicians. So, they are part of the political process, and in a democratic system of government, they are supposed to be responsive to the wishes of the public. If they are not themselves politicians, they may well be directed by politicians or operate within organizational and budgetary frameworks created by politicians. In their interactions with politicians, the strategic leaders may have varying orientations to the legal and political mandates that they are meant to follow. For example, in a democracy they may see themselves as servants of a democratic political process and the decisions of politicians as legitimate orders. However, this is not to be taken for granted. They may see political decisions as ill informed and irredeemably short-term, and politicians may be seen as careerist and opportunistic.

They may see themselves as required to act neutrally in the implementation of political decisions, or they may welcome the role of working as the partners of politicians (maybe the junior partners) in leading the public services.

Then there is the public and the pressure groups to consider. The former – the public in general – may be important to strategic leaders because they form the consumers of public services. If not consumers as such, the public may be affected by the activities of the public services organization. Strategic leaders may also see the public as important in the decision making process, for example, important in refining the thinking in strategic plans produced by ministers. Pressure groups may be important because they influence the politicians who then author policies for implementation by strategic leaders. Or the pressure groups may be brought into direct involvement in strategic planning by strategic leaders seeking partnership, working with organizations in civil society to address community problems.

This is by no means exhaustive of the salient factors to be considered in the political context of strategic leaders, nor of the types of relationships that may be developed by strategic leaders with politicians, the public, and pressure groups. The bare bones of the parties and processes that need to be comprehended in exploring the importance of the political context are represented in the diagram at Figure 4.1, which cannot do justice to the institutional and cultural variations and evolutionary changes that impinge on strategic leadership in the public services. For example, a minimalist definition of democracy might say it is a political system that has universal suffrage, but democratic systems evolve and mature, entailing changes in their structures and culture. So the experiences of a strategic leader, in the context of a bureaucratic culture and paternalistic attitudes to the relationship with citizens (especially the less well off), might be vastly different from a strategic leader in a post-bureaucratic culture in

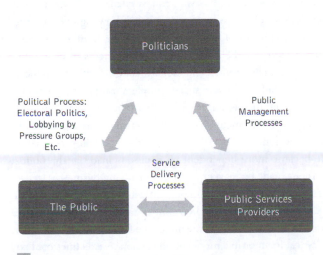

Figure 4.1 *Politics and public services*

which empowerment of the public was stressed and the state adopted more of a 'steering role' function than a provision of public services function (Osborne and Gaebler 1992; OECD 2000).

In this chapter, the aim is to increase our awareness of the nature and effects of the political context on strategic leaders in public services. In the course of it we will look at systems of government and public services, volatility in public concerns, and the interface between politicians on one hand and civil servants and executive managers of public services on the other. Also in this chapter, we consider how issues of concern to the public relate to political priorities and how policy making as a process (see Concept Box 4.1) relates to strategic management in government.

CONCEPT BOX 4.1   POLICY MAKING

Policy making – meaning the manner in which ministers interpret the programme for government, identify priority areas of public need, and resolve competing service demands in a resource constrained environment.

(PA Consulting 2002: 5)

SYSTEMS OF GOVERNMENT AND PUBLIC SERVICES

Sometimes it is necessary to take a very long-term view of the changes within government systems in order to appreciate the impact of fundamental changes in their institutions and culture. One of the clearest examples of this is provided by the smaller democracies of northern Europe (Denmark, Norway, and Sweden). Only when their history was reviewed over decades did it become apparent just how significant were the changes that had taken place in terms of the relationships between interest groups in society (Hibbs 1976, 1978; Korpi and Shalev 1979). In the process of evolution, these societies developed large public sectors and welfare states. Critical for these developments were the post-second world war success in electoral politics of Social Democratic and Labour parties and the organizational unity of the labour movements in these countries. Left of centre governments increased government expenditure (as a percentage of GDP (gross domestic product)) and the standard of living and quality of life of ordinary people became more dependent on decisions made in the political process, as against decisions made by market processes involving businesses, trade unions, and customers. These welfare states could be contrasted with countries such as the United States and Canada, sometimes labelled 'Anglo-Saxon' countries, where the market remained a more central institution in terms of the fate of ordinary people. The welfare state, in its classical form or in a modernized version, is a distinct context for strategic leadership in the public services.

The welfare state has tended to come under pressure in northern Europe. This could have been triggered by the changing attitudes of the public. It should be noted that the average tax rates for blue collar or industrial workers in welfare states was higher in percentage terms than in the other countries (Hibbs 1978). Arguably, the high direct personal taxation of these groups changed their attitude towards the performance and costs of the welfare state in the 1970s and in later years. This had repercussions electorally. Political parties that stood on anti-welfare state policies grew in popularity. In Denmark, in the 1973 election, the Progress party stood on a programme of 'reductions in the state bureaucracy, social expenditure and taxation' (Hibbs 1978: 174). An anti-welfare state political party also emerged in Norway in the same year. In Sweden, there was a growth of opposition to welfare policies and the Social Democrat Party suffered its first defeat in nearly 50 years in the elections of 1976. This evidence led Hibbs to conclude that the political base of the welfare state was crumbling. The obvious point is that democratic societies are evolving social organisms, and strategic leaders in public services inevitably have an important part to play in these evolutions.

The changes in public attitudes to the welfare state surely create complex dilemmas and tensions not only for politicians, but also for all strategic leaders in public services. This is because the driver of change may not be a carefully calibrated change of position by the public so much as the interaction between a basically contradictory set of public attitudes to spending on public services and taxes. This may explain the fluctuating fortunes of political parties of the right and the left who overplay their hand at times on tax cuts and reductions in public services, and at other times on investment in public services. The existence of contradictory attitudes certainly appeared to be the case in Britain during the election in 2005 (see Research Box 4.1).

RESEARCH BOX 4.1   ON-LINE ARTICLE BY ANTHONY KING, PROFESSOR OF GOVERNMENT AT ESSEX UNIVERSITY

Professor Anthony King discussed the findings of a YouGov survey for The Telegraph during the run up to the 2005 General Election in Britain:

[...] the belief persists that Britain is a highly taxed country by European standards. In fact, the tax take in Britain is somewhat below the west European average. Be that as it may, people's conviction that they are over-taxed cries out from YouGov's findings. Between half and two thirds of people, 59 per cent, believe that they personally pay too much in tax. Only about half that proportion, 28 per cent, reckon they pay about the right amount. Almost no one reckons he or she pays too little. [...] A large majority,

71 per cent, agree with the Conservatives that 'a considerable proportion of the money that the Government raises in taxes is wasted'. Moreover, they are confident they can identify how the money is wasted: on incompetent and redundant managers, excessive form-filling, needless duplication and excessive regulation. [. . .] People usually say they want service improvements even if it means higher taxes. As the figures in the section of the chart headed 'Taxes vs. spending' indicate, twice as many people currently opt for higher taxes as opt for cuts. [. . .] YouGov asked bluntly: 'Would you support a policy which required you personally to pay higher taxes in order to increase spending on public services?' . . . the majority response is 'No'. Well over half, 53 per cent, would oppose any such tax-raising policy. Fewer than a third, 29 per cent, would support it. The message is clear. A lot of people want higher taxes to pay for better services – so long as others pay.

Source: The Telegraph on-line http://www.telegraph.co.uk/news/main.jhtml?xml=/news/2005/04/18/nelec118.xml Downloaded on 9 May 2005

In the context of these contradictory public attitudes, politicians and strategic leaders in public services may see innovation, modernization, and reform as a way of reconciling the desire for lower taxes and better public services at the same time. The processes of innovation, modernization, and reform can originate in a straightforward way from public pressure through electoral politics, then through the making of policy on public services, and finally through plans and actions to change public services systems and organizations. However, not all attempts at reform and modernization can be understood in this way. There are other motives and pressures at play, and it might be predicted that different systems of government and different political contexts might require different interpretations of the causes of reform and modernization.

A significantly different government system from that of the small democracies of northern Europe is to be found in countries with arrangements that correspond more or less closely to what Pollitt and Bouckaert (2004) call the Neo-Weberian state. These countries include Belgium, France, Germany, and Italy, which are said to be structurally and culturally very different from 'Anglo-Saxon' countries such as Australia, New Zealand, the UK, the USA, and Canada. The Neo-Weberian state countries are said to have strong administrative traditions. Arguably, these Neo-Weberian states are characterized by a style of bureaucratic impersonality in the design and provision of services, an emphasis on a legal framework to govern the activities and conduct of public servants, and a focus on policy making and implementation as a legally-oriented activity. Maybe we could also include Turkey in this grouping, not only because it was in the past influenced by the French experience of government and public administration, but also because its civil service is very concerned with law making processes and providing civil servants with legal mandates for their actions.

Neo-Weberian, or bureaucratic, states have also engaged with reform and modernization. Perhaps sometimes it has been to emulate the example set by reforming politicians in other countries. Sometimes it may even be seen as reinforcing the effectiveness of bureaucratic mechanisms (such as the LOLF (*Loi Organique relative aux Lois de Finances*) Constitutional Bylaw on Budget Acts reforms in France). In some cases countries have reformed and modernized their public administration as part of a process of accession to the European Union (e.g. Turkey). The motivation to modernize and reform public service cannot all be put down to politicians reacting to ordinary tax payers wanting both better services and lower taxes at the same time.

Again, this is far from exhaustive as a discussion of government systems and political context, but the point being made is that the strategic leader in public services could be operating in very different states, including a welfare state, a modernized welfare state, a Neo-Weberian state, a more private market-oriented state, and so on. Moreover, the strategic leader could be in a state that is in an evolutionary phase requiring adaptation and adjustments in the size and pattern of public services.

PUBLIC NEED VOLATILITY

Some years ago Nutt and Backoff (1992: 420) provided the following rationale for the use of continuous strategic management by leaders:

> In the future, the leaders of public and third sector organizations must find a way to create and manage transformations. Transformation is required continuously . . . in response to dynamically changing needs that will characterize the future of most organizations with public features. Turbulent environments have high need for action and call for collaborative responses . . . This process calls for continuous strategic management that is carried out by the organizational leader . . .

The reality of dynamically changing needs can be evidenced by looking at how the public's perceptions of what are the big issues changes in just a short space of time. Take the case of the UK. When the Blair Administration was elected in 1997, the two biggest issues according to the public were the NHS and education (including schools). Twelve years later in the last year of the Labour Government, the two biggest issues according to the public were the economy and crime. In fact, the economy was way out in front as an issue, and unemployment had resurfaced as an issue after eight years of being relatively unimportant. Maybe some of these changes can be seen as resulting from the success of the government's investment and reform policies, but the explosion of concern about the economy in 2008 was a result of the banking crisis. So, not only have governments that wish to be responsive to public concerns got to keep an eye on changing attitudes among the public, they have also to be ready to respond to a crisis that has not been anticipated (see Figure 4.2 and Table 4.1).

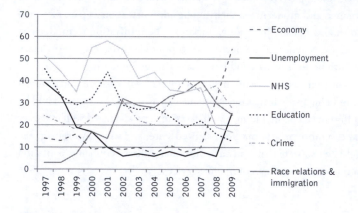

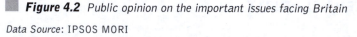

Figure 4.2 *Public opinion on the important issues facing Britain*

Data Source: IPSOS MORI

Table 4.1 *Percentage of the public thinking an issue facing Britain was important, 1997–2009*

	Economy	Unemployment	NHS	Education	Crime	Race relations & immigration
1997	14	39	51	45	24	3
1998	13	33	44	33	21	3
1999	16	19	35	29	18	7
2000	9	17	55	32	23	17
2001	10	10	58	44	29	14
2002	9	6	54	29	31	32
2003	10	7	41	27	22	29
2004	7	6	44	28	20	28
2005	11	8	36	24	30	33
2006	8	6	35	19	41	35
2007	10	8	37	22	35	40
2008	32	6	19	16	38	30
2009	54	25	17	13	28	25

POLITICIANS AND PRIORITIES

If the government of a country wishes to act on the basis of strategic thinking, where is the correct starting point? One possible answer is that it needs to start with a strategic vision. The centrality and usefulness of a vision is made clear in the following statement (OECD 2000: 13):

> A common vision serves to unify political leaders, senior officials, front-line workers and the general public. It also provides a guideline for choosing goals, for developing strategies to achieve those goals and for measuring results. In order to articulate a common vision, government should learn to consult with stakeholders and bring together their many, varied visions.

While it may be tempting to begin strategic planning and management with the formulation of a strategic vision, political leaders in the public services seem to be more comfortable in using priorities as a starting point. For elected politicians, it seems, 'priorities' carries the weight that 'visions' and 'missions' do in the private sector. 'In any government you need to ensure there are ways of setting the overall strategy, what you are trying to achieve, why and what is a priority and what is not' (Mulgan 2007: Ev11) (evidence given to Public Administration Select Committee). Politicians often use the word priority. Before he became Prime Minister, Tony Blair (1996: xi) said: 'Government can give a lead, set priorities, work in partnership with private and voluntary sectors, stand up for the majority and not just the few.' Gordon Brown used the word priority in his first major speech on the NHS as the UK's Prime Minister. In early 2008 he said: 'It is because the NHS has been a central priority since June that we have made immediate changes to improve safety and cleanliness in every hospital – beginning the deep cleaning of our wards, making provision for MRSA screening for all patients entering hospital, and giving matrons new powers to report safety concerns direct to the Care Quality Commission.' (http://www.number-10.gov.uk/output/Page14171.asp; accessed 25 January 2008). The word priority is so often used by politicians that we might say that successful politicians naturally speak the language of priorities.

Politicians may arrive at their overall priorities through consideration of the findings of surveys and focus groups. Some priorities may come from more direct interaction with the public. For instance, it has been said that public concern about anti-social behaviour came to the notice of MPs in the UK through their constituency work. MPs were told of this problem directly and face to face by citizens whom they met in their constituencies.

Setting priorities is, arguably, inevitably a very political process in which both values and interests are involved. Politicians who espouse a democratic relationship to society or a community may see in priority-setting an opportunity to draw on the values of the society or the community, and we often look to politicians to resolve issues of priority-setting created by the existence of competing interest groups. Moreover, it is sometimes obvious that elected politicians at local government level adopt, or are influenced in their priorities by, those priorities established by elected politicians at national level, perhaps reflecting an assumption about the mandates of local and national politicians.

Priorities may be seen as equivalent to the concept of key performance areas as used in strategic management. Duncan *et al.* (1995: 198) define key performance areas as a few key areas of activity necessary for an organization to achieve its purpose. Textbooks might suggest that key performance areas can be best identified after a mission statement has been clarified. But as used by contemporary politicians, key performance areas are priorities that represent a focused expression of their political values. An example of this would be the UK government's overall political priorities from 2001–07 which were health, education, crime and transport (Seldon 2007: 19). These key performance areas reflected a set of political values, and they also clearly aligned to the top issues as seen by the public between 1997 and 2005. For a government interested in 'the many and not the few', and aware of dissatisfaction of many ordinary people with the service they were getting from the NHS and state schools, these priorities provided the first clear statement of strategic intent. They provided the framework for a set of national performance indicators that were monitored, reported to the media, and discussed in progress reports and discussion documents.

Obviously, it is important that once the overall priorities are set by a government or an organization that they are actually the basis for strategic planning. Conversely, because strategic planning will involve situational analysis, there is potential for strategic planning to generate an implicit set of priorities that are in conflict with those of the politicians. This means that politicians may worry that their support for strategic planning by senior civil servants or top managers may backfire and produce goals that are not aligned to their political priorities. In effect, there is a danger that strategic thinking in the civil service or by top managers may lead to rival strategic agendas. Presumably, politicians will be happier about supporting strategic planning if they believe that it will advance achievement of their political priorities and not get in the way of them.

The problem of linking political priorities to strategic thinking and planning may be part of what Mulgan had in mind when giving evidence to a House of Commons Public Administration Select Committee (Mulgan 2007: Ev3):

> What has happened in the last eight years is some basic bits of machinery which make government more inherently long term . . . They include the creation of strategic capacity . . . We have seen a big improvement in the methods being used to think about the future . . . None of this is easy. It is bound to clash often with political priorities. It only works if the top politicians really want it to happen . . .

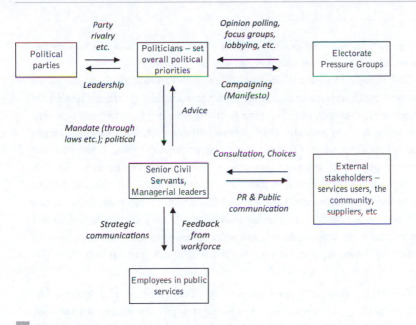

Figure 4.3 *Influences on the formation and impact of political priorities*

As Figure 4.3 shows, overall political priorities are potentially influenced by the electorate, senior civil servants, political parties, pressure groups, public service users, and many more groups and organizations.

Geoff Mulgan, in evidence to the UK's House of Commons Public Administration Select Committee in 2005, also pointed out the need for government departments to understand such priorities, and how special advisers could help with this (Mulgan 2007: Ev3): 'Where special advisers are doing their job well, they generally oil the wheels, getting things done, or helping departments understand ministers' priorities and so on.' In the UK, the special advisers have played a crucial role in relaying and interpreting political priorities to senior civil servants. (Evidence given to Public Administration Select Committee, 'Governing the Future' – second report of session 2006–7, volume 2, Ev3)

THINK POINT: WHY IS SETTING PRIORITIES SO IMPORTANT?

Setting priorities is about making choices. Governments and individual public service organizations confront situations that appear to offer a multitude of problems and opportunities. Strategic management is about making changes to achieve better futures, but what problems and what opportunities should be addressed? So many different lines of action seem possible, so where should government or the individual organization make a start?

Choices have to be made because of resource rationing. This is true of all sectors – public, private, and voluntary – but perhaps this is more challenging for government organizations because their activity is funded from tax, and thus they are always faced by pressures from citizens and interest groups wanting a larger share of public spending. There is a general appreciation nowadays that there will be a constant search in government services for savings and efficiency gains. We can support this contention with some findings of the OECD. After two decades of public services reforms, the OECD (2005) found that, although governments had a larger not a smaller role, general government primary outlays had remained broadly the same when looked at in cyclically adjusted terms and that upward pressure on expenditure remained. The OECD (2005: 21) concluded:

> For OECD countries, improving the cost-effectiveness and performance of their public sectors will help to reduce pressure on spending. As the past decade has shown, however, this in itself is unlikely to stem the continued upward pressure on expenditure generated by social entitlement programmes and social transfers. Public sector reform is not a substitute for the hard and, in many cases, unpopular choices that politicians have to make in some countries if long-term difficulties are to be avoided.

Summing up, setting overall priorities is made essential because there is a limit to the availability of a range of critical resources, not just money, but also resources such as management attention, public support, expertize, etc. 'If resources were unlimited, priorities would not need to be set because all needs could be met' (York 1982: 92).

THE INTERFACE BETWEEN POLITICIANS AND CIVIL SERVANTS AND PUBLIC MANAGERS

In a very responsive and democratic system of government we could expect politicians to make promises to the public in political manifestos. These promises would identify priorities and maybe even policies designed to address issues that are at the top of public concerns. Only after a few years in government would the politicians be able to know if their policies were the right ones and were having an effect that would be noticed and appreciated by the public. It might be hoped, if the policies were right, that the issues would be fading as public concerns and satisfaction with the government would be increasing. If the policies were wrong, then maybe criticisms of the government from the public would be increasing. These feedback loops could, theoretically speaking, drive policy learning by politicians.

Establishing priorities and defining key desired outcomes can be seen as part of the policy making process. It can also be useful to see setting priorities as a stage preceding policy making. One good reason for doing this is that priorities are key performance areas, and areas where governments intend to make a difference, but the policy represents (at least logically speaking) solutions to the issues concerning the public. The politicians may be offering to make an issue a priority, but may not at the outset have identified or even know a solution. The solutions may not be immediately obvious and may require politicians to learn from experience of applying new policies. Early on, a government may think it knows the solutions and confidently attempts to implement them only to discover they fail to have the required impact. If policy failures cannot be attributed to failures in planning and executing implementation, then they may be caused by the wrong policies. It may be simply that the policies are just not big enough to address fully the problems, and then politicians may have to find new policies with a bigger impact.

Such learning by politicians must be quite complex. It would not just be a matter of finding out about and evaluating the consequences of policies. The mechanisms by which policies succeeded or failed would also need to be understood. What were the institutional factors? What pressures to maintain the status quo were at work? How were expectations of the public changing? What was a realistic time frame to achieve success with a new policy? And so on.

Policies may be turned into strategies by civil servants. This is the view contained in the following remarks by Perrott (1996: 338) on the relationship between strategy and policy in the public sector of Western countries:

> In the Western model a public sector organization's primary focus and raison d'être is to effectively deliver a range of services to nominated consumer groups. Strategies regarding the nature, pricing, distribution and communication of the services offered, initially stems from the policy formulated by the ministers in charge of the particular service portfolio. Ministers are elected representatives of the people and supervise a specified portfolio of public services under an Act of Parliament, e.g. Consumer Affairs, Education etc.

These remarks of Perrott are a useful starting point for looking at the relationship between politicians and civil servants, and between policy making and strategy. In his view, policy comes first and is formulated by ministers. Then, second, strategy stems from policy, or we might say policy is then embedded in a strategic plan. Perrott goes on to remark that it is becoming more common that public sector organizations have to get their strategic plans approved by ministers. So, the elected politicians formulate

policies and top civil servants and public sector managers formulate strategies. However, in practice this simple division of labour may be giving way to more complex
fusions of policy making and strategy making as the elected politicians attempt to
develop long-term thinking (see Figure 4.4).

Boyle (1995a: 39–40) writing with reference to the Irish civil service, shortly after
an attempt to introduce strategic management into the work of the civil service, also
endorsed the strategic dimension to the work of civil service leaders: 'It is clear however, particularly from the strategic management initiative, that civil servants have
a major role to play in developing strategic thinking and processes in the civil service . . . the task of the civil servant is to stimulate strategic thinking and operationalize
strategic processes. . . .'

Also with reference to the Irish situation, PA Consulting Group summarized the
requirement of the Delivering Better Government (DBG) programme as follows
(2002: 26):

> It is important to clarify the role of Ministers and civil servants in the prepara-
> tion of Statements of Strategy. DBG is clear on the point that 'responsibility for
> the formulation of policy and for ensuring appropriate arrangements lies with the
> Minister/Minister of State'. Equally it is argued that the outcomes of such policies
> must be determined by the political level. Thereafter, once policy (and its associ-
> ated outcomes) have been established as a 'given', it becomes the responsibility of
> civil servants to identify and select strategies which will produce a set of outputs

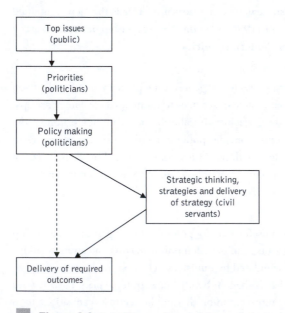

 **Figure 4.4** *Priorities, policy making and strategic thinking*

which will in turn deliver the policy outcomes required. This process rests on the supposition that clearly defined policies and outcomes are in place prior to the preparation of the Strategy Statement. Our discussions with both politicians and with senior civil servants lead us to believe that this is not always necessarily the case, and that to some extent at least the process of policy development can become 'bundled up' with that of strategy making.

Figure 4.5 is broadly consistent with these remarks about how policy making and strategic management was supposed to work in Ireland.

The picture so far is only one possible way in which politicians and civil servants may operate in relation to public management. First, there are examples in which the strategic planning is led by the politicians and it is fully justified to describe the role of civil servants as delivering the strategic plans of government ministers. Second, it is arguable that, because of their role in implementation, civil servants are becoming more political. Kooiman and van Vliet (1993: 65) see this as a trend in a number of societies:

> In modern society with all its new problems and opportunities (due to complex-
> ity, dynamics and diversity), the traditional Weberian distinction between the
> political system and the administrative apparatus can no longer be contained. In
> societies where policy making and policy implementation are interactive and can
> be seen as co-products of governmental agencies and their clientele groups, pub-
> lic managing is more and more 'political' in the traditional sense. Also the civil
> servant sets the agenda, promotes or hampers consensus, wins social support and
> makes bargains.

Third, the activities of politicians and civil servants in policy making is a much more negotiated, confusing, and even chaotic experience than might be suggested by some

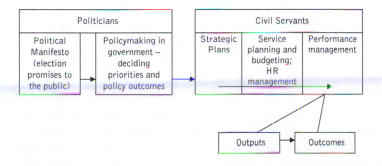

Figure 4.5 *Politicians and civil servants*

89

of the models of it as a linear or cyclical process. These are just models representing reality and not the reality itself.

Negotiations over policy go on between members of government, between government departments, and even between elected politicians and their parties. Some of the confusion occurs where the political leadership is fractured too deeply by factionalism and cohesion is lost. For example, individual ministers and their departments may find themselves confused about the actual direction of government, and even whom they should follow in the leadership.

Some sense of this, at times, chaotic nature emerged in a 2005 session of a Select Committee of the House of Commons in the UK. Gordon Prentice, a Labour Member of Parliament, said in the Select Committee that he sometimes did not know where policies came from and he asked Geoff Mulgan, previously head of policy in the Prime Minister's office, had he ever been surprised and not known something was government policy. Geoff Mulgan confirmed that there were times when both ministers and civil servants were surprised:

> When I was head of policy at Number 10 and running the Strategy Unit I did get a huge flow over my desk of what was in the pipeline for white papers and legislation and media announcements and so on. For any modern government the sheer volume of decision making taking place in departments and in bits of departments means that no human being can ever be completely on the top of every detail of every issue and they do experience surprise when they come across things happening. (Evidence given to House of Commons Public Administration Select Committee, 'Governing the Future' – second report of session 2006–7, volume 2, Ev9)

New policy can come from a political manifesto from an election campaign, but it can also emerge in other ways. Policy that is put into a manifesto can even emerge from government strategic planning, as it did in the UK in 2003–4. It can also be partly the result of work and advice by civil servants in specific departments during a period of government. We have probably not acknowledged sufficiently the influential role of senior civil servants and public services executives in deciding priorities and formulating policies. The matrix in Figure 4.6 (which has been adapted from the original) suggests how this influence might be framed bearing in mind that giving advice needs to take account of the strength of feeling of the politicians on one hand, and the assessment of the needs of the public on the other. This matrix is applicable to evaluations of government policies (defined in this case as government programmes and public services), but is interesting for its implication that politicians and the public should be of most importance in the role network of the civil servants and public services executives. In practice, of course, their advice and influence might on occasions also be heavily weighted towards the concerns of those who work in the civil service or public service organization.

Adapted from matrix of Les Prince and Ray Puffitt (2001)

High	Advise Programme/ Service not Needed	Recommend Maintain Programme/ Service
Level of politicians' concern (priority)	Recommend End Programme/ Service	Advise Case for Importance of Programme/ Service
	Low	**High**

Needs of the 'client group'

Figure 4.6 Matrix – working with politicians

IMPROVING WORKING ACROSS THE PUBLIC MANAGEMENT INTERFACE

In the case of central government departments, civil servants may wonder how they can ensure they have effective working relationships with ministers on strategy. Where there is an improvement in working with ministers, civil servants may find they can more easily move forward with strategy, as appears to have happened recently in the case of the UK's DfES (Capability Reviews Team 2007: 33).

The view taken in the PA Consulting Group report on the Irish situation (referred to above) was that the processes linking policy formulation and strategy design could be improved. In other words, the PA Consulting Group report expressed concern about the way in which the process of policy making turned into strategy. It was argued that it was possible to get a much better connection between the policy formulation work of the elected politicians and the management work of the senior civil servants in terms of strategy formulation.

It can be noted that there is a more subtle view of the relationship between politicians and civil servants than the one that identifies elected politicians as responsible for policy and concerned with outcomes, and senior civil servants as responsible for strategies to deliver the policies and concerned with outputs. Arguably, there is a case for a crossover of responsibilities with civil servants being junior partners in policy making and elected politicians needing to be more actively interested in policy implementation through some involvement in strategic planning. The elected politicians and senior civil servants both need to work together across the interface between them, so that politicians feel they have an ability to shape day to day operations and the civil servants feel they have a policy framework they can implement effectively.

91

POLICY MAKING WHICH IS ITSELF STRATEGIC

When politicians become strategic leaders themselves, the traditional notion of policy making may itself have to change. This is suggested by the following argument for a more strategic and innovative approach to policy, outlined in a speech by Tony Blair in 2004 on civil service reform:

> Strategic policy making is a professional discipline in itself involving serious analysis of the current state of affairs, scanning future trends and seeking out developments elsewhere to generate options; and then thinking through rigorously the steps it would take to get from here to there. I find too often that civil servants have not put forward a proposal either because they thought it would not be acceptable politically or because it simply seemed too radical. I always say be bold in putting forward proposals; don't be afraid to recommend ideal solutions that look impractical; it is my job and the job of ministers to decide whether something can and should be done but our thinking will be the poorer if too many ideas are ruled out before they get to us. Both the DfES and the Department of Health are currently seeking to recruit professional heads of strategy to strengthen this function.
>
> (http://www.number10.gov.uk/output/Page5399.asp;
> accessed on 4 December 2007)

Traditional policy making by government could be defined as being a decision making process about how a governmental priority area (such as the economy or education) or a political issue (e.g. rising levels of unemployment or literacy) will be addressed. For example, policies may identify programmes or projects that will be set up to deal with them. However, when policy making becomes strategic it is developed, enriched, because policy makers give special attention to looking ahead ('scanning future trends'), and to assessing the feasibility of planned action and the likelihood of successful outcomes ('thinking through rigorously the steps it would take to get from here to there').

An important UK development in terms of both policy making and the strategic capability of government in recent years has been the creation of central units at the heart of government. Such units can prepare reports that are then considered by ministers, and become the basis of government decisions. In April 2006, Lord Birt told a House of Commons Select Committee about one of these units that was responsible for taking a long-term view and thus enabling future policy to be developed:

> . . . the Strategy Unit has been supporting the Cabinet committee system . . . The Strategy Unit is a major unit, not only valued by the Prime Minister but I think by

all ministers who encounter it, and the unit is responsible for a very large body of work . . . They are not in any sense marginal, they are absolutely central to the formulation of government policy. (Evidence given to House of Commons Public Administration Select Committee, 'Governing the Future' – second report of session 2006–7, volume 2, Ev47)

Obviously, a key question here is who or what determines the work of the central units? The Strategy Unit, set up under the Blair Government, was said by Geoff Mulgan to have had a fairly open process, and this meant that the work it did might be instigated by the Prime Minister, but might also originate from members of the Unit and others.

THE PUBLIC

In the 1990s Mark Moore (1995) popularized the notion of public value in his book on strategic management in government. He suggested that public value is activity by government organizations that satisfies the desires of citizens and clients (Moore 1995: 53). How can this public value be measured? There are many options, and he said one approach is to measure customer satisfaction (Moore 1995: 22), but however it is measured, at the end of the day, judging public value is down to politics (Moore 1995: 38). This seems to mean that public value in a democratic society has to be judged by politicians, and not by market forces.

A recurrent aspiration in many countries has been to empower the public in relation to the design and reshaping of public services. Essentially, there is often a concern that voting in elections every few years is not enough power for the public, and that other channels for 'empowerment' of the public are also desirable. These other channels include involving members of the public in policy making, in strategic planning, and in choosing as consumers the providers of public services.

Taking the involvement in policy making first, Geoff Mulgan, previously head of the UK government's Policy Unit and Forward Strategy Unit, drew attention to the importance of involving the public for purposes of building support for reforms and made the following negative appraisal of success so far in attempts to be inclusive in the formulation of policy on illegal drugs:

. . . there have been many expert commissions and reviews, but not ones which actually have involved large sections of the public who remain quite resistant to many reforms which otherwise rational people who study the issues in detail support and that therefore creates a blockage in terms of political possibilities and creates a rationale for the media often to take up very knee-jerk positions on drugs. That is probably an example of the sort of issue where we need to think much more radically about ways of involving large sections of the public in the policy process and not just officials, ministers and experts. (Evidence given to House of Commons Public Administration Select Committee, 'Governing the Future' – second report of session 2006–7, volume 2, Ev6)

Attempts to engage the public with strategy and long-term thinking have been conducted by individual government departments. The UK's DfES, for example, planned regional events in late 2006 to find out the views of partners and service users on a strategy document. The Department also invited comments to be sent direct to the Strategy Unit of the DfES.

It has been argued many times that younger generations of the population in society expect more ability to make choices according to their own individual priorities and that the public generally has learnt from experiences of being a consumer in the private sector that it wants greater choice. A policy review process by the UK government a few years ago covered the public services and presented some evidence on the popularity of the choice approach to public empowerment (Prime Minister's Strategy Unit, Cabinet Office 2007a: 34):

Citizens want to have a greater ability to take important decisions that directly affect their lives. For example, 63 per cent of people believe that they should have 'a great deal' or 'quite a lot' of choice over which hospital they go to for treatment. People from lower socio-economic groups are the most in favour of more choice. A MORI poll in 2004 found that people in social classes D and E were most likely to consider choice 'absolutely essential' . . . This finding is supported by the British Social Attitudes Survey.

The degree of public empowerment through public channels may still be modest, but the public is not without power and some of its power is the power of public opinion. Politicians may encounter the power of public opinion when attempts are being made to design and implement programmes based on government's official political priorities. Government has to have an expectation that it can deliver improvements in its performance in the priority area in question and also maintain public support for it as a priority. When this is not the case, a priority may get sidelined. This conclusion seems consistent with developments in the UK over the period 2000–05 specifically in respect of transport as a key performance area of the government. So, it looks as though doubts about the feasibility and public acceptability of ideas for strategic actions to make improvements (e.g. road pricing), and also disappointing delivery results against performance targets (e.g. road congestion), may cause politicians to downgrade an area as a priority.

CASE STUDY

Transport Policy in the UK 2000–05

In 2001, transport was one of four priority areas for the UK government. It was hoping to improve both road congestion and rail punctuality. Over the next three or four years the focus of government on this transport area was changed. Not only was a road congestion target dropped in 2002 (Barber 2007: 389), but also transport's importance as a key performance area seemed to have faded by 2004.

Why did the focus on transport as a key performance area change? Even before the UK government had sorted out ways of measuring its performance on transport in 2001, events showed that transport could become a political hot potato. In September 2000 there was a campaign of protests at fuel prices by UK hauliers. The hauliers achieved an enormous impact for their protests by blockading oil refineries. The Prime Minister apparently saw these protests as political in nature, expressing the view that 'a lot of the forces at work were political' (Campbell and Stott 2007: 470). During the protests and blockades, which lasted for a number of days until the middle of September, a keen interest was taken by the government in how the media reported what was happening. Was this a mass protest by the public or the actions of a tiny minority? To what extent were the hauliers protesting on behalf of taxpayers generally, or to what extent were they a small group of people with only their own vested interests in mind? At the same time, the government had to communicate with the public in a way that maintained public support for the government's line. The Prime Minister evidently told Alistair Campbell that, 'on the question of tax and spend, we had to broaden it out, make it about schools and hospitals, and the cuts they would threaten' (Campbell and Stott 2007: 473). At the end of the protests against fuel prices, there was a political stock-take: 'Though some of the papers were willing to acknowledge TB [the Prime Minister] had stood firm, the sense nonetheless of a victory of sorts for the protesters and a defeat for TB. Philip [Gould, adviser to the Prime Minister,] did some [focus] groups last night which were not as bad as they might have been' (Campbell and Stott 2007: 473).

What happened next might be interpreted as a failure of confidence among politicians in radical ideas for modernization of transport, such as the idea of road pricing for current capacity. A report on feasibility was published in 2004, but a 5-year strategy for transport, also published in 2004, merely said the time had come to consider seriously road pricing policy for current capacity. It also proposed that government would be leading the debate on road pricing and seeking to build a public consensus around the objectives of road charging. This seems to suggest that government was now doubtful about the public acceptability of road pricing in respect of current capacity.

95

In the light of the political protests over fuel prices by hauliers in 2000, and concerns about the feasibility and acceptability of road pricing, it is interesting that transport as a key performance area had been understood in 2001 as entailing performance goals in respect of road as well as rail transport, but by 2005 the Prime Minister's Strategy Unit was carrying out a strategic audit in which progress on government delivery in the transport area was focused on rail patronage and rail punctuality (Prime Ministers' Strategy Unit, Cabinet Office 2005). Barber (2007: 389) suggests that performance on road congestion in July 2005 was no better than in 1997 or 2001, and was not heading in the right direction. Also interesting is an assessment of how the Prime Minister worked during 2004 on the idea of each government department producing his five-year plans (Seldon 2007: 288):

> He did not want them to be seen as something driven from the centre: the goal was to secure far broader 'buy-in'. A heavy reliance on three Cabinet ministers was a crucial component of these efforts: Reid at Health, Clarke at Education, and Blunkett at the Home Office (his fourth 'key' department of 2001, Transport, had fallen by the wayside).

Seldon (2007) also reports that the Prime Minister gave most of his attention to 5-year strategies for health, education, and law and order in 2004. The marginalization of transport was also evident in the 2005 General Election manifesto. According to Seldon (2007: 334) he leaned towards road pricing, but the manifesto said only that the idea would be examined.

In the light of the case study of transport policy in the UK over the period 2000–05 we can suggest that politicians could set their agenda in terms of government priorities by reference to the matrix in Table 4.2. Having said this, it must be acknowledged that it assumes a certain type of political context and a certain style of political leadership.

Table 4.2 *Agenda setting*

	Not a major concern of the public	Yes, a major concern of the public
Chances of success low (uncertain feasibility of strategic action, not acceptable to public)	Do not make it a priority – assign to Minister who is 'safe pair of hands'	Keep eye on it
Chances of success high (proposed strategic action is highly feasible, and acceptable to public)	Market the importance of the area	Top priority

 96

Table 4.3 *Morphological Box – Politicians and the Public in Strategic Planning*

Component	Possible Options (may be combined)		
	1	2	3
Focus of strategy process	Influencing or steering budget decisions	Ensuring agreed purpose (mission) of organization (or community) is realised	Solving strategic issues
Role of politicians	Setting major objectives and choosing between competing objectives	To provide political oversight and to hold managerial leadership accountable	To provide strategic leadership and negotiate trade-offs within the planning process
Status of the public	Citizens (voters, pressure groups)	Service users ('customers')	Partners (empowerment of the public)
Role of management	To provide politicians with data on the needs of the public, costs of activities and likely results	To develop strategic plans and seek support of politicians for strategic plans	To facilitate strategic decision making by politicians, partners and the involvement of the community in the strategic planning process
Analytical and planning activities	Cost benefit analysis	Performance planning	Problem solving and creative techniques, scenarios, simulations
Focus of efforts in managing implementation	Ensuring strategies and budget decisions are integrated	Culture management – ensuring staff are motivated to deliver the mission statement	Maintaining support of partners and the public
Results sought	'Objective' and efficient allocation of budgets (possibly analysed by programme area)	High levels of satisfaction reported by service users (an organizational achievement)	Solution of community problems (a community achievement)
Achievement Orientation	Administrative achievement	Organizational achievement	Community achievement

THE VARIABILITY OF ROLES FOR POLITICIANS, PUBLIC SERVICES MANAGERS, AND PUBLIC

As we approach the end of this chapter, we have to acknowledge that we have covered a lot of ground and probably have not stressed enough the varying possibilities in terms of the roles of politicians, civil servants, public services managers, and the public. In some countries, and at some times, the strategic leaders have been elected politicians and civil servants have been expected to deliver the strategic plans of ministers. In other countries, at some times, it has been expected that strategic leadership is a professional responsibility of senior civil servants and top level public services executives, and that the role of ministers is somewhat arms-length to the process of creating and implementing strategies. Likewise the role of the public can be variously conceptualized as citizen, service user, or even partner. Some sense of the very many different possibilities is suggested in Table 4.3.

SUMMARY

We have argued in this chapter that setting overall priorities is very important to politicians. It has not been assumed that overall political priorities are derived purely from party political processes or political ideologies or doctrines. We have assumed that governments when setting priorities have to make sense of competing values and interests. It is likely that overall political priorities are potentially influenced by the electorate, senior civil servants, political parties, pressure groups, public service users, and many more groups and organizations.

Setting priorities is about making choices. This is important partly because governments and individual public service organizations confront situations that appear to offer a multitude of problems and opportunities. In fact, politicians seem quite comfortable with the language of priorities, perhaps reflecting their basic realization that government organizations cannot avoid the challenges of rationing.

Priorities may be treated as key performance areas. Sometimes politicians communicate their overall priorities to their top managers as a set of 'themes'. In this chapter, we have also explored some of the possibilities in terms of policy making processes and strategic management, and have not identified a single model of how they interact or interrelate.

Work-based assignment: priorities

The work-based assignments in this book are for civil servants and other public services staff who have four or more years of management experience.

Investigate the top priorities that are espoused in your own organization or an organization you know very well. Check to see if the espoused top priorities are all actually being vigorously pursued, and the reasons for any of them to be neglected. If there are strategic plans, research the extent to which they are being used to deliver these priorities. Comment on the need for changes in strategic plans and strategic planning to ensure more effective implementation of the priorities.

Work-based assignment: assessment

Use the morphological box in Table 4.3 to create a short written appreciation of the respective roles of politicians, senior civil servants/appointed managers, and the public in respect of your own public services organization or one that you know well. Comment on whether you think the roles should be changed and, again, relate this to the conceptual framework provided by the morphological box. Explain what advantages would be created by the changes you propose.

DISCUSSION QUESTIONS

1   What is policy making?
2   What is strategic policy making?
3   Should the elected politicians be the strategic leaders or is this role of strategic leadership best carried out by civil servants and appointed public services managers? What are the advantages and disadvantages of elected politicians being strategic leaders and the actual authors of strategic plans for government departments?
4   Can the public be empowered in relation to their public services? Why should they be empowered?

Group discussions: Managerial leaders and elected politicians

The senior civil servants and other senior managers who work in the public services may aspire to provide strategic leadership, but they can be successful strategic leaders only by recognizing that elected politicians confer democratic legitimacy on strategic visions and that managers need the support of elected politicians (Heymann 1987).

The following two mini-cases provide opportunities to have group discussions to think through some of the issues of leadership in a political context.

Mini-case 1: What is the responsibility of a civil servant for a strategic vision?

What would you do if you were a career civil servant who has just been appointed the chief executive of a new, large government agency that has been formed by merging two separate agencies, that have a branch in every town, and that has a total workforce numbering in the tens of thousands? What would you do if the government had already issued a statement in the national parliament explaining why the government had set up this new agency and explaining what it wanted to achieve in terms of its activities and in terms of the benefits and outcomes for the public? Given the existence of this political statement, would you begin by developing a formal statement of the strategic vision of the new agency? How does the existence of the political statement affect your leadership role as a civil servant?

Mini-case 2: A financial crisis – what would you do?

Imagine the following scenario. You are about to start a new job as a chief executive of a local government organization. You have been headhunted because you have a reputation for bringing about transformational change. You accepted the job because you are impressed by the desire on the part of the elected politicians to improve radically the performance of this particular local government organization. But before you have even started you have discovered there is a serious budgetary problem. You had asked the director of finance to provide you with background papers so you could get a detailed understanding of the financial situation of the organization. You have gone through these very carefully and you have found through your careful analysis that the organization is technically bankrupt. You have considered all sorts of solutions, but are coming to the opinion that the only way that financial stability can be achieved is by launching large-scale redundancies. It is a problem, however, because the elected councillors in this local government organization have long been on record as opposed to compulsory redundancies.

What will you do next? Will you now resign from the job you have not even started? If you do not resign, what will you do as the new chief executive? What do you expect to be the reactions of the key stakeholders? How will you handle their reactions?

FURTHER READING

Joyce, P. (2008) 'The Strategic, Enabling State: A Case Study of the UK, 1997–2007', *The International Journal of Leadership in Public Services*, 4, 3: 24–36.

Moore, M. (1995) *Creating Public Value: Strategic Management in Government*. London: Harvard University Press.

Chapter 5

Linear strategic thinking

LEARNING OBJECTIVES

- To appreciate the steps in a conventional model of strategic thinking as a linear process
- To outline some of the techniques that can be used as part of a strategic thinking process
- To consider the fact that strategic thinking occurs within organizational processes and organizational structures

I should say that what we are saying is that some strategic thinking — horrible phrase — needs to be going on across the democratic process, which of course involves political parties, involves Parliament and, in terms of them giving advice, involves the Civil Service too. — Sir Michael Bichard (former permanent secretary in the UK)

(Source: Evidence given to House of Commons Public Administration Select, Committee 'Governing the Future' — second report of session 2006–7, volume 2, Ev15)

INTRODUCTION

A few years ago, a UK initiative, Professional Skills for Government (PSG), made strategic thinking a core skill that was important for the senior civil service. What is meant by 'strategic thinking'? One definition of strategic thinking is that it is thinking ahead. This is a surprisingly rare activity in many public and private organizations with very many leaders focusing on the here and now, and on short-term matters. In contrast, strategic thinking pays a lot of attention to the future and thinking about long-term developments. This definition of strategic thinking is often implicit in the comments of politicians and civil servants. Arguably, it is a definition that has become more important over the last twenty years. There are also other definitions of strategic thinking. Strategic thinking may be defined as thinking clearly about goals, situations, alternative options, resources, costs, benefits, and the feasibility of the actions under consideration. In effect, this can be seen as a specific form of thinking ahead, one in which goals figure very prominently. If strategic thinking is thorough when looking at alternative options and feasibility, time and resources are not wasted on actions that make little difference; in this sense, strategic thinking can also be defined as thinking which finds good 'leverage points' for bringing about change. Strategic thinking may also be defined as thinking which pays attention to strategic issues, which are issues vital to the overall success or even survival of the public services organization. This type of strategic thinking means, first, posing questions about fundamental issues in the right way to facilitate the search for solutions and, second, thinking 'out of the box' to create new and novel solutions – and both of these steps in thinking are essential for strategic issue management (which we discuss in the next chapter). This view of strategic thinking, when the importance of clarifying the issues is stressed, may lead on to a concern to understand the interrelations between strategic issues. Strategic issue management is also endorsed by people who prize creativity in strategic thinking and the pursuit of innovation rather than simple efficiency.

The elaboration of what strategic thinking means in relation to a senior civil servant or top public manager is not just going into more detail about the thinking involved. The thinking has to be embedded in behaviour. So civil servants and public managers are encouraged to become more concerned with advising the politicians on strategic choices, addressing trade-offs and tensions, and communicating on strategy. They are encouraged to become more involved in long-term direction, working on strategic agendas across boundaries, and solving strategic issues or suggesting possible solutions. So, they are seen as having a role in increasing the responsiveness of the government, anticipating issues, risk management, and problem solving. (We return to this point later in the chapter.)

In this chapter we start off with a simple view of strategic thinking and then add some layers of complexity. We begin, in fact, with a linear model of strategic thinking. We then add some complexity by looking at techniques that may be used to inform strategic thinking. Finally, we acknowledge more complexity for other reasons, such as the way the real world of pluralism can muddy the clarity of the simple linear process, and as a result of the thinking being based within organizations that have levels of authority within them.

TYPES OF STRATEGIC THINKING

There is not just one type of strategic thinking. While not claiming there are no other types, we can identify the following three types. First, there is a type which may involve mission statements or vision statements, but which is essentially intended to produce improvements in performance. This is very much what was intended in the United States when a legal requirement for strategic management in federal agencies was developed in the early 1990s. Second, there is strategic issue management. This may be seen as requiring definite and formal management processes, but may also be seen as an individual capability and thus as requiring the personal development of senior civil servants or public service managers. This, arguably, is reflected in the call that we need more of our senior civil servants and public managers to be strategic thinkers. We can guess that lying behind this idea is a belief that having more resourceful and creative people heading up the management of the public services would result in more issues or dilemmas being tackled successfully. Third, there is also a type of strategic management that is multi-organizational and even multi-sector in nature. The English example of Local Strategic Partnerships illustrates this type. These different types address different outcomes, including performance, issue resolution, and community well-being. These types may be found at different levels of government.

In the next section we look at a linear model of strategic thinking which probably is most easily associated with the type of strategic thinking that is meant to produce improvements in performance. The linear model may also be used as a platform for creativity in strategic thinking and may help to produce innovations, but in practice it may be more conducive to a focus on performance improvements.

THE LINEAR STRATEGIC THINKING MODEL

According to John Kay (1993) there was a rationalist model of strategy that had, as a first stage, the analysis of an organization's environment. The second stage was when the executives of an organization decided on a strategy based on the analysis of the environment. The third stage was that of implementation of the strategy. He highlighted the many criticisms of the rationalist model, but noted that 'few firms, or their advisers, approach the strategy process in any different way' (Kay 1993: 336). Of course, while organizations may approach strategy in a rationalist way, how it turns out as a process could be very varied because of differing skills and circumstances.

The representation of the strategic planning process, consisting of three steps, more or less corresponds with the three component approach proposed by Johnson and Scholes (1989), which they labelled as involving strategic analysis, strategic choice, and strategic implementation (see Figure 5.1). They warned, however, that in practice the three components do not take a simple linear form (Johnson and Scholes 1989: 10): 'It is very likely that, far from being separate, the stages are very much involved with each other.'

Such simple overviews of a linear strategic planning process can be useful as a way of presenting ideas about strategy formulation and implementation, even if they are problematic in the presentation of stages as sequential.

103

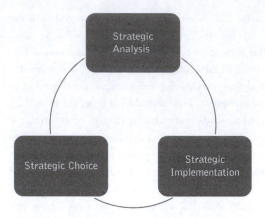

Figure 5.1 *The Johnson and Scholes (1989) model of strategic management*

For the time being, let us stick with the simplification of the process as a sequential one, but elaborate it by looking in more detail at what is involved in analysis, making strategic decisions, and implementation. The linear strategic planning process presented in the flow chart in Figure 5.2 displays the process as a series of steps that are followed in a linear sequence. Of course, we recognize that in practice an organization may deal with different stages more than once in producing a final draft of the strategic plan, and that, often, a sense of a clear sequence becomes compromised.

The process begins with the creation of a mission statement for the organization. This statement may prescribe who the intended beneficiaries of the activities of the organization are, and what activities the organization will carry out in order to provide the desired benefits. The next step in the process is to carry out a situational analysis, which can be composed of an external analysis and an internal analysis. The external analysis may identify and evaluate external trends and events, and assess the opportunities and threats for the organization posed by such developments. The internal analysis may focus on the capacity of the organization, mapping its values and capabilities. The data produced by the internal analysis may be critically evaluated, and strengths and weaknesses identified. Following on from this analysis of the external and internal environments, there can be an assessment of the organization's performance and an assessment of the programmes and services it delivers. In the light of the mission statement and the analysis of external and internal situations, as well as assessment of organizational performance and programmes and services, there can be a decision on the strategic objectives of the organization. Subsequently, the various strategic options available to the organization are identified. These options are evaluated in some systematic way, looking perhaps at feasibility of proposed actions, the risks and rewards of the actions, and perhaps the trade-off between risks and rewards. Following agreement on strategic action, work is carried out on planning the implementation

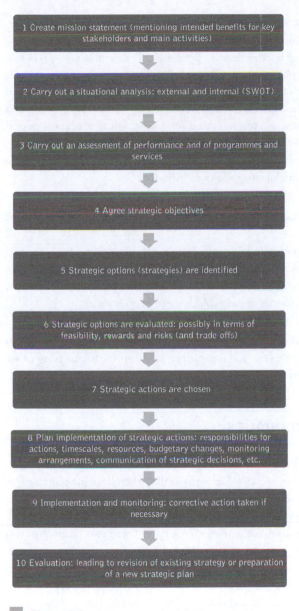

Figure 5.2 *Linear strategic thinking process*

of the strategic action. This may entail identifying and agreeing which individuals are responsible for managing actionable elements of the strategy, timescales, reporting arrangements, and resource plans. A key part of the resource plan will be decisions which have implications for budgetary allocations. A strategic plan that does not have budgetary proposals in the implementation section probably should be considered inadequate. The planning of implementation should also cover how the strategic decisions will be communicated to key stakeholders. Next, the strategic decisions are implemented and monitoring is carried out to determine if corrective action is necessary to ensure the strategic objectives are achieved. Finally, at some point there needs to be a thorough evaluation of the strategy – has it been fully implemented and has it been successful? This enables either a revision of the strategy or the preparation of a completely new strategy. The evaluation may be scheduled, but may occur sooner if circumstances change or there is an obvious failure of the existing strategy.

This simple linear process needs some revisions to make it more applicable to a public services situation. Some obvious additions include:

- Review of the organization's current mandate (e.g. legislation which has to be taken into account)
- Taking account of performance budgeting frameworks maintained by, for example, a Ministry of Finance or the Finance Department
- Consulting and researching stakeholders, especially the public (service users, clients), on their expectations of the public service in question.

The last of these, involving stakeholder identification and stakeholder analysis, is very important in the public services and is probably needed prior to clarifying either a mission statement or a strategic vision.

CONCEPTS AND TECHNIQUES

There are few reports of the concepts and techniques used in strategic planning by managers in public services. Smith (1994) informs us that when strategic planning was carried out in the UK by the Lord Chancellor's Department, two techniques were used: a SWOT (strengths, weaknesses, opportunities and threats) analysis and a PEST (Political, Economic, Social, and Technological) analysis. These two techniques will be quite familiar to students on postgraduate management programmes in universities. But what other techniques are used? UK local government managers surveyed in the 1990s were found to be using a variety of techniques including market research, SWOT analysis, cost benefit analysis, and risk analysis (Flynn and Talbot 1996).

Concepts and techniques that senior civil servants and public services managers might use include:

- Mission, vision, and values statements
- Forecasting
- Scenario planning
- Performance measurement

106

- Techniques for formulating performance indicators and targets (e.g. balanced scorecard)
- Techniques for identifying core competencies
- Situational analysis (e.g. SWOT)
- Techniques for identifying strategic issues
- Stakeholder analysis
- Resource analysis
- Risk analysis.

This is only a selection of the concepts and techniques available. We will look at some of these, but not all of them, below. Some we will look at in the next chapter.

Mission statements

A mission statement is a short statement of the aims of the organization. It should have been strongly influenced, or shaped, or directed, or mandated by elected politicians. The core components of an understanding of organizational mission may be set out in legislation passed by the elected politicians.

At the very least, a mission statement should spell out the intended beneficiaries of the organization's activities, what the intended benefits are, and the main categories of activities that will be used to deliver the intended benefits. The beneficiaries may be a specified group or section of the public who will receive a public service of some kind. (But not all activities will take the form of service provision and nor will all the stakeholders of a strategic plan be service users in an obvious sense.)

It is also possible to include in the mission statement other important information that helps to amplify the three core components. For example, the statement may indicate the geographical extent and location of its activities; for example, the statement may say that a service will be provided in a specific locality, or a specific country, or internationally. The statement may also elaborate on the beneficiaries, benefits, or the main activities of the organization in some way so as to draw attention to important principles it intends to follow in its operations and future developments. For example, a statement may say something about service user choice, or funding, or attitude to use of the latest technology (see Figure 5.3).

Perhaps the best preparation for answering the key questions used in drawing up a mission statement is a stakeholder analysis (a variant of which can also be used in thinking about and planning implementation). A study of stakeholders can help with identifying and understanding the intended beneficiaries of the organization's activities. It can be thought-provoking to consider not only who the powerful stakeholders are, but also who the important stakeholders are. There may need to be an appreciation in a public services organization that these two groups of stakeholders – the

107

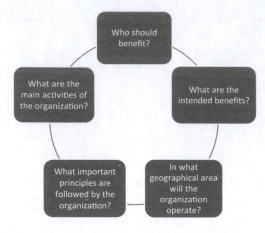

Figure 5.3 *Writing mission statements*

powerful ones and the important ones – may overlap but may not be identical. Some public services organizations are set up to serve groups of people who are not good at pressurizing or lobbying for what they want. The stakeholder analysis also needs to explore the values and interests of the important stakeholders and how they might make judgements (including their criteria) about the public services organization. The conclusions from these types of considerations of stakeholders can directly inform what is written in a mission statement, as well as prompting ideas about whom the leaders of the organization ought to consider involving or consulting when preparing strategic plans.

Strategic goals may be drawn from the mission statement. Whereas the mission statement is a declaration of the purpose of the organization, and, in that sense, will be setting out a positive and desirable agenda for a public service organization, the strategic goals are framed in the light of circumstances for the foreseeable future. In consequence, strategic goals are influenced by both aspiration and reality:

> Goals combine judgments about what is desirable and estimates about what is possible. It is generally wise to begin with an analysis of what is possible.
>
> (Heymann 1987: 19)

Mission statements also need to be written in a way that facilitates monitoring and evaluation of the strategic effectiveness of an organization.

Vision statements

The idea of vision statements may become confused with the concept of mission statements. We can define a vision statement to make the difference between them clear. A vision statement is a foresight or intention about the organization's future activities

 108

and achievements. Defined in this way, it is possible to have a situation in which a mission statement is kept the same, but a vision statement is changed to reflect new circumstances. Of course, in some circumstances, an organization may want to change both mission and vision statement.

The strategic vision sets a target for moving the organizations' capabilities, values, activities, etc., forward in time to, say, a future destination identified as five or maybe ten years ahead. Therefore, writing a strategic vision is the same as developing a point of view about the future.

We would expect that the overall direction in which the public service organization is travelling has in some way been defined for the managerial leadership by elected politicians.

Three different techniques for developing ideas for writing a vision statement are set out briefly below.

Technique 1: Empathy with service users and other stakeholders

This involves appreciating how the future could create more value for service users and other stakeholders. Having identified the powerful and the important stakeholders, having better understood their interests and values, the strategic leaders can ask: what would we need to be doing and achieving in the future to deliver the expectations and values of the most important stakeholders? What would our activities and accomplishments look like if we really met what they want from us? What capabilities would we have developed as an organization that would make these activities and accomplishments possible? What would be the delivery channels we would use?

The first step is therefore to carry out a stakeholder analysis. The leaders identify the key stakeholders of the organization by considering who is affected by the organization and who affects the organization. Next, they identify the top criteria by which each of the key stakeholders evaluates the organization. For example, service users might judge the organization favourably mainly on the basis of the reliability of the service. Finally, strategic leaders place themselves in the shoes of the most important stakeholder groups and consider the top criteria they have identified, and answer the question: what should the organization be doing in five years that would cause this stakeholder group to rate the organization more positively? The implication behind this technique is that the vision is a future scenario in which key stakeholders are more positive about the organization.

Technique 2: Challenging 'industry' assumptions

The first step is to identify all the current assumptions of how successful public service organizations in a particular part of the public sector operate, and then to imagine each one of the core assumptions no longer being true. If a core assumption was not true, what might be possible?

109

Technique 3: Exploring strategic issues

In this technique the strategic leader begins by listing the top strategic issues for the organization and then they identify those that have been issues for a considerable period of time. The next step is to answer the following questions: Why is this issue a concern? What is it making difficult for us, as an organization, to do? What might we do if we could solve this issue? The last question is obviously the question that gets to the heart of what might be a strategic vision for the organization.

How is vision used to produce strategy? There are at least two methods. You can brainstorm actions that move the organization from where it is currently to where it must be to deliver the vision. The actions comprise the strategy. Another method is to identify the issues that stand in the way of moving towards the vision and then carry out creative problem solving to identify strategic actions to solve the issues and realize the vision. I suspect that more people have used the first method. The second method is quite challenging, although it should be quite motivating. If an organization's leaders are optimistic, then identifying and resolving issues can be seen as an interesting and energising experience. However, if the leaders are pessimistic or cynical, then dwelling on strategic issues that are difficult to resolve can dissipate energy. (There is more on the creative approach to strategy formulation in the next chapter.)

Values statements

Values statements were probably in their heyday in the late 1980s and early 1990s. They were seen by some leaders as a list of explicit values that could be communicated to people who worked in the public services organization so as to influence their behaviour. For example, the values might relate to how the public were to be treated by staff during service interactions, the quality of the service, and the importance of equal opportunities both in relation to employment matters and the delivery of services.

The values could be identified by the top leadership team of an organization reflecting on their experiences in the organization and on the values in society (e.g. the rise of equal opportunities as an important value in society and as demonstrated through legislation). Sometimes it was considered possible to design training courses to instil these values throughout a public service organization.

These vision statements can be seen as important to back up strategic developments, but at times have also served in some way as statements of political priorities.

Forecasting

In the past, strategic management was often associated with forecasting. The strategist would attempt to model the future in some way, and then adjust the organization's trajectory to the outcomes of the forecast. Some years ago, organizations were inclined to favour forecasts based on past trends. A major problem with this type of analysis is that discontinuities may arise that throw out the existing trend. A good example of this is the 1973 oil crisis when OPEC (Organization of Petroleum Exporting Countries) managed to engineer a steep rise in oil prices by restricting supply.

There is still a place for trend projection despite the difficulty with forecasting. The difficulty is that we may confuse this with the ability to predict the future scientifically. Strategic leaders should look at history and should look at trends. They do, however, need to ask the question: will this trend continue as in the past or will there be a change in the future – are we approaching a turning point in this particular phenomenon?

Scenario planning

Scenario planning was a response to the rise of unpredictability in the 1970s that created severe problems for forecasting techniques. It is logically best suited to a situation where there would be confusion about what to do because of a small number of factors that are unpredictable. It would not be much use where there were a large number of important but unpredictable factors; this would overwhelm anyone trying to use scenario planning because there would be lots of possible scenarios. The point of scenario planning is to allow focused strategic thinking in the context of a *modest* degree of confusion.

Scenario planning creates scenarios of two or more different futures. It allows leaders to consider the 'best' way forward that maximizes the organization's future irrespective of which actual future occurs. For each scenario, leaders ask: If the future is going to be such and such, what do we need to put in place because of this? Through scenario planning the organization would start with a confused and unclear situation, but by identifying different possible futures and then describing them as scenarios, it would have a way of conversing about the future.

Scenarios are usually written as reports as if they had been written at a future time. The reports are produced using both analysis and imagination. Leaders can develop worst case, best case, and most likely case scenarios continually testing their assumptions about the future. They can use past data to extrapolate into the future, while being aware of the difficulties inherent in this.

Others could be involved by leaders through meetings and workshops. If leaders involve others it is possible that they find it easier to build understanding about the future and adaptability in the organization, and thus greater receptivity to change.

Scenarios are written in one or two paragraphs by encompassing the variables, assumptions, and the dependent variables within an appreciation of the organization's environment and how it had developed, written as if it is at the end of the selected planning horizon. One way of creating scenarios is to combine 'assumptions' and 'uncertainties' together and then add supplementary detail. The following 'analytical' approach is reasonably logical:

1 Select a planning horizon for the scenarios
2 Identify a set of assumptions for the scenarios
3 Identify a list of critical variables that feel very unpredictable (e.g. public expenditure plans)
4 Review the list of variables and eliminate those that (i) are thought to have a low potential impact *and* a low probability of occurrence, (ii) may not happen within the planning horizon, and (iii) are events which would be a total disaster
5 Distinguish the variables which are dependent on other variables in the list — use these to enrich the scenarios, but not to define the scenarios
6 Aggregate variables on the list into broader variables, aiming to end up with two to five key variables
7 Assign two or three realistic values to each of the key variables (e.g. change of government, no change of government)
8 List all possible combinations of the key variables (e.g. three key variables each with two values would generate eight scenarios)
9 Reject scenarios which are implausible and those scenarios which vary very little from other scenarios
10 End up with a final list of three scenarios, including the scenario that is the most probable case, and a worst case scenario.

Performance measurement

Performance measurement techniques include benchmarking, tracking, and the balanced scorecard.

Benchmarking has become a very popular technique worldwide in recent years. Public sector organizations have been using benchmarking for many years as part of the drive to modernize the management of services and increase performance. A few years ago, Poister and Streib (2005) reported that a third of city councils in their sample in the US, that had made strategic planning efforts in the preceding five years, were also benchmarking their performance against others to judge the effectiveness of their strategic initiatives. Benchmarking can be defined simply as comparisons of performance and other matters. It can also be defined more narrowly as a process where the managers of an organization measure their performance against the best performing organizations in an industry and make other comparisons (e.g. with internal processes, competencies, and costs) to explain the causes of the superior performance of the industry leaders. The purpose is often to arrive at an analysis of how the organization might improve its performance and catch up with industry leaders. Financial (and non-financial) data can be used to benchmark the organization's position and performance against its competitors.

Organizations can co-operate directly for the purposes of benchmarking studies. Public sector organizations have been co-operating extensively to generate more valid data for performance comparisons. Benchmarking can involve doing observations on the performance of rival organizations where the services are delivered publicly (e.g. refuse collection).

Another approach to performance measurement is to start with the organization's vision and mission statements and the associated strategic goals. Then the organization can track results against strategic goals using specially selected or specially designed measures. In practice this means setting up reporting systems so that results are reported on a regular basis to a strategic management group (see Figure 5.4).

The final technique considered here is that of the balanced scorecard. Kaplan and Norton (1992) argued that financial indicators of performance were more attuned to the needs of the industrial age, but today non-financial indicators (NFIs) are needed. They argued that performance should be evaluated using a combination of both kinds of indicators – financial and non-financial. The evaluation framework they proposed – the balanced scorecard – contains four categories of performance indicators, and these have been adapted for use in the public sector by many organizations:

1 Customer perspective: how do customers see us?
2 Internal perspective: what must we excel at?
3 Innovation and learning perspective: can we continue to improve and create value?
4 Financial perspective: how do we look to shareholders?

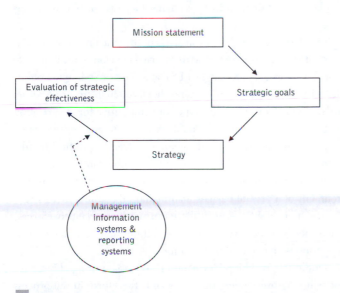

Figure 5.4 *Reporting systems*

Occasionally, organizations have spotted that there is an opportunity to study relationships between different performance indicators. For instance, a rise or fall in customer satisfaction may tend to precede a corresponding rise or fall in financial performance indicators, and improvements in performance on innovation may be followed in due course by improvements in financial indicators. It does not take much imagination to see how valuable it could be for strategic leaders to have a better understanding of such relationships – if they exist – and then how this could be the basis for continuous improvement as the organization learnt more and more about how to achieve better results.

Situational Analysis

A situational analysis is a major ingredient in strategic decision making. This type of analysis is an assessment of the current and the future situation of the organization. Such an assessment could involve studying:

1 current or future opportunities and threats;
2 organizational capabilities, values, and resources (including those resources owned by partner organizations); and
3 achievements and failures of the organization.

The strategic situation can be defined in a broad way to include internal and external environments, to include organizational values as well as capabilities, and to include recent performance of the organization. Analysis means breaking something up into its parts. Analysis can be useful for understanding not only the composition of something, but also understanding how something works by studying the ways in which various parts interrelate.

Commonly, strategic analysis is focused on the analysis of the situation of an organization, meaning both its external environment and its internal environment. In private sector management courses, managers are taught PEST analysis – standing for political, economic, social, and technological factors – and they are taught to use Michael Porter's five forces analysis, which examines five types of competitive force in relation to a specific industry. It can also be useful in the public services to analyse the external environment and to examine the social trends, economic trends, political trends, and technological trends. Among the social trends will be, importantly, changes in lifestyle, changes in values held by people in society. As we have noted, an analysis of the strategic environment of a private business can include the competitive structure of its specific industry. In the public services there can also be competitive forces, but, in addition, thought needs to be given to the possibilities and consequences of partnership and co-operation with external organizations.

As long ago as the middle 1980s, Philip Heymann (1987) was writing about public services organizations having overlapping mandates and, therefore, in the process of developing a strategic plan, he considered it important that there were some explorations of those overlaps of mandate in order to produce a good strategic plan. The same idea was followed up in the United States in the 1990s when evaluation criteria for the strategic plans produced under the GPRA 1993 were being devised for Congress – evaluation frameworks were created that included looking at what kind of consultation had taken place with other organizations where there were overlapping mandates.

The analysis of the internal environment will include reviewing assets, resources, strengths, and weaknesses of the organization. Assets, resources, and strengths can be used in taking successful strategic action. They are things which need to be considered when choosing courses of action. It is important to know the weaknesses of an organization – it would be foolish to take strategic action where the critical resource needed for a successful strategic action was missing, or which depended on an organizational activity that was currently weak. Of course, identifying a weakness relevant to an otherwise attractive strategic action might trigger a decision by the organization's top managers to develop the organization and overcome the weakness. So weaknesses can be a constraint on action, or have to be remedied.

There is not much discussion in strategic management textbooks of how to carry out strategic analysis of the values of the organization. And yet values are important. Values, just like capabilities, determine the capacity of an organization for taking strategic action.

Finally, some analysis of the organization's current or recent performance would be important as part of the overall strategic analysis of the current situation. This may be important in the sense of identifying any potential threat to the future survival of the organization. A downward trend in the numbers of service users, or a downward trend in income, or a deteriorating quality of service are just some examples of performance indicators that could spell future problems for the survival of the organization. Also a review of performance could be useful for setting ambitious, but realistic, performance targets.

Situation analysis is not restricted just to analyses of the current situation. Situation analysis can, for example, be useful in the selection of a course of action. The analysis in this case may involve risk assessments as well as an analysis of expected rewards from taking a course of action. Finally, situation analysis might also be useful in the planning of a strategic action. In order to make success more likely, situation analysis may be used to identify the resources that will be needed in strategic action, and to anticipate and manage the reactions of stakeholders to strategic action.

TREND ANALYSIS-HISTORY IS IMPORTANT IN MAKING CHOICES ABOUT THE FUTURE

Trend analysis may be seen as part of the analysis of the external environment. We can carry out a trend analysis using the PEST analysis as a starting point. This means

115

looking at political, economic, social, and technological factors. It can be useful to think about these external factors not simply as factors but as events, trends, and turning points. Public services managers can list all the events, trends, and turning points over, say, the last five years. This can be done through managers drawing on their personal experience. While this is subjective, it may also be argued that managers experience the trends, events, and turning points and they do think about these things and assess the evidence for their existence and seriousness. So we can argue that it is not unreasonable to ask managers to use their experience and judgement to identify and even rate them in terms of their importance for the organization.

As part of a strategic planning process, managers can then be asked to consider the possible future course of each of the top rated trends, events, and turning points over, say, the next five years. Will an important trend continue much as it has been continuing in the past, or will the trend accelerate, or slow down? Will the trend go through a major turning point in the next 3–7 years? Will an event be completed or will it still be in progress?

Some kind of a consideration of what might happen to trends, events, and turning points is very important. The manager drawing up strategic plans needs to make sense of the history of their organization, and this is largely a pragmatic process rather than a totally scientific one. We can usefully stress that making sense of the history of an organization by studying the trends occurring in its environment is even valued where strategic thinkers are exhorted to be very creative and imaginative in describing ideal futures for the organization. When thinking about the future it seems that it is good preparation to think about past trends. Although not concerned with the public services, Gary Hamel and C. K. Prahalad (1994) accepted that it could be useful to do trend analysis even when the intention is not to simply extrapolate the past, but to come up with something imaginative that will create entirely new strategic futures.

The anticipation of turning points in trends must be very important in the public services area. Take, for example, trends in public concerns; just because a specific concern has been growing year by year it should not be assumed that this concern will continue to grow. There is a degree of volatility in public concerns (Nutt and Backoff 1992) partly explained by the changing circumstances of society, and partly, hopefully, explained by the successes of government organizations. For example, public concerns about unemployment will, no doubt, increase during periods in which global economic activity is sluggish; and successful reforms of major public services may decrease public concerns over, for example, health and education.

CORE COMPETENCIES

Core competence became popular as a concept in the 1990s. Very broadly, as a first approximation, we can say that a core competence is something the organization is good at doing. A core competence is sometimes seen in strategic management as an advantage. An advantage can be defined as a competitive strength that allows one organization to triumph over rivals. We can also define core competence as something that makes it more likely that an organization will be successful in a strategic challenge – this may or may not involve beating competitor organizations.

So, core competencies are activities that the organization is very good at. It is also something that creates relatively high levels of satisfaction with the products or services the organization produces – we say it creates 'customer value'. In the private sector context we might restrict the term core competence to those activities that are not only done well and create relatively high levels of satisfaction for customers, but are also difficult for other companies to acquire or develop – not easily imitated. This last requirement reflects the definition of core competence as a competitive advantage as opposed to its definition as strength in relation to a strategic challenge.

Klein and Hiscocks (1994) provided a way of identifying 'skills' which might be seen as components of core competencies. Skills might be identified by asking the following questions:

1 What clues as to the skills of the company may be obtained by looking at the organization structure? Are there specialist units, for example, and what are their names?
2 What do members of the organization perceive to be the skills?
3 What will an examination of the products or services of the organization tell us about its skills?
4 What do customers and market watchers think the skills of the organization are?

The skills are thought to be woven or 'bundled' together to form core competencies.

Lewis and Gregory (1996) outlined an approach to identifying core competencies that involves reviewing and evaluating all the activities of the organization, and doing this in a way that requires working down through a hierarchy of activities and sub-activities. The main steps of a simplified version of their method are as follows:

Step 1: Top managers identify the main activities of the organization and then map their interdependencies and linkages.
Step 2: Each of the main activities is rated: how well is the activity done, how much does it contribute to customer satisfaction, and how easy is it to acquire or develop excellence in this activity?
Step 3: The top rated main activities are then broken down into their constituent activities and then the latter are rated (using same questions as in Step 2).
Step 4: The requirements of the top rated activities (as rated in Step 3) are identified in terms of equipment, machines, software, people skills, technology skills, and management.

117

SWOT ANALYSIS

The SWOT analysis may be the most commonly taught technique within short management courses or postgraduate manager education. Probably any sample of managers will include quite a few who have at some point in their careers used SWOT analysis. Very often SWOT analysis is thought of as being nothing more than a simple listing of strengths, weaknesses, opportunities, and threats facing an organization. But it may be better to think of the SWOT analysis as a way of summing up the work of situational analysis that has been based on the application of a whole set of techniques – trend analysis, core competence analysis, values analysis, etc.

Let us begin by providing a simple definition of each of the four key terms.

- Strengths – strengths enhance the performance of the organization
- Weaknesses – constrain performance
- Opportunities – are external events or trends that can be made to produce benefits if the organization takes action
- Threats – are also external events, or developments or trends, but these are ones that can damage the organization unless some action is taken by the organization

It might also be useful to make clear whether strengths and weaknesses are defined in absolute or relative terms. If defined in relative terms, relative to what? Is strength, for example, strength relative to other organizations or relative to a goal?

There is a need to think carefully about the items listed in a SWOT analysis. It is very easy, for example, to confuse an opportunity with an action. Sometimes people list an idea such as the launch of a new product or new service as an opportunity. Strictly speaking this is an action that is taken by the organization, possibly in response to an opportunity that has occurred. Sometimes people confuse performance with strength or weakness. So, sometimes a high level of customer satisfaction is taken as strength. Strictly speaking this could be taken as a performance variable and we should look for the cause of the customer satisfaction because it is the causal factor that should be listed as a strength.

Lists supplied as part of a SWOT analysis should also be scrutinized for duplication. This can occur where the same idea is expressed in different ways but is essentially the same idea. So it can be useful to go through the lists, grouping together all the items which are actually the same idea, but which are just expressed using different words.

Finally it can be useful to use a process of ranking all the strengths, ranking all the weaknesses, ranking all the opportunities, and ranking all the threats. The justification for this procedure of ranking is that, with limited managerial attention and capacity, management should be concentrating on the organization's most important strength, its most important weakness, etc, when trying to formulate strategic plans; and it may be argued that it is a mistake to be paying attention to less important strengths etc.

STRATEGIC CHOICES

There are at least two ways of deciding strategic actions. The first involves making a selection from a pre-determined and fairly familiar list of strategic options. Strategic decisions can be embedded in a more creative process so that it is not merely a matter of choosing from a pre-determined set of strategic options, but first involves creating a unique set of strategic options. Either way, there comes a point in the strategic planning process when strategic leaders decide to implement some options and reject others. In order to do this, they need to carry out an appraisal of the strategic options.

In practice, strategic choices may be made in a conversational way without great clarity about the criteria being used and with much being left as unspoken assumptions. Arguably, there is scope for more systematic approaches to evaluation, in which the options are laid out in detail and the criteria to be used are agreed in advance of the evaluation (see Bryson 2004: 218–9).

One of the most widely used frameworks for choosing action is based around the application of three criteria: suitability, feasibility, and acceptability. Suitable strategic action can be defined as action that looks like it offers a good fit between the action and the circumstances of the organization, and between the action and the desired outcome. So some strategic options may not be judged suitable because they are not suitable in the circumstances, or not suitable in the sense of being likely to produce the desired outcomes.

Feasible strategic action is action that looks capable of being carried out. This is not to be confused with the previous criterion. It is not a matter of whether the action will have positive consequences. It is a matter of whether we can complete the action at all. One aspect of judging feasibility is assessing whether we have or can get the resources needed to implement the proposed strategic action. Strategic actions may be judged to lack feasibility because the organization lacks the necessary money needed to take the course of action or because it requires certain skills not currently found in the organization and not easily obtained by recruiting people from the labour market.

Acceptable strategic action is action that looks as though it will be favoured or supported by all the powerful or important stakeholders. Stakeholders may react positively or negatively to a proposal to take a specific strategic action for a variety of reasons. These include their perception of the impact on their interests. However, they may find action acceptable or unacceptable because of their values, or their ethical standards, or because of their concern for its impact on a third party, and so on.

Two further comments might be made about the use of these three criteria. First, we could stretch the concept of feasibility to also take on the issue of political feasibility. For one interpretation of politically feasible action might be action that is acceptable to powerful stakeholder groups. On this basis, there is an overlap between feasibility and acceptability. Second, it does seem sensible to judge proposed action by its timeliness. An organization should think about timescales and about how long will it take to carry out proposed courses of action. For example, strategic leaders may worry about a development that could threaten the organization and may have estimated that the organization has only, say, two years to take action to counter the threat. Or, alternatively, there may be a political judgement that powerful stakeholders will allow the current leadership of the organization only so long to bring about an overall improvement in the performance of the organization. So, sensible leaders will assess options for action in terms of how long they will take to implement and produce their positive effects. Will the benefits flow within six months, two years, five years, or ten years? In some cases strategic options may be rejected because the benefits will take too long to flow. While it is possible that there may be some proposed strategic actions that are not timely because they will take too long to work, there may also be some actions that will impact too quickly. This seems less likely, but should not be ruled out as a possibility.

HOW SOUND IS THE INTELLECTUAL PROCESS FOR PRODUCING A STRATEGIC PLAN? – THE ISSUE OF FEASIBILITY

Nutt and Backoff (1992) stressed the importance of feasibility as a key concept in strategic thinking for public sector and third sector organizations. There is evidence from research into local government in the USA that feasibility assessment of proposed strategies is a very important element of a strategic planning process (Poister and Streib 2005). So, civil servants and public services managers should build into their strategic thinking a strong concern for the feasibility of the strategies they are thinking of adopting. How can this concern be acted upon?

It will be suggested here that civil servants and public services managers can do at least three things as part of their strategic thinking to show concern for feasibility:

1 Look at trends over previous years and consider their likely future development
2 Evaluate the feasibility of alternative courses of action before selecting the best course of action
3 Check out proposed actions in terms of resource availability and acceptability to powerful stakeholders.

So, we can ask if strategic thinking has included a trend analysis, if the best course of action has been selected after evaluation of the feasibility of alternatives, and if alternatives have been evaluated in terms of resource availability and acceptability to powerful stakeholders. If the answer in all three cases is yes, then we may guess that the selected strategic action is more likely to be successful.

The importance of examining trends prior to the selection of action can be argued in terms of an understanding of freedom to act. Any organization, in practice, has some choice about what it will do. But, in practice, an organization makes its choices in a set of circumstances. What someone can do nowadays is very different from what someone could do 2000 years ago. The difference is only partly explained by different inclinations on the part of the individual; it is also because of very different circumstances then and now. Anyone can choose to travel halfway around the world, but the experience will be entirely different in a world in which travelling by plane is commonplace from a world in which there are no planes. Therefore, specific action is a function of will and circumstances. To make decisions purely on the basis of will, ignoring the circumstances that prevail, surely must increase the likelihood of failure.

The circumstances of an organization can be examined by analysing the key trends. As suggested earlier, there need be no presumption that trends can be always extrapolated. When examining trends, managers should ask themselves whether the trends will continue as in the past, or whether there is any reason for suspecting that the trend will pass through a turning point.

The benefit of considering the feasibility of alternative courses of action before selecting the best course of action may seem so obvious that it warrants no further discussion. Surely, choosing to take some action simply because it is the first action thought of must lead (on average) to poorer results than tending to choose action only after the feasibility of alternatives have been considered and evaluated? If feasibility is not checked out in advance, we can guess that attempts to implement action will run into obstacles and there will be an implementation failure. This occurs quite often and it is widely accepted that implementation of strategic plans is very difficult.

Finally, we can simply assert the obvious point that managers can usefully look at the resources that are required, and how they can be obtained, and look at the likely reactions of various stakeholders (Nutt and Backoff 1992). These are both very important for planning the implementation of strategies.

RISK ASSESSMENT

A basic proposition we could make is that it is very hard for many people in public services to agree on the right goals for their organization, and then to think creatively about courses of action to pursue those goals. But it seems to be even more difficult to get people in public services to manage the risks of strategic action. In other words, risk assessment and then risk management does not necessarily come naturally or easily to public service leaders and others in the public services.

How can you conduct a risk assessment in relation to proposed strategic action in a reasonably coherent manner? One approach, outlined here, is to begin by identifying a number of environmental and organizational factors that might create barriers

121

to successful implementation of strategic action. One example might be a sudden announcement by national government that it is having budgetary problems and it has to implement, very rapidly, a series of spending cuts throughout the public services. An unexpected change of government as a result of a general election could herald changes of policy and funding part way through planned strategic change. An example of an internal development might be the sudden departure of a chief executive half way through the planned strategic change. It is often thought very difficult to maintain the momentum of strategic change when there is little continuity in who leads the organization – so the departure of a chief executive could be quite a blow to radical strategic action (Osborne and Gaebler 1992). If not the departure of the chief executive, it might be that there are two or three key managers or key professionals in a public service organization who might suddenly decide to take early retirement and their departure could have quite devastating effects on the organization's ability to implement a planned strategic action. Another possible factor could be a scandal about a public service in the media that makes a particular service suddenly become less popular.

Once the factors are identified, what then? The next thing to do is to calculate the probability of these various factors occurring during a specified time period. For example, how probable is it that there will be a change of government at a general election? The probability could be scored using a scale of zero to ten, with ten meaning that the factor is 'very probable' to occur and with zero meaning that the occurrence of the factor is 'very improbable'.

The third step is to estimate the impact of the factor on the strategic action. You consider: What would be the impact should this thing happen? Would the impact of this factor on the proposed strategic action be disastrous, would it block its realization? Or would it be less serious, possibly merely a minor effect, perhaps just slowing down the implementation of the strategic action? Impact could also be assessed using a points system. We could use a scale of zero to ten points, where ten points means that the impact is very likely to cause complete failure of the strategic action and a score of zero means the impact is negligible.

To determine the relative risk of each factor we multiply the probability by the impact. So we define risk specifically as the probability of an event occurring multiplied by the magnitude of its negative impact. If we add up all the risk figures for all the factors considered we can come up with a total risk score for each course of action.

The best public services leaders will encourage an entrepreneurial approach to strategic action. They will be ambitious for the improvement of the public services and be prepared to take risks to bring about radical improvements, but they will not want to take foolish and unnecessary risks. They will, therefore, want to remove as much risk as possible from strategic action so that only the unavoidable risks are left. They would use risk analysis and risk management to eliminate strategic actions that are dangerously risky and cannot be de-risked to acceptable levels of risk.

POINTS SYSTEMS FOR EVALUATING STRATEGIC OPTIONS

While they may be scientifically dubious, a good case can be made for the value of points based systems for promoting a thorough conversation about the strategic options among the strategic leadership.

The method of constructing a points based evaluation system is very simple. First, the strategic leadership decides on the number and nature of the criteria it wishes to use to evaluate the various strategic actions being actively considered. For example, they might select some of the following ten criteria:

1 Acceptability to key stakeholders
2 Acceptability to service users
3 Acceptability to the general public
4 User benefits
5 Consistency with mission
6 Technical feasibility
7 Cost of financing
8 Cost-effectiveness
9 Risk
10 Timeliness.

Next, the leadership decide if all the criteria are to be equally weighted, or whether some are considered of more importance in making a choice of which actions to implement and therefore need to be weighted accordingly. Proposed actions are then rated on each of the criteria on, say, a scale of zero to ten points. A course of action rated as zero out of ten points on one of the criteria would be judged to be totally unsatisfactory in this respect. Action rated ten out of ten points for a criterion would be judged to be highly satisfactory in that respect. The raw scores would then be adjusted according to the weightings and an aggregate score calculated for each course of action. If two or more courses of action are scored using this point system they can then be compared, both in terms of the overall score, and in terms of the scoring against specific criteria.

It is sometimes said to be a mistake for managers to simply decide on a course of action based upon which of several courses of action achieved the highest score under such a points based system. Instead it is suggested that strategic leaders and their teams might better debate the scoring and argue through their disagreements, and then take the score into account when making their final decision. So, the total scores are considered, but do not determine in a simple way the judgement made.

To repeat the point made at the beginning of this section, the process of scoring the different criteria, and deciding on weightings, should not be taken as a completely scientific process (in the sense of being completely 'objective'). It is a process that can help strategic leaders make sure there is a thorough and detailed consideration of all the alternative actions that might be approved.

USING A MATRIX TO DISPLAY TRADE-OFFS

If there is broad agreement between those involved in assessing the strategic actions that have been generated, and there are two key criteria – and only two criteria – perhaps a matrix provides a good way of displaying trade-offs when selecting action.

Consider the case of a trade-off between selecting actions that are popular with elected politicians that have a political oversight role, and actions that seem to offer more public value in the eyes of service users. If proposed strategic actions can be rated as low, medium or high in these terms we can draw up a three by three matrix (see Figure 5.5). The strategic options then can be placed in the matrix to facilitate the conversation among strategic leaders trying to choose between them.

There are two obvious decision zones in the matrix. Actions which are unlikely to be popular with the elected politicians, and create little value for service users, can be seen as an obvious rejection, whereas strategic actions that are highly popular with elected politicians, and would be perceived as very valuable by service users, can be seen as an obvious choice. The interesting cases occur where action is thought likely to be very popular with the elected politicians, but is expected to create little public value for service users, and the opposite situation where there is a clear case in terms of value for service users, but the politicians are not interested. It is more likely that cases will be clustered in the remaining cells of the matrix where actions are judged to be medium in popularity and/or value to service users.

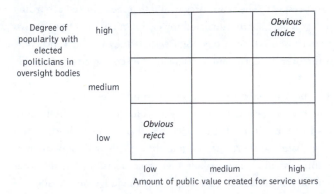

Figure 5.5 *Matrix to judge trade-offs*

STRATEGIC PROCESSES INVOLVE MORE THAN THINKING AND TAKE PLACE IN ORGANIZATIONAL STRUCTURES

According to Dyson (1990: 3) a strategic planning process is a 'management process involving consultation, negotiation and analysis which is aimed at ensuring effective strategic decision-making'. In this chapter we have largely addressed strategic thinking as a process involving analysis. This is the conception of the strategic thinking process that is most frequently assumed in formal education courses about strategic management. Students are largely taught that strategic planning is an analytical process aimed at producing rational decisions. Concerns that strategic management is not reducible to an analytical, or technical, process are rarely given much consideration in courses.

However, we should not assume thinking precedes communication. Sometimes we only clarify our own strategic thinking as we explain our ideas to others – our own implicit ideas suddenly come into mind as we talk. The implicit thinking can then become explicit. We sometimes only clarify our implicit strategic thinking as we react against other people's spoken ideas. So listening to others as part of strategic thinking processes and consultation, in which we explain proposals and seek the opinions of others, can be very important in the development of strategic thinking.

A consultation process may entail formal meetings between managers and others within organizations, but there can be consultation even when there is no formal process. As a low key and informal process, consultation may be found in everyday and ordinary conversations. Moreover, such conversations may be interwoven with many other types of conversations – so we should not assume that consultation is always an explicit and discrete activity. It may be, but in some organizations it may be occurring in a very 'natural way'.

It may not be just consultation that occurs through an informal conversational process – so may analysis and negotiation. In fact, the idea of strategic management taking place conversationally has been remarked on in recent years by Gary Hamel (2002). Although his book on strategy appears to be written primarily for the private sector reader, he provides food for thought about the strategic management process in any organization when he presents it as an ordinary conversational process rather than as a highly technical or analytical process based on using a whole set of techniques. This suggests we should look out for a fairly fluid strategic thinking process occurring through lots of conversations, including formal conversations in management meetings, casual conversations over tea, in fact, conversations taking place in a whole range of settings. Out of this, according to Hamel, we get strategic decisions. Out of this we may also get forward looking and strategic ideas about the future of an organization, and ideas about how the organization can get to the future.

When Dyson writes about the planning of strategy involving negotiation, this can serve to remind us that strategic management is partly about bringing about change, and we may then recall the discussion from an earlier chapter that change can affect many interest groups inside and outside the organization. Some groups may hope to gain an advantage from change, but some groups may stand to lose from a strategic change. Consequently we can think about groups that favour the status quo and other groups that form – or could form – a coalition for change around any specific strategic decision. So, strategic processes are fundamentally political in the sense of being laced with conflicts between groups with differential and fluctuating amounts of power. We might, here, think of organizations, therefore, as pluralistic coalitions of groups, some coalitions trying to impede changes and some coalitions trying to advance changes.

The various interest groups, and their perspectives and interests that form the organization and its environment, may be well understood. If an interest group has 'clout', this is a very important dimension to the nature of strategic thinking. Take the tendency of a Ministry of Finance (in a national government), or a finance department (in a single public services organization), to be a powerful voice in strategic conversations. They will have a lot of say in decisions not only on strategic investments, but also in what is a strategic priority because of the grip they have on the budgetary process. This can produce tensions between different parts of government or different parts of a public service organization. This came out very clearly in the United States when the federal budgetary process began to be seen as undermining the strategic planning of government agencies acting under the Government and Performance Results Act 1993 (a point to which we will return in a later chapter).

This view of strategic management as a political process underlines the reality that the arguments that go on about strategy are often not really arguments about what is in the best interests of the organization or the public, but rather arguments about how the interests of different groups are being affected. There is an important point here for strategic leaders in public services. While it is important to listen carefully to what different groups say in response to strategic ideas, it not wise to take what is said at face value (Heifetz and Linsky 2002).

Dyson's conception of strategic planning as having three elements (consultation, negotiation, and analysis) is important for a realistic view of what happens in practice, but it is difficult to keep all three elements in mind when we talk about strategic processes, and we may find ourselves drifting in to focusing on, say, the analytical element.

What else is there to say about strategic thinking processes? By looking at real examples we can see that thinking processes have an organizational aspect. For example, Smith (1994) reported on the corporate planning process used by the Countryside Commission in the 1990s (UK). In this case the strategic planning process had six stages. The first stage was the initial analysis; the second was top-down guidelines; the third was bottom-up proposals; the fourth was finalization of the plan; the fifth was submission of the plan to, and discussion with, government; and sixth was monitoring of the plan. In the outline of the Countryside Commission's process there is an obvious element not found in the flow chart presented earlier in this chapter – this is an indication of how strategic planning works organizationally and how it works between the organization and government. Specifically, the outline draws attention to the different roles or contributions of top management, more junior management, and government. So, the value of the description of the Countryside Commission's process provided by Smith (1994) is that it underlines the need to see strategic thinking as not merely a set of analytical steps, but also as being structured into relationships within and beyond public service organizations.

If we look again at the flow chart at Figure 5.2 we can imagine the whole process being conducted in various ways organizationally. For example, a centralized organization might have the whole plan being produced by a small group of top managers, but, in a more decentralized organization, we can imagine top management providing the managers of departments or parts of the organization with a mission statement and a written briefing setting out a strategic analysis and stating the corporate objectives. The top managers may then require lower levels of management to carry out strategic thinking to identify, evaluate, and propose actions to top management for approval. Once proposals have been approved by top managers, then lower level managers may be required to think about and produce implementation plans, which may then have to be referred up to top managers for approval especially in relation to changes in budgetary allocations. Monitoring may involve both top managers and lower level managers through reporting systems which allow the top managers to judge the success of implementation and the meeting of key milestones in the implementation of strategic decisions.

Even in a decentralized organization, we can expect variations in how the process works in practice, meaning that the distribution of power within the organization may affect how tightly or loosely bottom-up thinking and planning is controlled from above. The difference between centralized and decentralized systems also emerges in terms of the role of government in the approval of strategic plans of individual public services organizations. If finalized strategic plans have to be submitted to government, this might suggest a centralized system. Again, it is quite likely that the degree of centralization may vary even if strategic plans have to be submitted. Where public services organizations are very independent, then the submitted plans might be merely rubber-stamped. If government has a high degree of centralized control, then the submitted plans may be modified through serious bargaining between government and public service organizations.

Once we locate strategic thinking in organizational processes and organizational structures, and do not see it as a process that takes place as pure intellectual thought and contemplation, then strategic thinking becomes a skill involving communication and political skills. This is illustrated in the development of the concept of strategic thinking within the Professional Skills for Government (PSG) framework in the UK (see Concepts Box 5.1).

> ## CONCEPT BOX 5.1 A PRACTICAL VIEW OF STRATEGIC THINKING IN THE UK CIVIL SERVICE
>
> PSG was developed in the UK after 2003. One of the core skills needed at a senior level in this framework was strategic thinking.
>
> In 2010 strategic thinking was defined as:
>
> 1 Able to shape and set the long-term vision and direction for the department, taking into account both wider government priorities and delivery systems
> 2 Knows how to identify tensions, set priorities and make trade-offs between different policy areas and over different timescales (short, medium, and long-term)
> 3 Able to present Ministers and colleagues with key choices based on robust evidence and facilitate the strategic development process
> 4 Knows how to take a corporate perspective across government, pro-actively working as a team with Whitehall peers, influencing and shaping their strategic agendas and understanding key strategy and decision processes
> 5 Champions the role of strategic thinking in the organization, working effectively with relevant internal and external experts.
>
> Some of the behaviours entailed in this strategic thinking included:
>
> - Understanding and explaining the long-term vision and direction for the government department
> - Using the government's wider priorities to develop the long-term vision and direction for the department
> - Consideration of the trends relevant to the development of the long-term vision and direction of the department
> - Using focus groups, formal surveys, etc. to include views of people in department
> - Understanding and explaining strategic choices and the likely implications from pursuing the various strategic choices
> - Presenting Ministers and colleagues with key strategic choices
> - Using trends, scenarios, etc. to make judgements about strategic choices
> - Working across departmental boundaries on strategic agendas
> - Making use of internal strategy experts in strategic thinking

DO TECHNIQUES MATTER?

Hopefully the techniques we been reviewing in this chapter look plausible, but if strategic processes involve more than thinking, and they involve communication and negotiation, do we have an exaggerated sense of the value of techniques for strategic thinking? Surprisingly, few studies have been carried out to evaluate the use of strategic thinking techniques in a public services context. As John Bryson and a colleague remarked specifically about large-scale interactive methods of strategic planning, there are some very good descriptions of techniques, but very little systematic evaluation of the benefits of using them. This is generally true of strategic thinking techniques in the private and public sectors. There is little systematic evaluation of their benefits and advantages in practice.

SUMMARY

This chapter has mainly concentrated on strategic thinking as a rational process consisting of a sequence of steps. Despite objections that are frequently voiced about representing strategic thinking as a rational and linear process, it is worth remembering the point made by John Kay, who claimed that organizations generally do approach strategic thinking as a rational process.

Techniques were presented as additions to the process of strategic thinking, additions that provided structured ways of carrying out thinking as part of the overall strategy process. If we think of strategic thinking as akin to a craft, then the techniques are intellectual tools that can be selected and used to fashion ideas as a skilled accomplishment. In a sense, they are available to be used, not used, or used in a modified way. One example of this is the way the stakeholder analysis can be used to corroborate and refine ideas about the mission of a public services organization; and it can be used again for the purpose of thinking about how strategies can be implemented to minimize resistance to change. The specific form of the stakeholder analysis will probably change slightly depending on how it is to be used within strategic thinking.

Another view of strategic thinking is to consider it as embedded in organizational processes and in organizational structures. Reference was made to the ideas of Dyson, who referred to strategic planning as being a management process involving analysis, consultation, and negotiation. A key point about situating strategic thinking within consultation and negotiation processes, as well as within analytical processes, is to recognize that strategy is also subject to the effects of conflicting perspectives and interests.

Work-based assignment: core competencies analysis

The work-based assignments in this book are for civil servants and other public services staff who have four or more years of management experience.

Either use your own organization or select another organization you know very well and use the approach suggested by Klein and Hiscocks to identify its top skills. Use what you discover to make an assessment of the core competences of the organization.

129

Work-based assignment: feasibility assessment of strategies

Interview one or two people who were closely involved in writing your organization's current strategic plan, and ask them whether proposed strategies were assessed carefully for feasibility before they were chosen. Ask them if any strategies were dropped at the choice stage because they were not feasible. Ask them for their views on the importance of assessing feasibility before choosing between strategic options.

DISCUSSION QUESTIONS

1 Even though it may be hard to follow it exactly, should leaders in public services follow a linear model of strategic thinking and try to be as rational as possible?
2 Are there any techniques that you think are especially important in strategic thinking in the public services? What two or three techniques do you think are most useful in the public services?
3 What criteria should be used in making strategic choices and how important are assessments of feasibility?
4 Does strategic thinking in public services need to be developed in some way to cope better with the negotiation processes that may occur?

FURTHER READING

Nutt, P. (2008) 'Investigating the success of decision making processes', *Journal of Management Studies*, 45, 2: 425–55.
Prime Minister's Strategy Unit, Cabinet Office (2003) *Strategy Survival Guide*. London: Strategy Unit.

Chapter 6

Strategic issue management

LEARNING OBJECTIVES

- To understand the concept of strategic issues
- To explore strategic thinking used to identify and address strategic issues
- To appreciate methods that may be used to probe strategic issues and to generate ideas for action to solve issues

INTRODUCTION

The most direct way to uncover strategic issues is to ask two questions:

- What is making it difficult for this organization to achieve its top goals, or its mission, or its strategic vision?
- What would make it much easier for this organization to achieve its top goals, or its mission, or its strategic vision?

The answers we give to these questions can be called strategic issues. It is because an issue includes something that makes achieving a strategic vision easier, such as an opportunity or strength, that it is probably better to talk about 'addressing' a strategic issue rather than the more obvious phrase of 'solving' an issue, which implies an issue is always a problem (e.g. a threat or weakness). Sometimes issues might also be identified by observing and analysing conflicts or tensions between different stakeholder groups or interest groups.

By definition, a strategic issue is a development or event that has serious consequences for the likelihood that an organization (or a consortium) will achieve its strategic goals (or strategic vision, or strategic mission, etc.). Strategic issue management is a process in which such issues are first identified, and then action is taken to address them.

As long ago as 1983, Douglas Eadie in the United States was writing about the need for strategic issue management to be used in the public sector. His version of strategic issue management was very concerned with fostering creativity in strategic management, and innovation in terms of action. Overall, he was less concerned with efficiency and performance as such. Other leading American scholars gave their attention to strategic issue management in the 1980s and onwards; for example, Nutt and Backoff (1992, 1993) and John Bryson (1988, 1995, and 2004).

CONCEPT BOX 6.1   ISSUE MANAGEMENT

Nutt and Backoff (1993: 311) defined issue management as an approach that concentrates on issues, and involves thinking about the situation (through a SWOT analysis) in order to develop ideas for the organizations' strategic development:

> Issues are treated as emergent developments that are apt to influence the organization's ability to meet its goals. Issues can arise internally or externally and may have beneficial or negative effects. Issues are used to fill the gap between a SWOT analysis and strategic development. This approach allows for the continuous revision of SWOTs, suggesting a process that periodically updates strategy with the insights drawn from recent developments. Annual strategy sessions are planned to resolve a few pivotal issues, with SWOT review and revision done every five years. Using issues as the focus of inquiry allows strategic managers to become more flexible and responsive to emergent developments.

Some of the leading ideas in strategic issue management are, first, that strategic management revolves around addressing strategic issues; second, that leaders need to think about how to overcome barriers to action and use opportunities for the realization of strategic goals; and third, that leaders need to pay attention to implementation (see Figure 6.1). The last idea – the emphasis on paying attention to implementation – is linked to an awareness of the importance of conflict management, and stakeholder analysis and management. Nutt and Backoff (1992), for example, highlight the need to look at how various stakeholders will respond to proposals for new strategic actions.

Despite the focus on strategic issue management by influential leading scholars in the United States, when it came to reforming the public services in the US federal government in the early 1990s, the reforms did not emphasize strategic issue management, but instead focused on performance management and getting results. It is worth underlining the contrast between strategic issue management with its concerns for solutions and creativity, and the federal government reforms focused on strategic

Figure 6.1 *Strategic thinking using issues*
(Based on explanation of issue management by Nutt and Backoff (1993))

planning and performance measurement and management. As federal agencies moved towards the implementation of strategic planning linked to performance management, they worked on performance measurement and identifying performance indicators and performance targets linked to strategic goals. This seems diametrically opposed to the creative problem solving and coalition building efforts of strategic issue management. Of course, there is no logical reason why individual organizations should not design strategic management processes that attempt to do both – both concern themselves with long-term strategic goals and managing performance towards the achievement of those long-term goals, and, at the same time, the identification and management of strategic issues involving the handling and management of stakeholders and coalitions of interest groups.

STRATEGIC ISSUES

Some experts identify issues with developments or events that are threats or opportunities. Some imply that a strategic issue is not easy to resolve. In part, this might be because a solution is not immediately obvious and it takes some intellectual effort to work out what a solution might entail. Alternatively, as Nutt and Backoff (1992) argue, a strategic issue can be seen as a 'tension' that is formed by opposing forces pushing the organization in different directions. At one point (Nutt and Backoff 1992: 181), they suggest that strategic management groups who formulate issues as tensions 'begin to appreciate the need to reconcile contradictory pressures'.

Nutt and Backoff were not the first to think about strategic management in terms of contending forces and strategic issues. They outlined some of the antecedent ideas as follows (Nutt and Backoff 1992: 129):

> Treating issues as tensions is consistent with several schools of thought pertinent to strategy formation. Jantsch (1975) contends that strategic management should

balance opposing forces, such as budget cuts and the treatment of the disadvantaged needing care in a mental health center. Tensions are similar to the dialectical ideas used by Mitroff and Emshoff (1979) and Mason and Mitroff (1981) to frame needs in policy making as opposites. The opposing ideas produce strong claims and counterclaims that create tensions for which a response is devised. Cobb and Elder (1972) identify issues as conflicts between interest groups. Both Mason (1969) and Sussman and Herden (1985) found that exploring these opposing forces led to superior results in policy making. Strategic managers that deal with one of two opposing forces and ignore the other create potentially dangerous situations in which the barriers to action or opportunities posed by the unrecognized forces may be overlooked.

Perhaps an example will make this conception of a strategic issue as a tension clearer. Nutt and Backoff (1992: 127) provided the example of a hospital that had a low bed occupancy rate, was suffering a decline in revenue, and wanted to cut back on the numbers of employees, but at the time had a contract with a trade union that constrained its ability to do this. So, one implication of this idea of a strategic issue as a tension is that solving a strategic issue (low occupancy causing reductions in revenue) in an obvious way can cause side-effects which are serious and unwelcome (e.g. resistance to layoffs by the union). In this case, we can use the word dilemma to understand the subjective problems caused for leaders by a strategic issue. The resolution of the dilemma involves finding actions that solve the problem and avoid unwelcome side-effects (or take advantage of opportunities). This suggests that the definition of strategic issue can be formulated as being a special type of problem which exists when it is not easy to know immediately what the best solution might be, or a problem when it is difficult to see how to resolve it without creating further serious problems (or missing good opportunities). In addition, we can sometimes recognize this type of problem by the fact that leaders face fairly clear problems of mobilizing sufficient support behind obvious solutions and of dealing with resistance and opposition – and this can be both within and outside the organization. This may be the case when a strategic issue manifests itself as the site of a major conflict of interest.

One point stressed by some experts is that strategic issues often require urgent responses by leaders. On this basis, they point out the danger of trying to delay handling strategic issues caused by only considering them within an annual strategic planning cycle. If strategic issues tend to be very urgent in nature because they emerge suddenly, and require a very rapid response, then it may be necessary for an organization to develop a strategic management process for issue management that sits alongside the annual strategic planning process. On the other hand, perhaps there are some strategic issues that do not fit this pattern of sudden acute development, but are more chronic in nature and can be handled through the annual planning process.

There needs to be some clarity about how different types of problems – strategic issues and operational problems – are being processed. Where a problem is a strategic issue, then this is an issue that should be considered by the leaders of the organization (or by the leaders of the relevant part of the organization). The strategic leaders need to ensure issues are analysed and action taken to resolve them. If the problem is not a strategic issue, then it needs to be referred elsewhere – say to middle or front line management. So, the main practical justification for trying to be clear about what is a strategic issue and what is not a strategic issue is a matter of deciding who in management is responsible for dealing with which issues and problems.

If we assume that strategic leaders need to focus on the most important strategic issues otherwise their credibility as a leader will suffer and they may find themselves being sacked and replaced (Nutt and Backoff 1992), there is a need for leaders to be good at distinguishing top priority strategic issues from less important strategic issues. One way to define the top strategic issues is to evaluate the consequences for the organization if they are ignored. All strategic issues are of interest (positive) or cause concern (negative) because of their consequence for the future success and future viability of an organization. But the top strategic issues will be those that offer the biggest opportunities, or pose the biggest threats, to achieving the top strategic goals and the biggest opportunity for the success of the organization or the biggest threat to the survival of an organization. Therefore, perhaps every time a strategic issue comes along a leader should pose the question: What will be the consequence of us doing nothing about this issue? Will doing nothing about this issue mean we fail to achieve our long-term strategic goals (or, equivalently, will it mean that we fail to deliver our organizational mission, or stop us moving towards a strategic vision of the future of the organization?). Will doing nothing about it mean we are significantly less successful or even threaten our survival?

MORE ABOUT THE NATURE OF STRATEGIC ISSUES

We have laboured in the preceding paragraphs to express an important idea about strategic issues: and it is worth underlining this point. Specifically, many but not all strategic issues are 'problems' in the usual sense of the word. It is very easy to assume that strategic issues are always problems. However, arguably, there are some issues that are not problems but, as we have been saying already, are opportunities. We can define an opportunity as something that we can use to better achieve strategic goals (or to better deliver the mission of the organization, or to move more swiftly to realizing a desirable strategic vision). The issue is then one of exploiting an opportunity. In this case, we could still say we have a problem – but in the distinctive sense of we have the problem of not wasting an opportunity!

Some strategic issues may not actually be affecting current organizational results. Some could be issues because they will have an impact on the organization in five years' time or ten years' time. This, of course, requires that leaders who are interested in using strategic issue management are on their guard against merely reacting to their experiences of what is happening now. Leaders must also use their imagination, and develop their ability to anticipate issues, by looking at things that could impact on the organization in the future. Studying trends that are starting to emerge could be one way of strategic leaders sensitizing themselves to possible future strategic issues.

Perhaps most strategic issues concern the public services that the organization produces, and its success in meeting the needs of service users (or customers). If a public service is substantially failing to meet the needs of existing users, or if there is a key section of the public missing out on a service, for example, then this probably means the organization is failing in respect of its mission. And, of course, a failure in a serious way to deliver a mission is a strategic issue. But strategic issues may be found in other aspects of a public service organization – and not just in the public services it produces and whose needs it serves.

Some experts see strategic issues as originating in the external environment of the organization. Public services are continually faced with changing external environments. These changes may be economic and technological, and they may be political. Among the most important external developments are, however, changes in society, changes in lifestyles, and changes in public attitudes. Leaders of public services who overlook such changes fail to keep their organizations adapting to new requirements. As we saw in an earlier chapter, at one point in time, for example, there may be public concerns about the quality of educational and health services, and leaders will need to respond to this. Within a matter of a few years – five or ten years, maybe – such concerns may have receded and the public attention has turned to new concerns, such as community safety, personal safety, and the levels of immigration. It is a basic fact that society evolves all the time. Lifestyles change all the time and, in consequence, what the public wants from the public services also continues to change. Strategic issue management processes can, therefore, be useful in helping to adjust the organization, its values, and its capabilities to the new external realities.

Technological change is an important source of strategic issues. Governments all around the world have been coming to terms with the astonishing growth of the Internet since the mid 1990s and the way in which more and more of the daily lives of citizens are influenced by the Internet. People now frequently communicate by email. They often do their shopping on-line. They shop for holidays on-line. They book hotels and plane flights on-line. This technological development has also affected the business world. There are Internet-based retail businesses. Banks now offer to conduct their interactions with their customers on-line. Manufacturing businesses are using the Internet for procurement. And, inevitably, with the public using the Internet, and with businesses using the Internet, questions arise about on-line access to government services and citizens being able to carry out transactions with government using the Internet. Indeed governments all around the world made major efforts in the late 1990s and early years of the twenty first century to migrate government services to the Internet. This is an example of a technological change that was actually linked to lifestyle changes and economic changes, and posed a major challenge to government services.

So we could envisage strategic issues as emerging from the external environment of a public service organization and then, in a sense, there being an issue because the organization needs to adapt its strategy, its values and capabilities, and its alliances so as to continue to be a successful provider of services. By adapting the organization and thus addressing the issue, the leaders of public services create or renew satisfaction among service users and among politicians.

However, perhaps we should specify a second characteristic of strategic issues. They not only necessitate an ongoing 'dialectic' between the environment and the organization, but, in addition, they are determined by the strategic intent of those who lead the organization. This is because, in developing a strategic goal and thus a strategic intent, trends or events become issues by virtue of the fact that they impinge on this strategic intent. If, as a strategic leader, you have a clear strategic intent, then what is happening in the external environment may matter because it blocks or facilitates the realization of that intent. So there is a degree of relativism in a strategic issue. The significance of external developments depends in part on what it is the organization is trying to do in order to make the public services better in the future. But this relativism is limited by the public's experiences and judgements of the public services. A strategic issue cannot be reduced purely to a reflection of the intentions of strategic leaders within the public services. Issues are also partly a matter of what the public needs and wants.

STRATEGIC ISSUE AGENDA

Should public services organizations be systematic in considering the management of strategic issues? Some organizations may be in slow changing environments, and may feel able to deal with sporadic strategic issues on an ad-hoc basis. But if an environment is complex and dynamic, then an organization's strategic leaders have, at any point in time, to be concerned about its capacity to deliver its strategic vision if there is a stream of fairly tough or intractable strategic issues. Presumably that type of situation can overwhelm the capacity of many organizations to identify and resolve strategic issues. A key dimension of this capacity is the amount of attention strategic leaders can give. Leaders cannot give limitless attention to strategic issues.

The consideration of strategic issues is begun by the strategic leaders of an organization constantly monitoring their environment, reviewing their strategic goals and intentions, and therefore thinking about what strategic issues they are currently facing or will be facing. They evaluate these strategic issues in terms of their seriousness. This might be judged in terms of the consequences for their strategic goals or strategic visions of not solving the issues. They also need to evaluate their urgency. On this basis, strategic leaders form a ranking of the strategic issues, with serious and urgent issues being ranked most highly, and less serious and less urgent issues being ranked lower. Such a ranking of strategic issues is the essence of the formulation of a strategic issue agenda.

The strategic issue agenda, which should be reviewed fairly frequently, is used for structuring discussions about what to do. Decisions need to be made about what issues on the strategic issue agenda require action now or in the future. Strategic leaders may review the ranking of the issues and then consider each issue in turn and decide whether it is an issue that needs attention now and what action needs to be taken, or whether it is an issue that is serious but that they should continue to monitor and keep under surveillance. They might also decide that an issue is becoming less serious and less urgent, but decide to continue monitoring it for the time being. There may be some issues that are fading away or are judged now to be of no importance and may be dropped from the strategic issue agenda.

KEY CHARACTERISTICS OF STRATEGIC ISSUE MANAGEMENT

The design of the thinking aspects of a strategic planning process that can be used to manage strategic issues has been explored by Eadie (1983), Nutt and Backoff (1992), and Bryson (2004).

Eadie (1983) provided an early encouragement to recognize 'issues' as relevant to strategic thinking and planning in the public sector. Whereas a process of budget preparation and operational planning could be useful for productivity improvements, and strategic planning techniques could be applied in a process of mission and goal formulation that might be useful for organizational cohesion, he argued that the techniques of strategic planning were needed to deal with issues.

> Often important issues cannot be dealt with through operational planning because they cross too many intra-organizational lines, or are heavily influenced by a complex, changing environment – or, frequently, both. In this instance, the need is for innovation and creativity, which calls for applying the techniques of strategic planning.
>
> (Eadie 1983: 450)

As well as some case material, Eadie offered what was, in effect, an eight step process for strategic planning in which environmental scanning and opportunities loomed large (see Figure 6.2). Implicitly, this suggested that environmental scanning was a key technique for identifying strategic issues, and that the issues took the form of opportunities.

Eadie (1983) suggested starting strategic planning on a limited basis and widening its use as an organization's capability in strategic planning developed. Perhaps

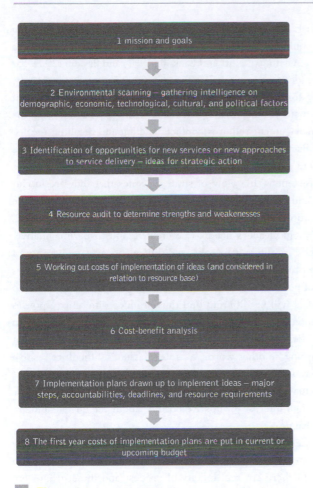

Figure 6.2 *Eadie (1983) steps in strategic planning (to deal with issues)*

an organization should start with one strategic issue, tackle that, learn from the experience, and thus establish the credibility of thinking strategically and not just operationally. Logically, of course, if you establish the credibility of strategic management through strategic issue management, you also establish the credibility of the strategic leaders who use strategic issue management. The implication of Eadie's views is that strategic issue management which is focused on one or two issues only will be particularly useful in an organization with no past history of strategic management. Likewise, the leader who is new and has no history with an organization can use strategic issue management to show that they can make things better and, therefore, they are worthy of the trust for which they are asking when they put forward an ambitious long-term strategic plan (Joyce 2000).

Writers who came after Eadie were to offer more detailed advice on how thinking within strategic planning could be applied to issues and their solutions. However, a constant theme, found in the writing of Nutt and Backoff (1992) and Bryson (2004), as well as Eadie (1983), is the idea that strategic issue management is aimed at creativity, and this involves searching for and creating less obvious solutions. It is also evident from the attention given to stakeholder management that Nutt and Backoff take the view that strategic issue management requires conflict handling and resolution skills. John Bryson and Nutt and Backoff have also described the processes for strategic issue management in ways that put a lot of stress on fairly participative approaches.

These remarks are consistent with a view of strategic issues that they are intrinsically difficult to address and resolve partly because they involve analysing strategic situations in which the solutions are not immediately obvious and not to hand ready-made. This means that strategic leaders need to be creative and to be imaginative. Furthermore strategic issues are difficult to solve and difficult to manage because of the multiplicity of interests present in the situation. Thus the need for strategic leaders to understand the impact of possible solutions on stakeholder groups, and the need to appreciate that these impacts will be different and thus produce different responses by stakeholders. Some responses will be ones of resistance to attempted solutions to strategic issues. Other responses will be ones of active or passive support for what strategic leaders are attempting. In other words, a strategic issue is difficult to resolve and requires some considerable effort – both intellectual and leadership – because it is a combination of intellectual challenge (of knowing what to do) and leadership challenge (of ensuring that enough interest groups are positive about the change and are mobilized to support the change).

The Nutt and Backoff view of strategic issue management sits very comfortably with a pluralist view of strategic management – the idea that inside the organization and outside the organization there are multiplicity of groups, and these groups are defined by their different interests. They may have related interests, but possibly we should stress the differences of interest they have about particular issues.

Why might a participative approach to strategic issue management be stressed? Strategic leaders may adopt a participative approach because they wish to engage people with the strategic management process, and the reason they want to engage people with the strategic management process is possibly based around a very simple idea that involving people in analysing issues and then coming up with solutions produces more support for change. So, it could be argued that a participative approach is intended to ease the problems of implementing strategic solutions. However, this probably does not mean that the process will be conflict-free. There will still be potential clashes between different interests, and thus the need for good conflict handling and resolution skills.

Finally, we should note here that strategic issue management, as described by Nutt and Backoff (1992) and by Bryson (2004), with an emphasis on participative approaches, also leads quite naturally to the design of large-scale planning events (including what are named whole systems development events). These large-scale events provide one way of creating a participative approach to strategic issue management. However, we should note the findings of an evaluation by Bryson and Anderson (2000) of these large-scale events. Their overall conclusion is that, while there are some good descriptions about what these large-scale approaches are, there is a lack of evidence about the consequences of using these methods.

A METHOD FOR IDENTIFYING AND UNDERSTANDING ISSUES

It was suggested above that leaders can experience strategic issues as dilemmas. Other, similar, words that come to mind are paradox and contradiction. All of these words suggest the need for creativity. Apart from an injunction to be creative, or possibly to think intuitively, is it possible to think of a way of developing creative solutions that overcome the dilemmas of strategic issues?

We can distinguish between methods of deepening an understanding of an issue and methods of finding a creative solution to that issue. Nutt and Backoff (1992) provide some interesting ideas for both of these – identifying and clarifying the nature of a strategic issue, and then structuring the use of a creative imagination. In this section we concentrate on some ideas for identifying and appreciating strategic issues.

Nutt and Backoff say that developments that signal the need for strategic action (i.e. one part of a strategic issue) can be classified into one of four types. These include both internal and external developments, and are labelled by them as follows: equity, preservation, transition, and productivity (see Figure 6.3). Equity developments include human resource developments within the organization that raise questions about the fairness with which people are treated. (Of course, there are also fairness questions about who is receiving a service and what benefits are being delivered to service recipients.) Developments which are classified as preservation ones could be internal to the organization, and these are ones that serve to maintain traditions by preserving cultures, practices, or agreements. Transition developments might occur in the external environment, and can be illustrated by the emergence of new needs and new opportunities. In response to the development of new needs, a public service organization may consider developing new services. Other external developments may pressurize the organization to improve its productivity.

Nutt and Backoff suggest using this framework of four types of developments to specify issues as tensions. This involves first of all identifying the development signalling the need for action (e.g. the emergence of a new need) as a particular type of development (e.g. a transition development), and then trying to see if it can be paired

141

Figure 6.3 *Specifying issues as tensions*

with one of the remaining three development types. If the triggering development was 'transition', this step would yield the following three tensions:

- Transition-equity
- Transition-preservation
- Transition-productivity.

The point would be to describe each of the tensions using data from the situation under consideration. To explain this, let us consider a development triggered by, say, a new need. This may be paired with a pressure to increase productivity. This is labelled a 'transition-productivity tension'. Nutt and Backoff give as an example of this the continuing need by a hospital to produce cash flow (which will depend on productivity), while implementing a planned expansion of services (which is a response to a transition development). As this example seems to indicate, a pole of the tension may be described in terms of an organizational action (such as planned expansion) rather than in terms of the development that signals the need for organizational action (such as a growth of external demand for the service). We could say that the immediately obvious action in the face of increased external demand is to expand the service, but this could be a problem if we concentrate too much on change management and neglect the need to manage delivery to existing service users while the change is being implemented. Thus, the framework can be used to guide the search for tensions in actual situations.

The next step in using the framework, having already paired the triggering development with the three other development types, is to consider the remaining combinations of development types. So, if the triggering development was the emergence of a new need (a transition development), then the remaining combinations of developments would be:

- Equity-preservation
- Equity-productivity
- Tradition-productivity.

In this second step, the three tensions, according to Nutt and Backoff, are examined with the triggering development regarded as a 'moderator', which they define as relaxing an issue or stressing the issue further.

Logically, given four types of development, these two steps suggest six types of tension. In fact, Nutt and Backoff (1992: 134) suggest that 'an issue is connected or implicated in all six tensions'. The six issue tensions, which emerge from their exploration of the framework, are all plausible in the context of the modernization of public services. These are paraphrased as follows:

1 Continuing to meet service user demands during a change programme
2 Ensuring there is some fairness (between and among winners and losers) as a result of a planned change
3 Respecting traditional cultures/practices/agreements while ensuring fairness
4 Getting a productivity increase from a public service that is already feeling under a great deal of stress and is resisting pressure to abandon its traditional cultures/practices/agreements
5 Dealing with inertia during a change programme
6 Having regard to fairness within the system while making changes to increase productivity.

The value of using this framework is, in part, the production of fresh insights that might occur as a result of trying to reframe known facts and experiences in terms of these fairly abstract categorizations of developments. It is important, however, that the strategic leader feels comfortable moving backwards and forwards between 'data' about the real strategic situation and the more abstract schema offered by Nutt and Backoff. It is no use thinking only at the level of the more abstract schema. By moving from situational data to the framework and then back to the situational data, the strategic leader gains a more considered (and hopefully more complete and balanced) appreciation of the situation.

It is probably important at this point to stress again the integral nature of conflicts of interest to this process. On one hand, what we have described is an intellectual technique and may give the impression that issue identification is an intellectual or even analytical process. But the framework also potentially highlights the range of interest groups that may be contending for influence in the definition of issues. This is

143

obvious in the case of looking at equity developments and traditional developments. Consideration of equity (and thus who are the winners and losers) in planned change, or in action to improve productivity, should highlight some of the key stakeholder groups. Likewise, consideration of who is opposing or resisting change or productivity improvements again will highlight key stakeholder groups.

There are conflicts between the providers and service users and there are conflicts between different groups of service providers about both the issues and the data to show there is an issue. We can illustrate both of these with examples from the public services.

An example of a modest service issue relates to pressure to improve swimming pools in public leisure services. The providers may stress the use of 'scientific data' to judge the adequacy of water cleanliness. Based on professionally or technically excellent standards the water may be judged to be clean. The situation may appear quite different to members of the public using the swimming pool. They may say there is too much chlorine in the water, or the water looks cloudy and could be dirty. This shows the potential conflict between those providing the service and those using it.

An example of conflicts between providers can be taken from public art galleries where the public has free admission because the galleries are funded out of taxation. There can be an argument between different groups of professional employees within the art galleries about the issues that need addressing. One simple distinction is between professionals involved in acquiring and looking after the art collection, and those involved in engaging the public with the consumption of the services of the galleries. The former group may work in rooms not open to public, and rooms where the art collection is stored until it is put on public display. They include art historians and those involved in the preservation and protection of the paintings, and who, therefore, have scientific-technical skills to do with looking after paintings. The latter group include people employed in art galleries who are concerned with, for example, the design and running of exhibitions and shows. They are interested in putting together paintings in a particular way, and advertising the exhibitions and shows to the public. They may think about featuring a particular painter or perhaps a particular theme. They are mostly concerned with how the paintings are being experienced by the public – how to put on a good exhibition. Those involved in the marketing function within the art galleries are also thinking about how they can perhaps draw in sections of the public to the art gallery, including types of people who are rare visitors, so that the art gallery becomes busier than in the past. But if the public come in larger numbers to view the paintings, some of the professionals who are responsible for preserving and protecting the collection may worry about the increased threat to the paintings because people may touch them more. So, perhaps those who are more concerned with the technical side of the art gallery may have mixed feelings about increasing the numbers of the members of public attending the art gallery, whereas those involved in exhibition work and marketing may feel that is a really good thing.

Similarly, the professionals who want to make the art galleries more popular to wider sections of the population may think they can make exhibitions and shows even more interesting by borrowing paintings from other galleries in other countries. They will support the idea of forming a set of alliances with other major art galleries around the world, so that they can now draw on a bigger collection than that owned by their own gallery. For others, such alliances would potentially be a problem since the paintings in their collection would have to be sent to other galleries, and might be damaged when being moved around the world.

However appealing the analytical framework offered by Nutt and Backoff, it is also important to remember their continual point that the tensions can be materialized in conflicts between different parties and different interest groups. Strategic issue management is never a purely analytical exercise.

A METHOD FOR FORMULATING ACTION IN RESPONSE TO STRATEGIC ISSUES

We turn again to Nutt and Backoff (1992), this time for a method to formulate strategic action. They suggest a useful set of steps for structuring the use of imagination and intuition to identify suitable strategic actions to address strategic issues. First, they recommend the use of SWOT analysis to identify strengths, weaknesses, opportunities, and threats. Second, they suggest stating issues as tensions and then assessing the significance of issues for the organization. In outlining a recommended strategic management process, Nutt and Backoff (1992: 434) suggest that issues are recognized by their effect on organizational functioning or ability to achieve a desired future, and they suggest looking for the 'most significant factor pulling in the opposite direction and pair the issue with this factor'. They go on (Ibid 1992: 435) to advise the use of a discursive approach to establish an issue's significance: this involves 'identifying its important features and why it merits the organization's attention'. Third, they say that the top priority issue can be selected for the process of issue management. Fourth, they propose that the results of the SWOT analysis are used to identify actions that will address the top priority strategic issue in such a way as to move the organization towards its strategic vision. For example, proposals for action which use a top strength of the organization to address an issue, and that moves the organization closer to a desired future state (strategic vision), would be noted for subsequent evaluation of feasibility. But ideas for action do not have to make use of a single strength or address a single opportunity. The ideas may address a combination of strengths or a mix of strengths, weaknesses, etc. Indeed, Nutt and Backoff suggest that there may be proposals for action that address a strength, a weakness, an opportunity, and a threat all at the same time! Fifth, ideas for action that have a common theme are grouped and labelled as a strategy (see Figure 6.4).

145

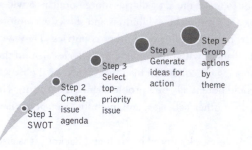

Figure 6.4 *Formulation process*

Their framework of six types of tensions, which was outlined in the previous section of this chapter, can be used in step two as a way of checking that all relevant tensions have been identified. This would be done before the discursive assessment of the significance of issues. One approach to the discursive assessment of an issue might be to consider two questions (Eadie 1983):

- What would be the perceived cost of not dealing with the issue?
- Will addressing the issue be complex because of the likely reactions of powerful stakeholders to obvious actions that might be taken to address it?

The fourth step in this process involves a 'sensitized' brainstorming which can be represented by Figure 6.5. This means that you remind yourself of all the top items in the SWOT, the strategic vision, and the issue immediately prior to brainstorming, and if all these elements are in your mind then they may automatically inform the brainstorming. The brainstorming might be 'cued' using the following type of question in respect of each of the top issues:

- What action using our top strength can we take to address the issue in order that the organization moves closer towards its strategic vision?

The question can be altered to make use of other items in the SWOT – for example, the top weakness, the top opportunity, and the top threat. The wording has to be altered to make the question read correctly with these other items. So the question might be rephrased, for example, what action overcoming or mitigating the top weakness can we take to address the issue in order that the organization moves closer towards its strategic vision? What action taking advantage of our top opportunity can we take to address the issue in order that the organization moves closer towards its strategic vision? What action blocking or avoiding the top threat can we take to address the issue in order that the organization moves closer towards its strategic vision?

Cued brainstorming is definitely not easy to do and can quickly produce a lot of ideas for action that will not stand scrutiny in terms of their feasibility. However, the

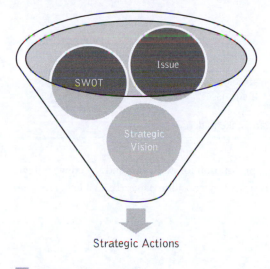

Strategic Actions

Figure 6.5 *Cued brainstorming*

best thing to do is to generate as many ideas as possible without being critical of any of them until all the ideas are expressed and captured, and only afterwards should you begin the process of sifting through them for their feasibility.

This process sounds easy to follow, but the idea of treating the issue as a tension makes it more difficult than it sounds. This is so even if we try to create a strategy for an issue analysed as a tension made up of a contradiction between two developments, which is one way that Nutt and Backoff see the task of strategy formulation. Nutt and Backoff (1992: 145) say: 'Strategy is sought that attempts to balance the opposing forces in a high-priority issue tension so that strategic action is taken to deal with one development in the tension while being cognizant of the other.' Above we noted their view that an issue is connected or implicated in all six types of tension. Trying to develop a single strategy that consciously dealt with all six types of tensions implicated in an issue would be very complex!

Nutt and Backoff have many useful ideas for checking out the ideas and strategies produced in the process described above and then planning their implementation, but steps one to five above contain the essence of their method for strategy formulation.

A final practical point concerns how to document the results of strategic thinking about issues. One approach is to use 'issue briefs' and 'issue position papers' (Heath 1997). The first of these, the issue brief, can be used to record thinking which defines and explains a strategic issue, establishes the cost of not addressing the issue (the consequences and timescales of the consequences of doing nothing about the issue), discusses options, and analyses the interests and power of stakeholders in respect of the issue. The issue brief is, more than anything else, a summary of strategic thinking on

147

Table 6.1 *Issue brief*

Issue brief
1   Definition and explanation of the strategic issue
2   The cost of not addressing the strategic issue
3   Options
4   The interests and power of relevant stakeholders

the issue and options. It is, therefore, preparation for evaluating and selecting strategic actions to address the issue, which is set out in a position paper (see Table 6.1).

SUMMARY

Strategic issues may be positive or negative events, or developments that can be identified by scanning internal and external environments. They may be identified as issues on the basis that they have important consequences for the mission or vision, or strategic goals of a public service organization. It is often suggested that strategic issue management requires creativity and innovation by strategic leaders, but it is also critical to remember that such management needs effective conflict handling and resolution skills, and may be usefully enhanced through stakeholder analysis and management.

Nutt and Backoff (1992) have provided some useful ideas and frameworks for understanding strategic issues and the underlying nature of strategic issues and for using them to generate ideas for strategic action.

Work-based assignment: formulating an issue agenda

The work-based assignments in this book are for civil servants and other public services staff who have four or more years of management experience.

This assignment is designed to enable you to practice thinking about strategic issues. Please carry this out on your own organization or select an organization that you know well. This could be an organization from which you receive a service. It could be an organization that you have researched.

First of all, think about any concerns you might have about the future success of this organization. If you can, list up to eight concerns.

Second, remind yourself of the definition of a strategic issue and then evaluate each of the concerns you have listed. Check that they are actually strategic issues. Remember, a strategic issue is one that should be referred to the leaders of the organization for solution. Other kinds of management problems that are not strategic issues need to be referred elsewhere. Only keep strategic issues in your list. Delete the others.

Third, have a go at ranking them in order of importance. Do this by asking what would be the consequence of not solving this issue. What would be the consequence for strategic goals? What would be the consequence for the future success or survival of the organization? Try if you can to justify your judgement of the seriousness of the consequences with some evidence.

Fourth, rate the urgency of each of the issues on the list (which should now be in rank order of importance). You could rate each issue on a scale of 0–10, where you would rate an issue as 10 if you think that it is very urgent and action should be taken immediately, and as 0 if it is something that does not require action now but should be kept under surveillance.

Finally, identify the strategic issues which are both important and urgent.

Work-based assignment: assessing issues

Identify six strategic issues in your own organization or an organization you know well. Then choose one of them as the top strategic issue based on the consideration of the following criteria:

- What would be the perceived cost of not dealing with the issue?
- The complex consequences of likely reactions from powerful stakeholders to obvious actions that might be taken to solve the issue.

Prepare a one-page issue brief (see Table 6.1 for format).

Work-based assignment: creative ideas

This assignment is based on the method of Nutt and Backoff for generating ideas for strategic action. First, carry this out in your own organization, or select a public service organization you know reasonably well because you were employed by it, or now use its services, or have researched it. Second, carry out a SWOT analysis and rank all the strengths, weaknesses, threats, and opportunities so you can identify the organization's top strength, the top weakness, the top opportunity, and top threat. Third, pick the top strength and generate a number of ideas for actions in which this strength would be exploited. Try to generate ideas for action that simultaneously address the top strategic issue, and move the organization towards achieving its strategic goals or vision. Repeat this but using the top weakness/top opportunity/top threat. Try to generate a large number of ideas and do not be disappointed if many of them prove, on further consideration, to be either not feasible or not suitable. This methodology is bound to create a large number of ideas that are not good enough, but if there is at least one really good idea, then the whole exercise proves to be very worthwhile.

149

DISCUSSION QUESTIONS

1   In what circumstances should strategic leaders use the type of strategic thinking that has been considered in this chapter?
2   What are the advantages and disadvantages of using the methods proposed by Nutt and Backoff to probe the nature of strategic issues and to generate ideas for action?
3   What is the essence of 'creativity' in strategic thinking and how important is it for a strategic leader to be creative?
4   What techniques can strategic leaders use to think about the conflicts and tensions between interest groups that are a manifestation of strategic issues?

FURTHER READING

Nutt, P.C. and Backoff, R.W. (1992) *Strategic Management of Public and Third Sector Organizations*. San Francisco: Jossey-Bass.
Nutt, P.C. and Backoff, R.W. (1993) 'Transforming public organizations with strategic management and strategic leadership', *Journal of Management*, 19: 299–347.

Chapter 7

Strategic planning and management

LEARNING OBJECTIVES

- To appreciate the nature of strategic planning and management in the public services
- To review the benefits of strategic planning
- To consider the issue of responsiveness to the public

INTRODUCTION

The public services in the United States and the United Kingdom experimented in the late 1960s and early 1970s with the idea of programming, planning, and budgeting systems (PPB), which can be seen as an ancestor of the strategic planning systems that were subsequently developed in the late 1980s and 1990s. There were also attempts by the United Nations during the 1970s to encourage the use of planning based on objective setting to produce improvements in performance. Again this can be seen as a precursor to contemporary strategic management practices in the public services.

In the early 1980s, the diffusion of strategic planning into government and public services was still limited. Douglas Eadie (1983: 447) wrote that 'there is ample evidence that strategic planning of some kind is widely practised by large business . . . Strategic planning has barely penetrated the collective consciousness of the public sector'. Over the next twenty years, the use of strategic planning spread, and more and more public services organizations wrote strategic plans. Berry and Wechsler (1995: 159) remarked, 'since the early 1980s, strategic planning has been one of the "hot" innovations in public administration, promising public agencies the benefits of a rational and highly structured, future-oriented management technique borrowed from the best run private sector companies'.

A strategic plan can be defined as a formal statement of strategy, that is, a written document setting out a strategy. A strategy for a public service organization (or a consortium of organizations) may be defined as comprising strategic goals and a plan of action to achieve those goals (Heymann 1987). Formulating a strategy tends to involve making decisions that affect who benefits from the organization's activities, and what these benefits are. A strategy tends to have effects that are wide-ranging in their impact across the organization. Also, in consequence, a strategy tends to involve decisions with significant resource (money, people, etc.) implications.

Strategic plans come in a variety of shapes and sizes. They can be quite lengthy, comprising many pages. They can go into great detail on services and programmes. They can vary in the degree to which they are produced as working documents for the management team, or as public relations (PR) documents for external stakeholders. In fact, individual organizations may find it useful to produce several versions of the strategic plan for different stakeholders. For example, one version of a strategic plan may be in use as a working document of the management, another version may be distributed to the public, a third version may be distributed to employees, and a fourth version might contain suitable performance and financial data so that it can be used in reporting to oversight bodies. The different versions might have different functions; from reassuring the public to mobilizing support of politicians and employees, from an inspiring but real plan for future activity to a compulsory report to oversight bodies.

In this chapter we will look at types of strategic planning process in the public services and its benefits. We will also consider how strategic planning can be more responsive to the wishes and needs of the public. We finish the chapter with a brief discussion of the difference between strategic planning and management that, to some extent, acts as an introduction to the following chapter, which has a focus on implementation.

TYPES OF STRATEGIC PLANNING PROCESS IN PUBLIC SERVICES

There can be a variety of motives for producing strategic plans, and a whole variety of types of strategic planning in public services. In terms of motivation, for example, strategic planning can be initiated voluntarily (Berry and Wechsler 1995) and then the contents of strategic documents may be designed by the top management of the public service organization to meet its own purposes. Thus a strategic plan that contains objectives, identifies planned actions, and allocates management responsibilities for these actions would be useful for those managing strategic action. Other strategic plans may be more like bilateral agreements between central government and the department or agency or a local authority. In such a case, the contents may focus on financial aspects and performance, which implicitly challenges the provider organization to deliver a required level of performance in return for the stated volume of revenue.

Evidence from the private sector suggests that some organizations are highly successful because they concentrate on efficient performance, whereas other organizations are likewise highly successful because they concentrate on innovation (Miles and Snow 1978). If we extrapolate this to the public services, it might be suggested that some organizations use strategic plans to achieve performance and results, and some use strategic plans to facilitate change and innovation. If the organization puts an emphasis on both performance and change, we can expect to find not only performance measures in strategic plans, but also strategic projects that are concerned with new developments.

The strategic planning that was fostered in US federal agencies by the Government Performance and Results Act (GPRA) of 1993 was, formally anyway, very focused on performance and results. The US General Accounting Office (1996) believed that their studies had shown that results-oriented public services did three things: define mission and desired outcomes, measure performance, and use performance information (see Figure 7.1). The US General Accounting Office (GAO) suggested that the GPRA required these three steps of federal agencies. It argued that, as a result of the GPRA, federal agencies were required to create strategic plans that had mission statements, to create annual performance plans containing annual performance goals and indicators, and to write annual performance reports about the achievement of the annual performance goals.

Osborne and Gaebler (1992) summarized the strategic planning process in a way that is concerned with performance and results, but also mentions issues and vision. So this is a model that might be seen as applicable for those organizations interested in both performance and change.

In essence, strategic planning is the process of examining an organization's or community's current situation and future trajectory, setting goals, developing

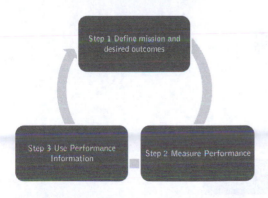

Figure 7.1 *Key steps in implementing GPRA (Based on a figure in US General Accounting Office (1996) p. 10)*

a strategy to achieve those goals, and measuring the results. Different strategic planning processes have different wrinkles, but most involve a number of basic steps:

- analysis of the situation, both internal and external;
- diagnosis, or identification of the key issues facing the organization;
- definition of the organization's fundamental mission;
- articulation of the organization's basic goals;
- creation of a vision: what success looks like;
- development of a strategy to realize the vision and goals;
- development of a timetable for that strategy;
- measurement and evaluation of results.

(Osborne and Gaebler 1992: 232–33)

It is not clear that there is anything distinctive to the public services about this summary of strategic planning by Osborne and Gaebler. There is another model of strategic planning which may be more tailored to suit the public sector environment. This was first outlined by Heymann (1987) and then again by Moore (1995) (see Figure 7.2). Arguably, it is more tailored also to discussions of strategic change and innovation.

Heymann (1987) used his model of strategic planning to understand and analyse US government agencies. In what respect did his model suggest that strategic planning for these organizations was different from the private sector version? He argued that managers in public services needed the support of others outside the organization more than did their counterparts in the private sector:

To a far greater extent in government than in a private corporation, the power to control major management decisions is shared not only with superiors,

Figure 7.2 *The Heymann–Moore model of strategy and strategic planning*

154

colleagues, and subordinates but also with others outside the organization who also have power to shape its future and its goals. That is called democracy. Each of these outsiders has his own views of what should be done and how.

(Heymann 1987: 13)

This suggests an important point about all organizations that are more exposed to the pressures of democratic processes; the strategic thinking of their leaders should benefit from expertize in stakeholder analysis, and implementation of their strategic plans may require more use of stakeholder management. So, arguably, stakeholder analysis and management may be more salient for leaders in public services than private sector business leaders.

Heymann put forward a series of propositions that have a great deal of plausibility. While he expressed these in relation to federal agencies, they are presented here as hypothetically relevant for all public services leaders. There are eight identified:

1 The strategic leader needs to get the support of others outside such as political bodies (for resources and authority), private businesses and individuals, special interest constituencies, the media, other public services organizations, etc.
2 The leader has to communicate and implement desirable goals that get the external support needed to secure the required authority, resources, and co-operation and collaboration
3 The outside interests will support or oppose the organization's strategic statements and actions depending on their interests
4 The strategic leader will not manage to satisfy all of the outside interests
5 The strategic goals need to be credible in terms of the organization's capacities: 'The staff must include people able and willing to work for these goals, and the organizational structures, resources, and authority must be adequate to the task' (Heymann 1987: 14)
6 The strategic goals need to be aligned to organizational values (to ensure there is energy to deliver the goals)
7 The desirable goals must be defined by the strategic leader to meet social needs that superiors (including political superiors) see as important
8 The leader needs a strategic plan containing actions to deliver the goals by ensuring there are the right amounts and types of capacity, and the right external support.

This model is summarized by Heymann (1987: 15) succinctly: 'Thus the central challenge of strategy is to make desirable goals, external support, and organizational capacities fit together.'

The purpose of the strategic plan is, as we have seen, to identify the organizational steps needed to develop additional capacity, and to generate external support to deliver desirable goals. But, according to Heymann, the strategic plan also indicates

155

priorities and provides guidance on various matters. This guidance helps individuals frame their actions to support the overall goals and plan of actions. Logically, of course, when the leader of a public services organization articulates new strategic goals they will then need to develop a new strategic plan to develop new organizational capabilities and structures and new external support.

We came across the research of Moore (1995) already in an earlier chapter, and noted his analysis of two case studies on Boston Housing Authority (BHA) and the Houston Police Department (HPD). Some echoes of the Heymann model of strategic planning can be found in his findings. First, it may be recalled that the leaders studied by Moore paid a great deal of attention to getting external support. In these cases, it was external support from political management that they sought because they wanted resources and authorization. Second, they worked on organizational capacity in various ways. They took action to improve the effectiveness of the top management team (in one case bringing in new subordinates, and in the other making responsibilities clearer); they addressed internal accountability; and they re-engineered operational procedures. Third, they were concerned with the fit between strategic purpose (desirable goals) and structure (organizational capacities). Fourth, they signalled priorities in respect of the important jobs that needed to be done.

Moore called the model of the organizational strategy 'the strategic triangle' and also suggested it was a model adapted for the public sector. He did evolve the concepts, but they were recognizably the same as Heymann's. Most notably, whereas Heymann suggested that the desirable goals not only needed to be consistent with organizational values, but also meet social needs that superiors (including political superiors) saw as important, Moore suggested (1995: 71): '... the strategy must be substantively valuable in the sense that the organization produces things of value to overseers, clients, and beneficiaries at low cost in terms of money and authority.' This nuancing of the nature of desirable goals brings us to the concept of 'public value'. Moore's discussion of public value has been widely noticed and appreciated (see Concept Box 7.1).

CONCEPT BOX 7.1   PUBLIC VALUE

First, an axiom: value is rooted in the desires and perceptions of individuals.... [Some desires] are for things produced by public organizations and are (more or less imperfect) reflections of the desires that citizens express through institutions of representative government. Citizens' aspirations, expressed through representative government, are the central concerns of public managers.

...managers can create value (in the sense of satisfying the desires of citizens and clients) through two different activities...[First] to produce things of value to particular clients and beneficiaries: they can establish clean parks to be used by families; they can provide treatment to heroin addicts; they can deploy military forces to make individuals secure and confident in the future. We can call this creating value through public sector production...

Public managers can also create value by establishing and operating an institution that meets citizens' (and their representatives') desire for properly ordered and productive public institutions.

...the world in which a public manager operates will change. Citizens' aspirations will change...new problems may crop up...It is not enough, then, that managers simply maintain the continuity of their organizations, or even that the organizations become efficient in current tasks. It is also important that the enterprise is adaptable to new purposes and that it be innovative and experimental.

(Moore 1995: 52–5)

Both Heymann and Moore put forward their ideas on strategy in the public sector with an appreciation that things change. As we have seen, the concept of public value was an element of Moore's model, and so he emphasized the usefulness of the 'strategic triangle' for helping public managers to cope with change and continue to create public value.

In short, the concept [of the strategic triangle] focuses managerial attention outward, to the value of the organization's production, upward, toward the political definition of value, and downward and inward, to the organization's current performance. To the extent that this review reveals important incongruities in the position of an organization, then the manager of that organization would be encouraged to rethink his or her basic strategy until it was once more properly aligned.

(Moore 1995: 73)

For many years this was a problem for many public sector academics and for some public services practitioners. They were suspicious of anything that was copied from the private sector, but it is not necessary to either simply copy private sector strategic management, or flatly reject it in total. The Heymann and Moore model of strategy in the public services shows how the general idea of strategic planning, as developed in the private sector, can be adjusted to make it useful for strategic leaders in public services. Strikingly, both Heymann and Moore ultimately ground their adjustments to organizational strategy in assumptions about the public services situation created by democracy. These assumptions include the nature of power relationships in public services (which lead to an emphasis on the strategic leader's need for external support), and the nature of value created by public services (and thus the importance of receptivity to strategic change).

157

ACADEMIC STUDIES OF STRATEGIC PLANNING

Academics have produced some important insights into the nature of strategic planning processes and how they can be made more effective.

At least one study has found that there are many commonalities between the public and private sectors in how strategy is developed. This is a study by Collier, Fishwick, and Johnson (2001). Their study makes use of survey data from over 1,000 respondents in the public sector and over 4,000 respondents in the private sector. They used their data to characterize the strategic development processes used by public and private sector managers, and found evidence in both sectors of the use of a command style of process. This is where a single senior individual, such as the chief executive, determines the vision of the future, is associated with the strategy, and makes the strategic decisions. They comment (2001: 19): 'The strategy can become so intrinsically linked with the senior figure that he or she is often perceived as the embodiment of the strategy.' Collier and colleagues also found the use of a planning approach in both sectors. This is where strategy development is a rational and analytical process that involves making an analysis of the environment, evaluating options against strategic objectives, and expressing the strategy in plans. A third approach, named an incremental approach, was also widely found and involved experimental, small steps with strategy emerging as an adaptive response to the need to change. Both sectors contained strategy development with a political dimension, where strategy emerges from the interplay of power, bargaining, compromise, blocking, and so on, and where there are internal interest groups who compete for influence over strategy. Finally, they report two other approaches, which they named a cultural one and an enforced choice one. In the case of the cultural approach, a strategy is developed in line with the taken for granted beliefs, assumptions, etc. They defined enforced choice as strategy development processes that are constrained by external forces. It should be noted that these six different approaches to strategy development were not mutually exclusive; individual organizations could have varying amounts of each approach. (They refer to these different approaches as dimensions of the strategy development process.)

They did find some variations, however, in terms of the prevalence of these different approaches to strategy development. They said that public sector managers were less likely than private sector managers to use a command style development process, more likely to report a political process, and almost as likely to use a planning development process. These differences were less startling, however, than the findings in respect of which sector's respondents experienced strategy development as being most constrained. This particular difference is, arguably, consistent with Heymann's case study conclusions in the US, which were that public sector leaders were more dependent on external support than their private sector counterparts. Those dependent on a group often found that they had to make compromises or adjustments to get their support, which could be seen as, in effect, an experience of being constrained.

158

While the findings of Collier and colleagues did suggest that the public sector managers were substantially more likely to report external constraint, meaning that forces outside the organization determined their strategic direction and strategy, overall this research showed a big overlap in the management experience of strategy development in the two sectors. Arguably, the key finding is that much of what happens around strategy development appears to be the same in both the public and private sectors.

Quite a different approach to the study of strategic processes was taken by Frost-Kumpf and colleagues (1993). Their study was essentially a case study using qualitative data and inductive analysis of strategic change in a state agency in the United States. In their research they identified three streams of strategic actions. One stream concerned the leadership's use of strategic language to set out a new strategic direction for the agency. This action appears to have stimulated action by those working in the agency, and this action aggregated into a strategic transformation of the agency. A second stream of strategic actions was concerned with the capability of the agency, and included the development of management, participatory and planning abilities through collaborative planning efforts, and training. This second stream involved other stakeholders outside the agency, including the consumers. A third stream of actions was made up of actions creating co-operative ventures with other government agencies. In some ways, these findings reflect those of Heymann (1987) on strategic planning in government, and his isolation of the importance of planning to integrate changes in the strategic direction of a public services organization with its organizational capacity and external support.

The inductive analysis of Frost-Kumpf and his colleagues also identified nine thematic patterns among the strategic actions. These patterns were:

1 taking symbolic actions
2 developing new programme thrusts
3 empowering key constituencies
4 developing alternative sources of revenue
5 responding to opposition
6 building internal capacity
7 developing technical expertize
8 utilizing training, and
9 gaining external cooperation.

These seem to provide a finer grain view of the three streams of action, but at the same time provide a checklist of the elements of a strategic process that can be usefully compared and contrasted to the evaluation worksheet developed for the US Congress, which we will look at in a later chapter.

The two empirical research studies reviewed above have both been descriptive and analytical. They have been aimed at understanding strategic processes.

Empirical research that can tell us about what strategic processes work best in what circumstances appears to be very unusual.

A recent empirical study has gone further than most studies in trying to use quantitative methods to establish the causal factors in the effectiveness of strategic planning processes. This is a study we will make use of several times in this book. It is the study by Poister and Streib (2005) of strategic planning in municipal government in the United States. They carried out a postal survey of senior officials in cities with populations of over 25,000 people – getting over 500 completed surveys and producing, in their judgement, a highly representative sample of US cities. They note a finding that 44 per cent of those surveyed by them reported the use of strategic planning on a citywide basis, which they suggest indicated a modest spread in strategic planning when compared to earlier studies. Most of the strategic plans contained a review of the mission of the organization, a vision for the future, strategic goals, and action plans.

Were the strategic plans working? Most of the respondents in cities with strategic planning appeared to be satisfied with the results being achieved. This did not mean that all the municipal authorities with strategic plans were achieving all their strategic goals. But more than 40 per cent of the strategic goals were being achieved. Interestingly, there were some lessons from the Poister and Streib study about how to increase the impact of strategic planning. These are some of the lessons (we will repeat some of these points elsewhere):

1 Involve citizens and other stakeholders in developing the strategic plan
2 Carry out feasibility assessments of proposed strategic actions
3 Set annual objectives for managers (for example, department heads) based on the strategic plan
4 Make sure new money in the budget is targeted on strategic goals and objectives
5 Report performance measures to the public on a regular basis
6 Use annual reviews of managers to check that they are accomplishing the strategic plan
7 When evaluating strategic effectiveness, organizations should track performance data over time. It is not enough just to compare the actual performance against target performance.

Some of these lessons can be linked to the observations made by Gordon (2005) about developments in strategic planning in US local government. Specifically, Gordon referred to performance measurement (checking performance over time), and performance management (linking individual objective setting and performance review for managers to the strategic plan), and also making the connection between strategic plans and budgetary decisions (making sure new money is targeted on strategic goals). In other words, there is evidence from the Poister and Streib study that strategic planning should be integrated with performance management and budgetary systems. We return to this again in the next chapter on implementation.

The final verdict of Poister and Streib (2005: 54) is quite upbeat: '... our study does show continuing growth and development in the field — a raising of the bar — with leading-edge jurisdictions that are broadening their strategic planning efforts into more sophisticated and comprehensive, and reportedly more effective, strategic management approaches.'

BENEFITS OF STRATEGIC PLANNING IN PRACTICE

Much time, effort, and expense can go into the production of a formal and written strategic plan for a public service organization. One worry that is sometimes expressed by senior managers in the public services is that they will go to all the trouble of creating a strategic plan only for it to be ignored, for it to gather dust on a shelf. So, what is the evidence that strategic planning in the public services is worthwhile? This is the question being considered in this section.

Berry and Wechsler (1995) reported survey findings showing that US state agencies had begun to use strategic planning for a variety of reasons. The chief benefits intended by the state agencies in using strategic planning appear to have been to set a direction for policies and programmes, and to help them manage pressures to reduce spending and resolve competing resource allocation priorities. So, strategic planning is a process that supports management decision making. The planning process helps managers think about where they are trying to get to, know what warrants most attention, and make policy and budget decisions. It would seem likely from this that strategic planning would be most attractive to managers in times that were characterized by change and discontinuity. If there were no changes or discontinuities — and no prospects of them occurring — and organizations were in a steady state, then perhaps strategic planning would be less attractive because managers would operate on the basis of habit rather than purposeful decision making. So, providing there were not excessive costs or disadvantages involved in carrying out strategic planning, it would seem likely that it would be most used in periods of change and uncertainty.

RESEARCH BOX 7.1   BERRY AND WECHSLER (1995)

Strategic planning in government organizations emerged and spread in some countries as a voluntary innovation. This is illustrated by the case of state government in the US; a national study of strategic planning carried out in the spring of 1992 found most state agencies had introduced it in the preceding eight years (Berry and Wechsler 1995).

They noticed, as a result of their survey of state government in North America, that a minority of agencies had initiated it because of some top-down process such as a statutory requirement or a mandate from the state governor. Instead, the survey found that 88 per cent of the cases were the result of a leadership decision (Berry and Wechsler 1995: 160). Common factors in the introduction of strategic planning were the chief executive's experience in another agency and the recommendation of an internal planning officer. In fact, a quarter of agencies said that these were the most important factors in the decision to introduce strategic planning. Another one in ten said that the most important factor was the desire of agency leaders to have a framework for setting priorities. And a further set of responses – nearly a tenth – said the most important factor was to improve management and improve performance. So it was often a voluntary decision of management to adopt strategic planning; this presumably meant that leaders thought it helped them do their job and deliver on their responsibilities.

A UK study of public services managers also suggested that strategic planning supports management decision making. Very many of the respondents claimed that strategic planning helped with achieving goals, helped with setting milestones, allowed better use of resources, and gave staff a unified vision (Flynn and Talbot 1996). Helping with setting milestones and using resources better both seem to suggest that strategic planning supports management decision making.

Flynn and Talbot's finding that strategic planning helped by giving staff a unified vision, and in achieving goals, is very interesting. Not all forms of strategic planning and management entail a step of preparing a formal strategic vision, which may be defined as a representation of a desired future state that acts as a goal for strategic action. However, when a public services organization is under pressure to make radical changes, then the idea of an explicit strategic vision becomes more and more useful. The usefulness is not restricted to helping leaders of the organization to make decisions about strategic actions and investments, but also potentially as a basis for mobilizing commitment and initiative throughout the organization. It could be assumed that the top leaders of the organization would spend time communicating this vision to managers and other employees and explaining the rationale for the vision. If successful, and if managers and others had authority to make decisions and take action, it might be claimed that using strategic planning for the purpose of 'giving staff a unified vision' would be part of a process of empowering people within the organization.

We return again to the survey of strategic planning in municipal authorities in the US by Poister and Streib (2005). The respondents in cities with strategic planning were generally satisfied with the implementation and achievement of strategic

Table 7.1 *Impacts of strategic planning*

Rank	Impact	Per cent
1	Delivering high-quality public services	89
2	Defining clear program priorities	86
3	Focusing the city council's agenda on the important issues	85
4	Orienting the city to a genuine sense of mission	85
5	Making sound decisions regarding programs, systems and resources	83
6	Enhancing employees' focus on organizational goals	80
7	Communicating with citizen groups and other external stakeholders	79
8	Building a positive organizational culture in the city	75

$N = 225$ respondents in municipalities with strategic planning efforts in the last 5 years

Table Top Ranked Impacts of Strategic planning in US Municipal Authorities (Poister and Streib 2005)

goals. Respondents that had one strategic plan had accomplished on average about 40 per cent of their goals, and those that had completed more than one round of strategic planning were reporting 60 per cent of their goals being accomplished. The vast majority said that the time and effort put into strategic planning had been worthwhile.

Most of the respondents said strategic planning had a positive impact on producing high quality public services. There were also impacts in terms of focus and mission, improved decision making, organizational culture and employee focus, and external communications with the public and others (see Table 7.1). The reports of negative impacts of strategic planning were insignificant.

The Poister and Streib survey suggests, therefore, that the experience of strategic planning was very positive in US cities. The satisfaction levels with the implementation of strategic goals is high, the proportion of goals accomplished is very respectable, and the positive impacts of strategic planning are extremely widely reported, with benefits for service delivery and the internal management and functioning of public services organizations.

DESIGNING A STRATEGY PROCESS IN PRACTICE

An early model of a public strategic planning process specified the first step as 'organization' (Sorkin *et al.* 1985). Toft (2000: 8) justified this on the basis that public organizations at the time were new to strategic planning and needed a first step, which was a 'plan to plan'. He explained that the plan to carry out strategic planning was critical to the effectiveness of the whole process, and suggested the formation of a steering committee consisting of both staff and external stakeholders.

Even though strategic planning is no longer so new in the public services, there is still an argument for making the first step one in which the design of strategic planning process is agreed. Bryson (2004: 35) advises:

> Obviously, some person or group must initiate the process. One of the initiator's first tasks is to identify exactly who the key decision makers are. The next task is to identify which persons, groups, units or organizations should be involved in the effort.

Bryson also supports the idea of a policy making body to oversee the effort, which is similar to Toft's suggestion of a steering committee.

How might such a policy making body or steering committee proceed in preparing a plan for carrying out strategic planning? First, the body or committee could carry out a stakeholder analysis and use the results to decide who needs to be involved in the strategy process and decide how they need to be involved. There are several different ways to involve stakeholders or their representatives in the strategic planning process. For example, they could be part of the decision making, or they could be consulted, or, perhaps, they could be just kept informed. One possible result of the stakeholder analysis could be a decision to redefine the membership of the policy body or steering committee with a view to building wider sponsorship or commitment to the idea of carrying out a strategic planning cycle.

Second, the body or group could assess organizational readiness to engage in strategic planning. This assessment may even trigger some organizational development before strategic planning can be feasible (Joyce 2000: 82):

> So, a chief executive with a healthily functioning organization, which is running smoothly, may still need to develop strategic foresight, set a strategic direction, and bring about strategic changes. On the other hand, a poorly functioning organization may be in such bad shape that attempts to introduce strategic management processes would get nowhere. Thus, we are making the point that individual organizations in the public sector may need organizational development plans if they are to stand a reasonable chance of successful strategic management.

Bryson (2004: 82) recommends the assessment of organizational readiness should cover 'current mission; its budget, financial management, human resource, information technology, and communications systems; its leadership and management capabilities; the expected costs and benefits of a strategic planning process; and ways of overcoming any expected barriers'. He also suggests three possible options at the end of the assessment; proceed with strategic planning, improve the organization's readiness, or choose to give up on the idea of strategic planning.

Third, the body or committee should consider, in general terms, what type of strategic planning process it thinks will suit the circumstances. It could, for example, consider emphasizing strategic performance management or strategic issue management. It could consider some form of inter-organizational strategic planning. For a public services organization that is relatively inexperienced in the use of strategic processes, it may be unwise to go immediately to a process involving scenario planning and comprehensive corporate planning. It may be better to start off with strategic issue management, use it to solve a visible strategic issue successfully, and thereby build the credibility of strategic processes in the eyes of organizational members. At the same time, of course, success in strategic issue management builds the credibility of the strategic leaders of the organization, so that when they say they want to engage in some longer term, more comprehensive, strategic planning there is some confidence built up within the organization that these leaders are capable of successfully leading a strategy process.

RESPONSIVE STRATEGIC PLANNING

As a result of public services reforms, more and more strategic leaders want to ensure that what their organization delivers is not only important to politicians, but also creates public value in the eyes of those who use the services. Strategic planning needs to be adapted to suit this more responsive posture for the public services. How can more account be taken of service users for strategic planning in public services? First, there are lessons from private sector approaches that are customer centred. Second, there is expeditionary marketing. Third, there is a programme planning model. Fourth, there is the use of a whole systems development model. Each of these is described in a little more detail.

LESSONS FROM THE PRIVATE SECTOR

One lesson is to make more use of data on service users. Public services organizations are often poor at using data on service users even if the data actually exists and even if public services managers say they understand the importance of collecting it and using it. It is not clear why it is so difficult to get public services managers to use data on those who use the service for strategic planning purposes. Perhaps it is because, in practice, many of them see the service primarily from the perspective of the provider, do this as a matter of habit, and simply forget to empathize with the service user.

Asking the right questions is the key in getting the right data and making the most of it. So what questions should be asked about service users? Osborne and Gaebler (1992: 174) present a set of questions which they attributed to an American police service chief called David Coupar. His questions have been generalized for use by any strategic leader in the public services.

165

1   What important service user needs are there in your area?
2   How do you find out what they are?
3   What methods can you use to find out?
4   What are you going to do to address problems identified by service users?
5   How successful have you been in solving the problems and meeting the needs?

When looking at service user needs it is important not to take at face value what the public say they want of a service (or does not want). When the analysis of the data produces an answer on what the public wants, the next step in strategic thinking is to ask 'why?' This will produce an answer in the form of 'the public wants this in order to . . .'. The next step is to repeat the 'why?' question, but now in respect of the new answer. Again, this produces yet another statement of what it is the public wants (the public want this in order to . . .). The process is repeated until no more new answers can be generated. As a result, the strategic leader will have a more complex view of the structure of what the public wants. For example, members of the public may object to planning permission being given to replace a single family home on a large plot of land by a block of flats. In this case we know what the public does not want, but why do they feel like this? It may be that the public who are objecting are worrying about the extra traffic congestion it will produce. By eliciting the underlying concern, the public service authority then has an additional range of possibilities for handling this situation. For example, perhaps there needs to be action to reduce traffic congestion?

It is also useful to think about what the private sector calls customer segmentation. It is useful because it helps those doing strategic planning to avoid unwarranted assumptions that each public service satisfies an obvious and single standard need. A customer segment is a group of customers who are of the same type. The type may be defined using personal characteristics that are familiar to planners of public services (gender, age, disability), but perhaps identifying customer segments should be approached with more of an open mind about the relevant characteristics. Having identified groups of customers the next step is to check out the distinct needs of each group in relation to a specific service. For example, it is sometimes said that women have a different interest in good street lighting than do men because of women's frequent concerns about their safety in using the streets of cities at night. People using a free public library, to take another example, might have very different motives depending on the type of person they are. Some library users may be students who need a quiet place to study, whereas retired people may want to borrow books to entertain themselves.

It is possible to build on customer segmentation to develop a 'customer service matrix'. This matrix cross-tabulates customer segments and public services. Customer segments may form the columns and services form the rows. This can be used in a range of ways. For example, it is possible to map which services are delivered to which customer segments. It will then be obvious if there are gaps in the services that are provided to some of the segments. The obvious follow up questions are: (1) would a specific type of customer benefit from having a service that it does not currently receive; and (2) is it feasible to extend this service to this group of customers?

This focus on the needs of the service users can be built into strategic planning in the following way. The process of strategic planning can start off by a search which involves market research and includes looking at what customer needs are and what the future social trends are. In this model of strategic planning, market research is really the first step. This is followed by a visioning step. At the third step the leaders involve employees. Then the planning turns to the creation of new standards and new services. Fifth, implementation planning is carried out in respect of roles, skills, organizational structures, etc. When the change has been implemented, the final step is the evaluation of the results. This is a fairly logical and straightforward approach to strategic planning, but it begins with getting and analysing data on customer needs (Thurley and Wirdenius 1989).

EXPEDITIONARY MARKETING

The expeditionary marketing approach is based on trying out a strategic action that has not had the benefit of market research, but has been through a strategic planning process to identify feasible strategic action. After the strategic plan has been implemented, the organization carries out research into the reactions of the users of the public services affected by the strategic action. This is a simple reversal of the conventional model where the research is done first and then comes the strategic plan. This approach is potentially useful where the services are innovative ones and the service users find it difficult to articulate their needs and yet are able to give an opinion based on experiences of actual services. For example, the approach might be tried for services aimed at some specific groups such as people with learning disabilities.

PROGRAMME PLANNING MODEL

The programme planning model was used in the 1970s. In this approach, the public services begins with a step in which service users (that is, customers) are helped in a workshop to identify and rank the problems that they are having with a service. The next step is to present the problems to the professionals who deliver the services. Importantly, sessions in which the professionals try to find solutions are attended by some external experts to bring a more detached view to the process of trying to identify solutions. The solutions generated by the professionals are then tested for their acceptability to the top decision makers who are responsible for the policies, strategies, and budgetary decisions of the organization. If the solutions are not acceptable to these resource controllers, because of clashes with policies and strategies of the organization, these are dropped from further consideration. If any of the solutions are

167

considered good ones, this process makes it possible for the organization to modify the strategic plan or strategic goals to make them compatible with the solutions. This kind of approach is consistent with what John Bryson called backward mapping. The backward mapping is essentially starting from an initiative to solve a problem (being proposed by professionals at or near the front-line of service delivery) and mapping back to strategies and the policies, and then making adjustments in them.

WHOLE SYSTEMS DEVELOPMENT

The increasing realization that good strategic decisions are based on as much consensus as possible has led some public service organizations to experiment with whole system events or large-scale strategic planning events to make a direct bid for a consensus. Such events can involve members of the public, representatives of partner organizations, as well as professionals and front-line staff. Mulgan (2007: Ev13) has made a specific statement in support of involving front-line staff, '. . . in all strategy work I would certainly encourage the close involvement of front-line staff, the people who have to live with it . . .'. A strong plea for involving a wide range of people was made by Sir Michael Bichard (2007: Ev17), who told a Parliamentary Select Committee, '. . . strategic thinking happens when you involve a wide range of people with different experiences and approaches, because every strategic issue is a function of connectivity and it should not be a black art and it should not be done behind closed doors and public servants should be accountable'.

Whole systems development events are interesting large-scale interactions of key stakeholder groups, in this case aimed at agreeing a strategic plan for a public services organization. They can be carried out with 200 or 300 people. The key stakeholders can include, taking the example of a local authority, elected politicians, managers, professionals, front-line staff, representatives of organizations with overlapping mandates, and members of the public. The event might last one or more days. It could begin with the presentation of a draft strategic plan, including strategic vision and strategic goals. The various stakeholders, internal and external, could then be asked to react or respond to what they have heard. In turn, the top leaders of the organization are asked to respond to the views and judgements of professionals, front-line staff, those who use the services covered by the strategic plan, etc. The response of the leaders should take the form of proposals to revise the strategic vision and plan in order to take account of the stakeholders' contributions. In this way whole systems development planning enables service users to be involved at a very early stage, and actually involved in the development of strategic visions and plans. If the users are involved before strategic vision and plans are fixed, and if they are involved when ideas are still very fluid, it may be hoped that their voice would influence in a significant way the development of the strategic vision and plans. Ideally, whole systems development events might be used to create strategic plans which are genuinely customer centric.

Whereas the programme planning model should ensure that strategic planning takes a consumer perspective, since it is focused on resolving the problems identified by service users, the whole system development event endeavours to modify the strategic visions and plans produced by leaders of the government organization by ensuring that stakeholders have their voices heard, and by ensuring the leaders respond to what they hear. Although it is very obvious if the strategic leaders in a whole systems development event are trying to avoid responding to uncomfortable feedback by stakeholders, the fact is that the leaders start the conversational process by outlining a leadership vision and plan. In this sense, these two techniques are quite different. On the face of it, it would seem that the programme planning model could support bottom-up innovation, whereas whole system development events could be seen as a more top-down approach, although it must be stressed that whole systems development processes do encourage the top strategic leaders managers to learn from those in front-line service delivery and from the public who use the services.

CASE STUDY

South Australia

The state of South Australia produced a strategic plan in 2004 called 'Creating Opportunity'. This plan had a number of sections to it: first, it set out objectives; second, it set out the current situation ('Where are we now'); third, it set out the targets the state wanted to achieve; fourth, it set out performance indicators; fifth, it set out priority actions; and, lastly, it set out who was responsible for the priority actions. So, the strategic plan provided not only a statement of strategic objectives, actions, and performance requirements, but also information important for the management of the implementation of the action.

The plan had six objectives and 79 targets. Its objectives were:

1 growing prosperity
2 improving well-being
3 attaining stability
4 fostering creativity
5 building communities
6 expanding opportunity.

These sound like desired outcomes rather than outputs.

Questions for discussion

1 Was anything important missing from the list of contents?
2 What do you think of the six objectives – do you think these were suitable for a state government in Australia?

169

FROM STRATEGIC PLANNING TO STRATEGIC MANAGEMENT

During the 1970s, books on private sector management began to use the term 'strategic management' in preference to 'strategic planning'. This was done by some writers to underline the need in the 1970s to pay attention to the management of implementation of strategy, as well as the goal setting and analysis used to select strategic action. The reason for this increased attention to implementation might be attributed to at least two separate concerns. First, the business environment of the 1970s was much more volatile than that which had existed in the 1950s and 1960s, which were generally years of growth. Simple extrapolations of trends in the 1970s were less useful than they had been for planning purposes, and strategic leaders had to cope with more unpredictable circumstances and discontinuities. Logically, this implied that implementation needed more attention as adjustments were needed during the implementation phase, and as lessons were learnt during implementation. Second, some of the early writers on strategic planning had also begun to realize that they had under-estimated the degree to which implementation was also affected by resistance to change. It might even be said by some that strategic implementation was the most important stage of the process. One way of summing this up is to say that strategic implementation processes needed to be taken seriously and that, therefore, strategic management was strategic planning processes plus strategic implementation processes.

In fact, many of those who talk about strategic planning in the public services context are also concerned about effective implementation, and may simply be choosing to use a more widely used and familiar term – they are probably not using the term 'strategic planning' to suggest that implementation is unimportant.

SUMMARY

In this chapter we have looked at the existence of different types of strategic planning. We noted the existence of a type concerned with performance and results, and a type that seemed to be more tailored to the public sector and which was suited to strategic change and innovation. In relation to the latter type of strategic planning, we briefly examined the concept of public value which was actually anchored within Moore's discussion of the strategic triangle with its three elements to be aligned through strategic planning.

We looked at the benefits of strategic planning and management in the public services, which include helping managers to set direction and milestones, to make budget decisions, and to improve the delivery of high quality public services.

The chapter briefly reviewed methods of achieving responsiveness to service users through strategic planning. There is more than one way of including them in strategic plan development in the public services. We first explored lessons from the private sector and its approach to understanding customer needs. The use of the word 'customer' in the public services is sometimes controversial. Of course, this word can even be confusing when describing those who consume public services, but it has been justified at times by the need to underline the point that public services should serve the public. Within the discussion of responsiveness, we emphasized the importance of careful study of the needs of the public, and the use of what is called customer segmentation, and on the back of this how to review services and beneficiaries using a 'customer service matrix'. We also considered expeditionary marketing, the programme planning model, and the whole systems development approach. The latter two were briefly described, and also compared with each other in terms of their approximation to bottom-up and top-down processes.

The chapter was concluded by drawing attention to the distinction between strategic management and strategic planning. In brief, it was argued that strategic management is concerned with the development of strategic plans (strategic planning) and their successful implementation.

Work-based assignment: evaluation of public value

The work-based assignments in this book are for civil servants and other public services staff who have four or more years of management experience.

This assignment is a qualitative study of the public value created by a public services organization you work for, or you know well. It has three stages. First, investigate the needs, desires, and aspirations of the service users who currently use the service or services. Second, assess the 'functionality' of the service or services – what needs, desires, or aspirations does it actually meet currently? Third, compare the findings of the first two stages and comment on the public value being produced by the public services organization.

Work-based assignment: evaluation of the current strategy of a public services organization

Investigate and write up the following aspects of the public service organization you work for, or you know well:

- The strategic goals of the organization and the social needs addressed
- The external support enjoyed by the organization
- The structure, culture, and capabilities of the organization
- The strategic plan.

Assess the effectiveness of the strategic plan in aligning the goals, external support, and capacities of the organization. Identify, if you can, any reasons for deficiencies in the alignments of these three aspects – is a reason, for example, a poorly designed strategic plan, or a poorly implemented strategic plan?

171

DISCUSSION QUESTIONS

1   Do public services require their own version of strategic planning? What should be different or special about strategic planning and management in the public services?
2   Is the concept of 'public value' useful, and how does it help in thinking about or doing strategic planning?
3   Is the evidence in favour of using strategic planning and management in the public services compelling? Please justify your opinion.
4   Is the public sufficiently involved with the process of strategic planning in public services? Are there viable methods for involving the public in strategic planning and could they be 'rolled out' generally?
5   Do we need to make a distinction between strategic planning and strategic management in the public services? If yes, what is the difference?

FURTHER READING

Gordon, G. (2005) 'From Vision to Implementation: The Changing State of Strategic Planning', *Public Management*, 87, 8: 26–8.

Poister, T.H. and Streib, G.D. (2005) 'Elements of Strategic Planning and Management in Municipal Government: Status after Two Decades', *Public Administration Review*, January/February 2005, 65, 1: 45–56.

Poister, T.H. (2010) 'The Future of Strategic Planning in the Public Sector: Linking Strategic Management and Performance', *Public Administration Review*, December, pp. S246–S254.

Chapter 8

Implementation

LEARNING OBJECTIVES

- To seek a better understanding of how to make strategic implementation successful
- To examine the planning of strategic implementation

INTRODUCTION

Nowadays, a frequently made assertion is that implementation of strategy is harder than strategy formulation. This assertion was supported by evidence from a survey of 11 national libraries, including those in Australia, Britain, Canada, France, Germany, Ireland, New Zealand, Malaysia, the Netherlands, Singapore, and the United States (Chalmers 1997). The most serious implementation problems appeared to be setting budget priorities in line with strategic priorities, and making changes in the competencies of staff and managers if required for the implementation of a strategy. So, two critical sets of resources (financial and human) were not easily aligned with strategy. Summing up the significance of the survey, the analytical aspects of strategy are easier than strategic implementation.

Implementing strategy is not only hard to do, it is often unsatisfactory as well. A recent review of civil service capability in the UK made the following generalization (Capability Reviews Team 2007: 44): 'The reviews found excellent practice in setting direction and in developing outcome-focused strategy, but poorer performance on translating this consistently into delivery.'

At the present time, there are civil servants and public services managers in a number of countries who are struggling with implementation of strategy. They may have a sophisticated or a rudimentary knowledge of how strategic planning is supposed to work on paper, but they know successful implementation is not easily achieved. They wonder what they need to do to make strategic implementation work in their own organization with its specific history, culture, habits, pressures, and problems. So, to some degree, they are struggling with not only understanding the theory of strategic planning, but, probably more importantly, they want to understand how they can deliver it in practice.

In private sector oriented management books the concern with implementation emerged in the 1970s, when the name 'strategic management' started to displace the earlier name of 'strategic planning'. Up until then books on corporate strategy focused on formulating strategies and gave little attention to the learning that could occur during implementation or the need to address conflicting interests and resistance to new strategies. It was later in the 1980s and 1990s that there was more appreciation of the importance of the work of turning strategic plans into concrete action. One response to this might be to call for the management of implementation, beginning with the planning in detail of the strategic actions, responsibilities for action, budgets, and the timing of actions. It could also require supporting the implementation of strategic action with communication by leaders, training, targets, and rewards. For example, Hussey (1999) gave the following advice for managing strategic implementation:

1　Provide a vision statement of what the business will be like after change
2　Involve others to get commitment to the changes; and do this by holding meetings to explain the vision and plan the detail of the change
3　Give support through training and coaching
4　Plan and manage the actions needed to implement the strategy, and align budgets and measure progress
5　Monitor and control and set up special systems to do this
6　Recognize those who make implementation successful by rewarding and thanking them.

Stonich (1982), basing an approach on consultancy experience, highlighted culture, organizational structure, management processes, and human resources as key areas for the implementation of strategy (see Figure 8.1).

CULTURE

Culture is a much used word by leaders in public services. There is some research on it in the public services. Arguably, Pettigrew and his colleagues (1992) identified organizational culture as one of the factors as they attempted to characterize receptive contexts. As stated in an earlier chapter, they did not think cultural change was easy to bring about, and they seemed to think that some organizational cultures enabled change, and some cultures were an impediment to change.

Usually, organizational culture is equated to beliefs, expectations, values, and norms. In former times there were public services leaders who were keen on employee

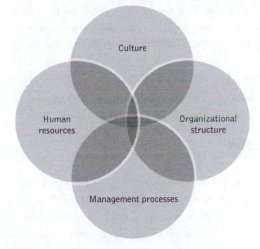

Figure 8.1 *Implementation factors*

programmes to inculcate new values and thus change the culture of the organization. Some saw the culture as the essence of the emotional life of an organization. If cultures develop over periods of time they can be seen as learnt from past experience, learnt from both successes and failures. Culture can also be seen as a factor in the capacity of a public service organization, sitting alongside capabilities, helping to shape what people in the organization are willing or unwilling to do on the basis of their taken for granted assumptions and values (Heymann 1987).

Conversations and meetings may provide strategic leaders with the data that they use to typify their organization's culture. It may be that often mentioned incidents from several years ago, or often repeated phrases that crop up over and over again in conversation, provide insights to the strategic leader on the nature of this culture. For example, the organization's top management may have taken a major decision five years ago with an impact on those who work in the organization, and people may often refer to this incident to explain or analyse everything that is happening now. The actions of top management may have been evaluated positively or negatively, but the incident is thought to say something important about the nature of the organization and how it can be expected to act. Front-line service managers may constantly, for example, use the word 'protective' to describe their responsibilities in relation to the staff; the word is repeated so often that it is clear that this is regarded as a norm for how front-line managers should behave.

What attitude could a leader have towards organizational culture during strategic implementation? Logically, the leader can ignore it and hope that it changes appropriately as a result of changes occurring because of strategic actions. If this approach is taken and the culture is a very strong impediment, a strategic leader may even feel during implementation that the culture is splintering the strategy. A second attitude is for the leader to make adjustments to the strategy to fit it to the existing culture, and, therefore, strategy is accommodating the culture. Third, the leader can try to change the culture using a range of methods including, for example, human resources (HR) systems for recruiting new individuals who have the desired values and beliefs, and using reward systems to alter what is perceived as valuable.

ORGANIZATIONAL DIMENSION

Bryson (2004: 270) defined strategic management systems as 'ongoing organizational mechanisms or arrangements for strategically managing the implementation of agreed-upon strategies, assessing the performance of those strategies, and formulating new or revised strategies'. He provided a sketch of six different types of strategic management system including ones we might say were appropriate for partnership situations and for use with market mechanisms. These were:

1 Integrated units of management
2 Strategic issues management
3 Contract
4 Collaboration
5 Portfolio management
6 Goal or benchmark.

The first of these systems seeks to integrate strategies at different levels and across functions. An overview of the second system type is described by Bryson (2004: 277) as follows:

> In this [strategic issues management] system, strategic guidance is issued at the top, and units further down are asked to identify issues they think are strategic. Leaders and managers at the top then select the issues they wish to have addressed, perhaps reframing the issues before passing them on to units or task forces. Task forces then present strategic alternatives to leaders and managers, who select which ones to pursue. Strategies are then implemented in the next phase. Each issue is managed separately, although it is important to make sure choices in one issue do not cause trouble in other issue areas.

The contract system is where one organization contracts other organizations to provide public services. Bryson suggests that strategic plans are used by both those commissioning and those providing public services. To Bryson's remarks on this type of system might be added the speculation that the concerns of the commissioning organizations' and providers' strategic plans are likely to be very different. For example, the commissioning organizations are likely to require strategic plans that maximize political support, and the provider organizations are likely to require strategic plans that focus on competitive advantage issues.

This contract system is also featured in Osborne and Gaebler's 1992 book, *Reinventing Government*. In that book, they suggested the need to split steering (in effect, strategic planning) from rowing (service delivery), and to split regulation from enforcement. This split of steering and rowing was supposed to enable a more holistic approach to be developed, and to enable the introduction of competition in the provision of public services. Essentially, they were arguing for more multi-organizational systems and a move away from hierarchical linkages to the use of other coordination mechanisms, including commissioning and contracting to deliver services. This movement from organization based on hierarchy, perhaps, is partially conveyed in words such as 'steering' (rather than top-down command and control forms of directing), and 'governance' (rather than government).

Bryson's fourth type of system, the collaboration approach, may be partially underpinned by contracts, but in this case the emphasis is not on competitive contracting and may involve no organization being 'fully in charge'.

The portfolio management system is where, for example, the organization treats its activities or units as independent and makes corporate judgements about them individually on the basis of their attractiveness and importance (e.g. market share).

The final system is termed a goal or benchmark model. Bryson sees this as a system in which there is only loose integration between a set of organizations. He thinks that this system is suited to shared power environments, and that it is used in most community strategic plans. It does offer some integration of participating organizations (Bryson 2004: 281):

> It is designed to gain reasonable agreement on overarching goals or indicators (benchmarks) toward which relatively independent groups, units, or organizations might then direct their energies. The consensual agreement on goals and indicators can function somewhat like the corporate control exercised in integrated models, although it is of course weaker.

Obviously, strategic implementation would be managed in very different ways for each of these six systems.

MANAGEMENT AND MANAGEMENT SYSTEMS

Management systems were highlighted by The PA Consulting Group when it evaluated the Strategic Management Initiative launched by the government in Ireland in 1994. PA Consulting Group identified three management systems: human resources management (HRM), financial management, and information systems (IS)

177

management. The report stressed the importance of improving all these three areas: 'These three components are critical enablers of change . . .' (PA Consulting Group 2002: 5). The systems had not been fully developed by the time of the evaluation. Taking the case of HRM first, some examples included failure to tackle under performance, and lack of ability to recognize and reward good performance. In the case of financial management systems, an example was the meagre financial commentary in Statements of Strategy. In the case of the IS management system, the report quotes the views of some of the managers in the Irish civil service that 'the part IT has to play in effecting change within SMI/DBG [i.e. two government reform programmes] is not fully appreciated at top management level' (ibid 2002: 77). Although not stated explicitly in the report, all of these management systems can be important for the implementation of strategy and/or public services reform.

Recognition of the importance of management systems can be seen in the approach taken by the United States government when introducing strategic planning into federal government on a systematic basis. In this case it was quite clear that the intention was to forge a strong bond between strategic planning and performance measurement and management. In the case of France, in recent years, the drive in the public services in central government has been to link performance measurement and budgeting on the basis of a focus on mission. The same trend towards linking and integrating management systems is to be found in local government in the United States. Gordon (2005), drawing on much practical experience from American local government, stressed the trend to integrate strategic plans with budgetary and performance measurement systems. Whereas, in the early 1990s, managers in local government in the United States were just beginning to use the concept of strategic planning in their services, a decade later, he reports 'local governments are becoming keenly aware that the vision and strategies of the strategic plan must be incorporated into budget preparation, review and approval' (Gordon 2005: 27).

Gordon illustrates this with the example of Worcester city government (Massachusetts):

> Simultaneous to the strategic planning initiative, a performance-based budgeting system was established internally for Worcester city government that identified service delivery inputs, outputs, and departmental outcomes. These were linked to departmental performance, budget priorities, and financial allocations. The system identified costs, benefits, efficiencies, and constraints of municipal dollars and services. Goals, objectives, and strategies of Strategic Plan 2000 were all tied to performance budgeting so that citizen priorities would be addressed when municipal departments established the annual agendas.
>
> (Gordon 2005: 27)

It is possible that some management systems are important in part because they ensure 'buy in' from managers in an organization, and their 'buy in' is important if implementation is going to be pursued with any vigour. For example, one way to get the managers motivated to implement strategic plans is to use the performance management system to integrate the individual objectives of managers and the strategic goals of the organization. This integration means at least two things: first, setting individual objectives for managers based on the strategic plan, and, second, basing annual evaluations of the performance of managers on the contribution they make to accomplish the strategic goals. There is evidence from strategic planning in local government that suggests these two things help to improve the impact of strategic plans (Poister and Streib 2005).

Strategic leaders must also take care how they integrate budgetary processes with strategic planning. Integration may be achieved by timing the budget decisions to follow shortly in time after strategic decisions in the strategic planning process. But then strategic leaders need to communicate the strategic decisions effectively to managers so that the tight time linkage of strategic and budget decisions is reinforced by budget decisions being better understood, and thus, hopefully, the budgets are well managed. If managers do not understand, or are unaware of, the strategic decisions, then there will be problems in how budget decisions are implemented. If there is no tight linkage between strategic and budget decisions, the evidence from a study by Goodwin and Kloot (1996) of six Australian and New Zealand local authorities suggests this may be a result of the organization having traditional incremental decision making with budget decisions shaping the strategy (see Research Box 8.1).

RESEARCH BOX 8.1   STRATEGIC PLANNING AND BUDGETING PROCESSES

Goodwin and Kloot (1996) carried out interviews in three New Zealand local authorities and three Australian local authorities to investigate the relationships between strategic communication, budgetary response attitude, and budgetary role ambiguity. They defined these concepts as follows:

- Strategic communication – this was communication of decisions made within the strategic process to managers.
- Budgetary response attitude – this attitude could be one of support, withheld support, or sabotage of the budget.
- Budgetary role ambiguity – this was not having the information needed to carry out the budgetary role.

In the Australian cases, strategic planning and budgetary processes were only loosely linked, with a time gap, and often with no link at all reported. In the three New Zealand cases, they found that there was a tight link between strategic planning and the budgetary process. They reported that the strategic plan was first revised, followed closely by changes to the budget.

Their analysis of the data for New Zealand cases (tight linkages between strategic and budgetary processes) indicated that strategic communication was positively associated with budgetary response attitude. This could mean that managers were more supportive of the budget when they had received more communication on the decisions made within the strategic process. Furthermore, this positive relationship appeared to exist because communications on strategic decisions reduced the ambiguity or uncertainty of the managers in how they should understand and manage budget decisions.

Their analysis of the Australian cases (loose linkages between strategic and budgetary processes) also found that strategic communication and supportive budgetary response attitudes were positively associated, but in these cases it did not occur because of a reduction in budgetary role ambiguity.

What sense can be made of this? Goodwin and Kloot (1996: 202) draw attention to the nature of the budgetary process in the Australian cases, suggesting that incremental budgeting explained the results observed, and pointing out that budgeting decisions were informing or shaping strategy:

> For the Australian setting, however, while the processes were not found to be as tightly linked as those in the New Zealand bodies, in each case the planning was incremental and budgeting led the development of strategy. So long as no information was received that suggested a change in strategic direction was needed, budgeting allocations were seemingly predictable.

To sum up, strategic communications to managers with budgetary management responsibilities seems like a good idea, and seems to foster positive attitudes on their part to the budget decisions. In the case of local authorities that have tight linkages between strategy and budget processes, and in which the strategy shapes the budget, the strategic communication reduces uncertainty and ambiguity in the minds of the managers about how they should manage their budgets, thereby creating positive attitudes towards the budget.

There is evidence from Poister and Streib's (2005) study that the budgeting process, performance measurement, and performance management were important influences on the impact of strategic planning. Conversely, their study implied that strategic plans have less impact if they are not integrated with budgetary decisions and performance measurement. This idea can be seen as implicit in Vinzant and Vinzant's (1996) model of four levels of strategic management capacity (see Figure 8.2).

180

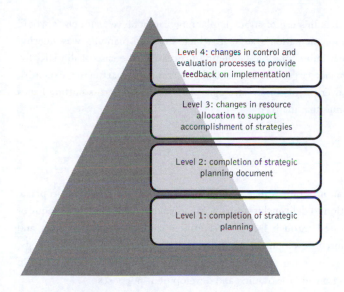

Figure 8.2 *Vinzant and Vinzant (1996) – levels of strategic management capacity*

In the Poister and Streib survey of US cities (2005: 49) only a third had got to level three as shown by having a budget tied to strategic priorities, and only a fifth had reached level four as indicated by using performance measures to track results against strategic goals and objectives.

There is also an issue about which of the systems (strategic planning, budgeting, and performance measurement and management) should take precedence over the others. So, even if the three are integrated, which system is determining or steering what is done? Ideally, strategic planning, with its concern for foresight and its concern for being clear about the benefits (outcomes) to be delivered to the public service users and others, together with its concern for basing planning of action on a robust strategic analysis of the situation, should be steering both the performance management system and the budget allocation system. Looking at some experiences of public services strategic planning, it is possible to imagine that strategic planning is being used to supplement old fashioned incremental budgeting or even new style performance budgeting. This is the case where central government departments and public service organizations are, first and foremost, given performance targets and budget allocations and told to deliver those performance targets with the budget allocated. With this as the central top-down pressure on departments and organizations, it leaves public services leaders, at best, trying to get extra 'leverage' in their efforts by drawing on strategic planning ideas and techniques. Even in this scenario, it may still be the case that strategic planning processes and techniques can make an important contribution to reform and improvement of the public services. But there is a question to be

181

answered about whether this use of strategic planning can achieve as much as would be achieved by an implementation system in which strategic planning was steering the performance management and the budgeting process. In the case of the UK, for example, are performance targets driving central government departments, executive agencies, and local government, or are strategic plans addressing cross-cutting issues and delivering outcomes that matter?

HRM

Strategic implementation requires that people in the organization have appropriate skills and the motivation to deliver the strategy. In larger organizations, these requirements may be addressed through formal recruitment and selection processes and through human resource development programmes. As a result of a new strategy, an organization may well prepare new job descriptions, and these would be used in recruitment and selection and for training and development purposes.

PROJECTS, PILOTS, LEARNING AND CONFLICT

Over the last decade project management became a more important tool as more managers in public services found themselves leading strategic changes. They turned to project management as a useful process for structuring the planning of implementation of strategic projects.

At face value, project management is a relatively simple process. It involves clarifying the project's goals, identifying the activities that make up the project, and allocating responsibility for each activity to a manager; setting the start and finish dates of each activity; and assessing the activities in terms of their budgetary implications, and, therefore, working out a project budget. It is quite possible that skills in executing project management have increased in recent years, especially in those public services organizations that have been at the forefront of modernization efforts.

Bryson (2004) provided a useful discussion about the use of different methods of strategic implementation in organizations with multiple sites. He drew attention to the fact that, in such organizations, it is possible to introduce strategic changes in one or more sites and then extend the implementation of the changes to the remaining sites later. As an example of this, when the US government passed legislation in 1993 requiring federal agencies to produce strategic and performance plans, the Act required that at least ten agencies or departments be pilots for the use of annual performance plans and programme performance reports. (Interestingly, there was no requirement for pilot projects for the strategic plans.) These pilots were to take place over the years 1994–96, prior to the requirement that all agencies submit strategic plans and annual performance plans in late 1997.

In essence, Bryson suggested designing the appropriate implementation process using one or more of the following: pilot projects, demonstration projects, and direct implementation. The choice and design of approach is based upon an assessment of the technical and political difficulty of the change process. In cases where the political difficulty of the change is relatively low, but there are significant technical difficulties, this could be a good situation for a pilot project. This allows changes to be tried out in one site, and then the experience of this first pilot project is studied and evaluated. Bryson (2004: 262) advised that 'in the early stages, when the practical nature of the changes still needs to be worked out, it is important to attract implementers with enough experience, skill and desire to make the changes work'. One way to attract implementers with the desire to make it work is to call for sites to volunteer as pilots. The lessons learnt from the pilot project may be incorporated in the proposed strategic change so that the technical difficulties are reduced when implementation is extended.

In cases where there is some modest level or low level of technical difficulty, but there is significant political difficulty (e.g. some groups have expressed some degree of opposition to the proposed strategic change), then leaders can consider a trial of the change in one site. As already noted, Bryson suggests careful attention to site selection. A site might be selected because it seemed to be the most likely to be receptive to the strategic change, and because it has the experience and capability of making a success of implementation. So, the strategic change is implemented at a favourable site, and then the project is used to reduce the opposition of those who were wavering or uncertain, for example, about the feasibility or its consequences. In other words, a demonstration project is carried out not so much because the organization does not know enough about how to carry out a strategic change, but because leaders want to prove to others that the strategic change is feasible and can be beneficial. Such a demonstration project is aimed, therefore, at overcoming some of the resistance to the change that exists.

In situations where the technical difficulty and the political difficulty of the change are both relatively low, then leaders should consider the use of direct implementation, which is where changes are implemented at all sites at the same time. If the amount of resistance to proposed changes is massive, leaders might still consider a direct implementation approach, the idea being that direct implementation right across the board, in all parts of the organization, means that the resistance or opposition cannot be concentrated on one site. So, the resistance has to be spread right across the board and may, therefore, be more easily overcome.

One final situation will be considered. This is where there is some political difficulty, but not a high level of political difficulty, and some technical difficulty as well. Leaders might consider starting with a pilot project, or a set of pilot projects, to learn the lessons necessary to reduce the technical difficulties involved. Then they could launch a demonstration project to show that it is possible to implement the change successfully. Finally, the change could be implemented in other sites.

183

Even where there is no formal piloting of strategic changes in order to learn lessons, there is an important argument that those responsible for strategy implementation should keep an open mind when monitoring the implementation process, and should be ready to learn as they implement:

> Is there a willingness to learn, during the process of implementation, by listening to stakeholders and revising the strategy as appropriate? The process of strategy implementation provides an ideal opportunity for learning and revising the strategy if management listens to staff and other stakeholders. Failure to do so can result in lost opportunity and may even prove more costly for the organization in the long term.
>
> (Tuohy 1996: 82)

FITTING IMPLEMENTATION TO LOCAL CIRCUMSTANCES

Both local government and nationally run services that are delivered at local level often find themselves responsible for implementing strategy that has been shaped or determined nationally. It is important in these circumstances that implementation decisions are used, in effect, to refine strategy to suit the local public. The process of implementation requires many decisions to be made because the concepts and ideas contained in national strategic thinking have to be interpreted and applied locally. Arguably, this fact alone means that the people who are responsible for implementing strategy locally are quite powerful in defining the actual strategy as it is being implemented. The strategy in operation is, therefore, the result of the intended strategy and its transformation into action through implementation. Seen in this way, implementation is not a neutral process of installation, but an active process of realization.

The importance of the local level is often recognized by public services managers. Many Chinese government managers, for example, are highly conscious of the differences between the populations of the city areas and the populations in rural areas, and of the differences between the needs of people in the west of China as compared with the people living around, say, Shanghai where economic growth has been relatively much faster. In the UK, there has been an issue of an urban-rural divide, with the public living in the rural areas having felt that their specific needs are neglected by governments that they thought were more interested in the needs of people living in the big cities. And, again in the UK, even populations in urban areas vary a great deal in their character and their needs – within London, for, example, the needs of people living in the East End of London are very different from those of people living in Kensington and Chelsea in the heart of London.

So, strategy needs to be implemented in a way that applies strategy differently in different localities.

TECHNIQUES FOR STRATEGIC LEADERS FOR USE IN RELATION TO IMPLEMENTATION

In this section of the chapter three very basic techniques that may be used by leaders for planning implementation of strategic actions are introduced. These techniques are stakeholder analysis, resource analysis, and risk management.

Stakeholder analysis

Stakeholder analysis is a very simple technique to outline. However that should not fool anyone into thinking that, because it is very simple, it does not have great value. It is hard to exaggerate the value of stakeholder analysis when planning the implementation of strategic action.

Stakeholder analysis can be carried out in many different ways, but when it is being used as part of the process of planning the implementation of strategic action, it needs to address some specific issues. First, what is the relevant set of stakeholders in the case of this proposed strategic action? The point is, of course, that the set of stakeholders will vary according to the strategic action being considered. Therefore, for every major strategic action planned, you probably need to carry out a separate stakeholder analysis. It should not be assumed that stakeholders will respond always in the same way to proposed strategic action irrespective of the content of the strategic action. So, it is obvious that we need to question how stakeholders groups will respond to the specific strategic action we are proposing to take. Will they like the proposed action and show support and commitment to it, or will they find the proposed strategic action undesirable from their point of view?

We can graph stakeholder positioning on a strategic action using two dimensions, attitude towards the proposed action in terms of whether they are likely to assist or block strategic action, and the power of the stakeholder group. In regard to the first dimension, we can use a scale of -10 to $+10$. If we rate a stakeholder group as -10, this would mean that they would be very unhappy about the proposed action, and $+10$ would signify that they would be delighted and very pleased with the proposed action. A score of zero would indicate that they are neither in favour nor against what is being proposed. In the case of the power of the stakeholder groups, we can use a very simple rating scale, say 1 to 10 points, where 1 means that the stakeholder group is very weak, and 10 would mean that they are a very powerful group. We can then plot all the stakeholders on a graph showing both how they are likely to feel about proposed action (against the action though to for it) and how powerful they are in relation to the proposed strategic action (see Table 8.1).

Making judgements about whether a stakeholder group is weak or powerful might involve a wide range of considerations. One might be the control a group has over a key resource that is needed for the successful implementation of the action. For example,

185

Table 8.1 Stakeholder Analysis

Stakeholder group	Attitude towards the proposed action (−10−+10)	Power of the stakeholder group (1−10)
1		
2		
3		
4		
5		
6		
7		
8		

many strategic actions need the support of the stakeholders who control the financial resources. Financial resources are often critical for the successful implementation of major strategic action. In the public services, elected politicians may be very important for this reason since it is they who have the power to approve budgetary allocations. Another key group might be professional staff working for the organization that has some special kind of expertize. This was discussed to some degree by Michel Crozier (1964) in his classic book, *The Bureaucratic Phenomenon*. Modern public health services contain high numbers of knowledgeable professional employees, and it is fairly obvious that governments are aware of the power and influence of such groups as doctors in health services. Such professionals are powerful, as we have said, by virtue of their professional expertize and they may feel very strongly that they have to be convinced about the need for strategic action before they will co-operate. So, strategic leaders cannot take their support for granted. In most countries strategic leaders cannot order highly skilled professional employees simply to implement proposed action, and time will have to be spent persuading the professionals. This is one reason why strategic planning in public services can be a slow and energy consuming process. But if this time is not invested in convincing professionals, strategic action may become stalled.

Professionals may sometimes appear individualistic, but they can also form powerful occupational groups and be very well organized. They, therefore, can respond not only individually, but also sometimes en masse to strategic change. Their power can also be expressed through their ability to lobby elected politicians through their networks. Their overall ability to exercise power and influence partly derives from the special knowledge base, partly from their high degree of organization, and partly as a result of their ability to lobby and pressurize politicians.

There may also be stakeholder groups in the community. They may have important political power bases exercised through the electoral process. Politicians may be very aware of this and nervous about ignoring the wishes of powerful constituencies in the electorate. Some groups in the public are very well organized, and capable of attracting media attention and putting pressure on the politicians through lobbying. In some localities, for example, voluntary organizations for physically disabled people can be very vocal in community level politics.

We are barely touching on the range and variety of ways in which individuals and groups can be influential and can be powerful. However rough and ready are the judgements made about the power and likely reactions of stakeholder groups to proposed strategic action, they are important so that leaders can think about their likely position on a strategic change, and think through the sorts of stakeholder management actions that might be deployed (Nutt and Backoff 1992).

Let us take the case of a stakeholder group that is both likely to be in opposition to a proposed strategic action, and also to have a high level of power or influence. One approach to stakeholder management in this case is to try to negotiate with the stakeholder group to see how much of an adjustment in the proposed course of action, or in the distribution of the benefits from the course of action, is needed to bring an adjustment in its likely reaction to the change. It should be stressed that stakeholder management could mean changing the planned strategic action. This may be needed to get a currently antagonistic group to become, if not supportive, at least less antagonistic.

Groups that are powerful or influential, and are likely to be supportive of the proposed course of action, could be valuable in the implementation process as advocates of the action. So the strategic leadership may concentrate on trying to get supportive groups to be active advocates. This might be possible by involving influential members of the stakeholder group, or representatives of the stakeholder group, in the planning of the implementation of the action. This should make them feel that they are part of the change process and willing to move behind efforts to implement the strategic action.

For stakeholder groups that are basically in favour of the proposed strategic actions, but that do not have a significant amount of power or influence, then perhaps stakeholder management is best kept low key and focused on keeping them informed, keeping them briefed. The idea in this case is to maintain their favourable attitude towards proposed strategic action. If there is a stakeholder group that is hostile to the proposed strategic actions, but does not currently have much power, stakeholder management may be aimed at not pushing them into the camp of powerful antagonistic stakeholder groups.

So, we see that stakeholder analysis and management can be used within the process of strategic implementation and is about defining the stakeholders, evaluating who they are, considering how they are likely to react, what their degree of power or influence is, and then, crucially, going on to plan specific implementation actions in relation to stakeholder groups. The aim is to maximize the chances of successful implementation and, as we have seen, this could include a decision to negotiate with antagonistic groups; a decision to call on active support of the spokespeople and representatives of positive stakeholder groups who support the proposed actions; a decision to keep some groups informed and briefed; and actions designed to reduce the chances of oppositional groups forming a coalition against strategic action (see Figure 8.3).

Figure 8.3 *Stakeholder assessment and possible tactics (based on Nutt and Backoff 1992)*

IMPORTANCE OF STAKEHOLDER	LIKELY RESPONSE TO STRATEGY	
	Opposition	*Support*
Low	Problematic stakeholders (take precautions)	Low priority stakeholders (educate them)
High	Antagonistic stakeholders (negotiate change with them)	Advocates (think about co-opting them)

Resource Analysis and Plan

A second aspect of planning implementation is planning the acquisition or deployment of resources as part of the realization of strategic action. Although there may have been some prior evaluation of the resources needed to make strategic action feasible – at the stage of choosing strategic action – the issue of resources has to be confronted again when planning implementation. Arguably, when it comes to planning implementation, even more work is needed to review and audit resources then when strategic choices are being made.

Some fairly simple questions need to be answered in order to provide the basis of an effective resource plan. As usual, the questions may seem simple, but arrival at the right answers may sometimes be more difficult. First, what types of resources are needed to implement the strategic action? The answer can take the form of a list of the basic resources that are needed. Second, what quantity of each of the resources is needed? We may have financing on our list, but how much money will be needed? In each case, we need a description of the resource and a calculation of how much of the resource is needed. Third, how important is the resource? If the resource is critical, it means that we cannot implement the action unless this resource is obtained. In some cases, the resource will not be critical. The resource may be just desirable and not essential. In other words, it is sometimes a matter of a leader feeling that ideally a specific resource is needed, but, if necessary, the action can still be implemented if the resource cannot be obtained. In some cases, the matter may be more complex – some level of availability of the resource is essential, but above this level the resource is desirable. For example, funding might be of this nature. Some level of funding could be critical, but we might be planning to obtain a level of funding beyond this because there are some desirable investments in the strategic action being planned. Fourth, how can we obtain (buy, redeploy, borrow, access) the resources we need for the strategic action? Sometimes, the resources may be obtained by bidding for funding from the organization's strategic budgets. With this funding we may then buy the needed resources from the current owners of the resources needed. Sometimes, it may be a matter of re-using resources, which may mean freeing them up from an existing use. Sometimes, the resources already exist as spare resources due to underutilized capacity, underemployed people, etc. Sometimes, organizations may look for partners and external support to supplement in-house resources.

What else is involved in obtaining resources for proposed strategic action? If we currently have the resource we need, but are using it in some other way, there will need to be some kind of judgement about the relative returns from its current deployment, and returns that we would get from redeployment. If the resources are held by stakeholders of the proposed strategic action, you may need to think through how to turn them into partners as opposed to just stakeholders. Partnerships provide the possibility of getting access to resources that you have no intention of owning or buying, but you do wish to see mobilized in support of the action you wish to take. Persuading other organizations to engage in partnership working so you can mobilize their resources may require discussions with them to show they share similar goals, and that it is feasible to create synergy by combining together to deliver the strategic action you are contemplating. If you can persuade or negotiate with stakeholders to become partners, and this allows you to mobilize the resources they control, you may then weave together the use of resources from different organizations in successful joint action.

So, summing up, the resource plan for strategic implementation begins with listing each of the resources that will be required. The plan then details how the resources might be sourced, how they might be obtained, through redeployment of existing internal resources; reallocation of budget; by buying; by working with partners, agreeing with partners to weave together their resources with yours because they share some overall goal.

The description just offered of resource analysis and planning probably makes it all sound too easy. There will be issues in trying to resource strategic action. How can we focus our attention on the most important resource issues in implementation? We could decide in relation to each resource, first, that it is easily obtained or not easily obtained and, second, whether it is desirable or critical in its importance (Nutt and Backoff 1992). Obviously planning needs to be most thorough, and action most determined, in relation to those resources that are not easily obtained, and which are of critical importance to the successful realization of the strategic plan (see Figure 8.4).

Risk Management

Risk analysis was discussed in an earlier chapter as part of a discussion about how to choose strategic action. The suggested technique for risk analysis could be repeated as part of the implementation planning process to carry out a check that the strategic action had been sufficiently de-risked, and to check on the extent to which residual risk could be handled by means of contingency planning.

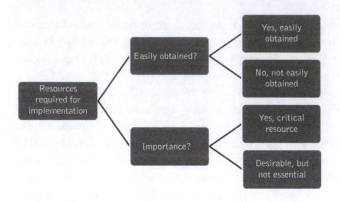

Figure 8.4 *Assessing resource requirements*

SUMMARY

As stated earlier in this chapter, implementation is not a neutral process of installation of strategy, but an active process of realization. In the end, the only strategic plan that matters is the one that is implemented, not the one that was intended. Interpreting the plan and making it concrete, inevitably, is more than simply imposing it as it is. Choices are always being made when making implementation decisions.

In looking at strategic implementation, this chapter looked at the familiar topics of culture, organization, management and management systems, and HRM. The discussion of the planning of implementation was explored in relation to projects and pilots, learning and conflict, and techniques for planning (stakeholder analysis, resource analysis and planning, and risk management).

Work-based assignment: planning implementation

The work-based assignments in this book are for civil servants and other public services staff who have four or more years of management experience.

In this assignment you practice drawing up an action plan to implement strategic action in your own organization (or an organization you know very well). Select an idea for a strategic action. Draw up a plan using the following questions:

1   What is the name of the organizational unit or units involved?
2   To whom should reports of progress on implementation be made?
3   What is the overall strategy of which this specific action is a part?
4   What is the specific strategic action, its objectives, and the details of how it will be carried out?
5   What support or resources are needed?
6   Who is responsible for the strategic action and its component parts?

7 Who else needs to be involved?

8 When does strategic action need to be started and completed?

9 What is the performance indicator(s) you would recommend for monitoring purposes?

10 Do the data/management information systems currently exist to measure performance and identify performance gaps?

When you have completed the preparation of this plan, prepare some ideas for how this would be best presented to top management of your organization for approval.

DISCUSSION QUESTIONS

1 Why is strategic implementation so difficult?

2 What can be done to increase the chances of successful implementation?

3 Does a strategic leader make their most important contribution to successful implementation through planning implementation, or communicating the need for the change and the benefits that will result?

4 In addition to ideas presented in this chapter, what other things might a strategic leader do in order to manage stakeholders in order to make implementation a success?

FURTHER READING

Bryson, J. (2004) *Strategic Planning for Public and Nonprofit Organizations: A Guide to Strengthening and Sustaining Organizational Achievement, 3rd Edition*. San Francisco: Jossey-Bass.

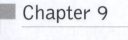

Chapter 9

Monitoring

> **LEARNING OBJECTIVES**
>
> - To investigate the nature of monitoring policies and strategies
> - To consider the trend towards outcome measures
> - To look at various techniques relevant to monitoring including performance planning, scorecards and programme assessment

INTRODUCTION

When politicians win elections in democratic systems and come into government, we expect them to bring with them new policies (on which they may have campaigned) and, especially as time goes on, to set about developing new policies in areas that had not featured in the elections. These policies may be informed by strategic thinking, and they may be turned into strategic plans and programmes set up under strategic plans. But whether the policies are strategic or not, politicians will want to know that the policies that they have decided on and expressed in legislation are being carried out. They will have allocated public money for their policies, and they will want to know that spending the money on the policies is achieving the results they wanted. These are key questions for politicians and are central to the process of monitoring. In other words, monitoring is about control. It is carried out over time during the implementation phase, which might, for example, be set at five years for many strategic plans. The need for monitoring may be partly based on concerns about the desire or capability of public service organizations to make the changes required by policy. So, strategic leaders want to know what is actually happening – is the policy/strategic plan being implemented? Expressed more negatively, is the civil service or specific public service organization making sufficient progress in implementation, or is implementation failing or going too slow?

In orthodox models of strategic planning, the monitoring of performance is a key part of a cycle of control. How does this cycle of control work? First, it assumed that the organization sets measurable strategic goals, linked to an organization's mission. These goals could be used as the basis for a gap analysis that feeds into the formulation of a strategic plan and its execution through budgetary and operational decisions. The analysis of current performance and past trends in performance would be needed to identify current or future performance gaps. So, in this way, performance assessment is an input to decisions on strategy and the strategic plan. The implementation of the strategic plan may then be followed up by measuring the impact of strategic decisions in terms of performance, and by reporting findings up the management line. On the basis of this reporting, top managers could consider whether or not strategic goals or decisions about strategy and operational matters need revision. So performance measurement matters both at the beginning and the end of the cycle of strategic management. See Figure 9.1 for a simplified representation of the control cycle.

Monitoring can also be useful for learning. Politicians and other public service leaders may hope that the strategic plans are right, but they might realize that they need refining. The monitoring may help with the work of refining policies/strategic plans. We might call this type of learning making mid-course corrections as it is discovered how to adjust strategic plans to make them more effective.

Evaluation may get muddled up in our minds with monitoring, but the timing and purposes of evaluation of strategy and strategic management are different. Strategic leaders should be evaluating strategies and strategic plans after implementation in

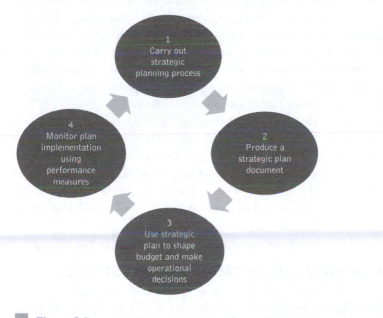

Figure 9.1 Performance measures and control cycle

order to decide if they have been worthwhile (what was the value of this strategy?). They may also want to know if the strategic plan still has value, or whether the time has arrived to move on and develop new policies and new strategic plans. Of course, evaluation can also feed into learning about policy and strategy as well.

Monitoring is not just an intellectual process. It needs to be organized and managed, and there needs to be skills and capabilities in monitoring. There has been much interest internationally in the development in the UK of a Delivery Unit, which was a small civil service unit set up to monitor and report on the results being achieved in priority areas of government. It also helped with the work of learning how to make refinements and adjustments needed to improve results.

We probably ought to distinguish the work of strategic monitoring of policies and strategic plans from the drive to improve performance through top-down performance management and performance budgeting. Strategic monitoring is concerned with checking on the implementation of new policies and strategic plans. Top-down performance management systems are an intervention in their own right to 'sweat the assets'. It is probably safe to say that the growth of activity in collecting and reporting performance information on public service outputs, and data on public service impact on clients or service users, has been mainly caused by performance management rather than strategic monitoring.

While, as it has just been argued, performance measurement and management within government can be developed as interventions in their own right, if they do exist they can be taken over and used for monitoring strategic plans. In the United States, performance management was a part of strategic planning reforms in the early 1990s. Under these reforms the US federal agencies were, in fact, required to produce strategic plans and then, on the basis of them, to produce performance plans. The basic idea of performance management integrated with strategic planning is quite simple. Performance data is produced and reported to the appropriate committees and forums in a timely manner so that the effectiveness of strategic plans can be evaluated, implementation of strategic plans can be checked, and poor performance can be challenged.

In this chapter, we will be looking at different approaches to performance measurement and reporting. These can be politically owned, or owned by top civil servants or appointed public managers. We will be looking at the significance of different types of performance indicators and targets, especially output and outcome indicators and targets. This is followed by a consideration of performance plans and programme assessment tools. Finally we look at how uncertainty issues and acceptability can be handled when setting performance targets.

POLITICALLY OWNED PERFORMANCE MEASUREMENT

When there are targets and performance measurement and reporting, elected politicians can begin to hold civil service leaders of government departments and managerial leaders of public service organizations to account. Where politicians want an effective system of accountability for civil service leaders and public managers, the politicians may want to use their political manifestos and campaigning documents as the source of their priorities and performance indicators.

There are some obvious points that can be made about politically generated performance measures. First, when they are very specific and easily measurable, they carry a political risk. There could be a big improvement in government performance that just falls short of the promised achievement – this is potentially dangerous as political opponents can draw attention to the failure to achieve what was promised, and portray the government as incompetent. It might seem much safer politically to make only vague promises.

Second, politicians are often accused of being short term in their thinking because they are always worrying about how they are going to get re-elected, or are prone to getting distracted by crises and unexpected developments. It might be thought, therefore, that any politically led approach to performance measurement and reporting will be very short term. In recent years, politicians appear to have become conscious of the dangers of short-term thinking. In the UK a new coalition government was elected in 2010, and their coalition agreement was very rapidly developed into structural reform plans that showed this longer time perspective. These structural reform plans were then made the basis of annual business plans by government departments. It was also true of earlier UK governments that there has been a desire to think long term. In May 2000, the then Prime Minister, Tony Blair, talked about the strategic direction of his government. He said:

> You may have heard me and my colleagues talking over the last few days about the need to keep focussed on the long-term – warning of the need not to get blown about by day to day events . . . what's important is to stay focussed on what really matters, on the fundamentals – on economy and jobs, welfare reform, on health, education, crime and transport . . . by concentrating on these fundamentals, I believe we've been able to make more progress than anyone would have thought possible two or three years ago.
>
> (Source: http://www.number-10.gov.uk/output/Page327.asp.
> Accessed 2 September 2005)

Third, just because performance measurement is based on the politician's priorities, it does not mean that they are without interest to the public. It is possible for a politically led approach to performance measurement and reporting to be also a public-responsive approach. This requires that priorities are based on the top concerns of the public. In the UK, the government's emphasis on education and health as key areas for performance improvements matched the prominence of these two areas in public perceptions of key issues in the decade from 1997. Arguably, elected politicians could order public opinion polling to track trends in public perceptions of national issues as a way of determining their strategic priorities and their selection of key performance indicators.

PERFORMANCE PLANS

Before we look at the long-running debate on whether you should monitor outputs or outcomes, let us first establish the idea of a performance plan that provides a simple way of thinking about how to monitor the implementation of, say, a five-year strategic plan. Looking at examples of strategic plans in the public sector, it is evident that they are sometimes looking for changes over a five-year period or, in some cases, over a longer period, such as 10 years. If the improvements in performance are to be monitored on an annual basis, the performance targets need to be set on an annual basis showing progress towards the achievement of the desired performance at the end of the planning period.

Table 9.1 is a performance plan chart, and it shows how performance information for such a plan can be set out. For each strategic goal, there may be one or more performance indicators, and for each performance indicator we can set targets on an annual basis.

The usual advice is to ensure performance targets are measurable and have timescales. An example of a set of performance targets follows. These are taken from South Australia's Strategic Plan for 2004. Let us look at them:

1　better the average Australian employment growth rate within 10 years
2　improve Adelaide's quality of life ranking on the William M. Mercer quality of life index to being in the top 20 cities in the world within 10 years

Table 9.1 *Performance plan chart*

Strategic goal	Performance indicator	Annual performance target				
		Year 1	Year 2	Year 3	Year 4	Year 5

3 achieve the Kyoto targets on greenhouse emissions during the first commitment period (2008–12)
4 increase patents applications to exceed a population share of all Australian applications within five years
5 increase the number of female members of Parliament to 50 per cent within 10 years
6 halve the number of rough sleepers in South Australia by 2010.

It is obvious that the South Australia strategic plan tries to specify performance targets using numbers and also to set timescales.

One final point about performance plans, is it enough to monitor actual performance against planned performance on a year by year basis? There is a little evidence that it is important to track changes over time in actual performance and not just compare actual and planned performance (see Research Box 9.1).

RESEARCH BOX 9.1 PERFORMANCE MEASUREMENT IN US LOCAL GOVERNMENT

Poister and Streib's (2005) analysis of the experience of over 200 cities in the United States that had undertaken strategic planning efforts over the preceding five years found that only 60 per cent of them used performance measures to track the accomplishment of goals and objectives in the strategic plan. Slightly less than half reported performance measures related to the strategic plan to the city council on a regular basis. Only a third reported performance measures associated with the strategic plan to the public on a regular basis.

Many of the city councils that did use performance measures to track delivery of strategic goals and objectives also reported using performance data to monitor improvements over time. In fact, there was evidence to suggest that this particular practice was associated with the impact of strategic plans. They also found that making regular reports to the public on performance measures associated with the strategic plan was another practice linked to strategic plan impact.

So, a hypothesis might be proposed: it is not enough simply to compare planned performance with actual, it is better to track performance over time and appreciate the trends in performance. A second hypothesis might be: it is not enough to be accountable upwards to politicians; it is better to make yourself also accountable directly to the public for your performance.

197

INPUTS, OUTPUTS, AND OUTCOMES

A key conceptual distinction in thinking about performance measurement in the public services is between outputs and outcomes. Ball (1994: 25), referring to New Zealand's public services reforms, said: 'We use these terms in a conventional fashion with outcomes being impacts on the community, such as a reduced level of crime, whereas outputs are services delivered by specific agencies, such as street patrolling, prosecutions and so on.'

The division of labour between politicians on one hand, and civil servants and public managers on the other hand, is often described as clear and reasonable. Politicians make policies, and civil servants and public managers deliver them. In practice, there are tensions between politicians and civil servants and public managers in terms of performance assessment, and these can emerge in the difference between outputs and outcomes. This has been noticed in the case of the New Zealand Government. Some years ago, management reforms were made that were designed to ensure the accountability of the top civil servants for outputs. The chief executives of government departments (i.e. the top civil servants) were party to performance agreements that reflected the services their ministers wanted delivered. The performance agreements were linked to contracts that were concerned with the outputs of the departments. Ball (1994: 25) made the following comment about the New Zealand public service system:

> While our system recognizes the critical nature of information relating outputs to outcomes in making policy decisions, there was a deliberate decision not to seek to use outcomes to define the accountability of chief executives and their departments. The reason for this is that the individual chief executive very rarely has sufficient control over outcomes to make accountability effective.

The distinction between outputs and outcomes, therefore, is partially important because of the accountability mechanisms and the incentives for senior civil servants and top managers in leadership positions in the civil service. The chief executives in New Zealand's public services clearly had an incentive to comply with their ministers. The ministers, as politicians, wanted outcomes really, but settled for outputs as the focus of accountability. The key point here is that politicians really wanted *outcomes* not *outputs*.

The importance of this point emerged a few years later when Schick (in 2001) wrote about the New Zealand government's introduction of strategic results areas (SRAs) and key results areas (KRAs). He suggested that they had only been partly successful in tackling weaknesses in directing budgetary allocations. He praised the New Zealand model for its focus on operational effectiveness but emphasized problems

198

in respect of policy and strategy. It appears that there was a difference of perspective and interest between elected politicians and civil servants. Schick wrote (2001: 4):

> One way of making this point is that chief executives and ministers have different perspectives and interests. Although chief executives may be interested in outcomes and results, the system impels them to focus on outputs for which they are accountable; and although ministers have an interest in inputs and outputs, their political goals impel them to focus on outcomes and objectives.

These references to problems of accountability in the New Zealand case can be contrasted with the growing use of outcome performance measures in the federal agencies of the United States government. A decade after the Government Performance and Results Act (GPRA) of 1993 became law, a report was produced by the United States General Accounting Office (GAO) which looked, first, into the effects of the 1993 Act in terms of an increasing focus by government on results. Second, it looked into the challenges of performance measurement and the use of performance information. Third, it looked at how the United States government could continue progress towards a more results oriented government. The GAO report said the 1993 Act 'had established a solid foundation' in terms of achieving 'results-oriented performance planning, measurement, and reporting in the Federal government' (General Accounting Office 2004). It also found that strategic and performance plans were getting better. But there were areas that needed more work, such as the linking of results to the allocation of resources. There were also reported difficulties in setting outcome oriented goals, collecting useful data on results, and linking performance measurement (at all levels from the institutional to the individual) to reward systems. Another issue was that the GAO believed there was an inadequate focus on cross-cutting issues that were of concern to more than one federal agency. The Obama administration responded to various concerns about how GPRA was working in practice with the GPRA Modernization Act, which introduced federal priority goals, adjusted the planning cycle to the political process and made other changes to strengthen political oversight.

The report summarized findings from surveys of federal managers for the years 1997, 2000, and 2003 showing that outcome-based performance measures were becoming more widespread in federal government. The evidence indicated that, whereas only a third of federal managers in 1997 had outcome performance measures, by 2003 just over half had outcome performance measures (see Table 9.2).

Table 9.2 *Outcome-based performance measures*

GAO Surveys	1997	2000	2003
Percentage of federal managers having outcome based performance measures	32%	44%	55%

It is worth mentioning here that elected politicians may sometimes also want input performance measures to be featured in reporting systems. This may seem surprising given the evident point that outcomes have an obvious merit in being results that the public might experience and credit to the politicians as achievements. If patients have shorter waiting times for hospital operations, or school children achieve better exam results, the public can conclude that the politicians have made public services better. But input performance measures can also be highly important in political terms. A Government may want to claim that it has made sure there are more doctors, teachers, and police, which should reassure the public that core public services are not being starved of funding and have the capacity to deliver more public services.

PROGRAMME ASSESSMENT

Monitoring can also be carried out on the performance of government programmes that form parts of strategic plans. Programme assessment is not new and predates the era of strategic planning. In the 1970s, for example, programmes were assessed to see if they were achieving their objectives, and to understand the causes of success or failure of programmes (York 1982). The process could involve identifying the programme, formulating criteria (e.g. efficiency, effectiveness, impact, quality), deciding on a method, collecting data, analysing the data, and then, finally, reporting.

In the United States in early 2002, the Office of Management and Budget (OMB) set up a task force to create a tool for assessing the performance of programmes – called the Program Assessment Rating Tool (PART). In the summer of 2002, OMB distributed the tool and instructions so that programmes carried out by federal agencies could be assessed by OMB. The assessments were made and sent to federal agencies, which were able to make written appeals to OMB in September of the same year. This process of programme assessment informed the President's budget for 2004, which was actually issued in February 2003. Subsequently, in 2004, an official of OMB said that the performance information from PART had been useful for making budget decisions and had helped to identify opportunities to improve programmes.

The tool comprises a set of questions. Those used in the 2004 PART are reproduced below (see Table 9.3). The possible answers to questions in the first, second and third sections are yes, no, or not applicable. The possible answers to section four are: yes, large extent, small extent, or no. (Specific questions according to the type of programme are ignored here.)

As can be seen by examining the contents of the PART, assessment is intended to be carried out in the context of the strategic plans for the federal agencies. This point was made, in effect, in guidance issued by the OMB. The OMB said that long-term performance measures and targets were the basis for assessing the results of programmes, and noted the strong focus on strategic planning in Section II of the tool. The linkage between strategic goals in the strategic plans of federal agencies and the outcome

Table 9.3 *Programme Assessment Rating Tool*

Section	Questions	Answer		
		Yes	No	N/A
Section I: Program Purpose & Design	1. Is the program purpose clear?			
	2. Does the program address a specific interest, problem or need?			
	3. Is the program designed to have a significant impact in addressing the interest, problem or need?			
	4. Is the program designed to make a unique contribution in addressing the interest, problem or need (i.e., not needlessly redundant of any other Federal, state, local or private efforts)?			
	5. Is the program optimally designed to address the interest, problem or need?			
Section II: Strategic Planning	1. Does the program have a limited number of specific, ambitious long-term performance goals that focus on outcomes and meaningfully reflect the purpose of the program?			
	2. Does the program have a limited number of annual performance goals that demonstrate progress toward achieving the long-term goals?			
	3. Do all partners (grantees, sub grantees, contractors, etc.) support program-planning efforts by committing to the annual and/or long-term goals of the program?			
	4. Does the program collaborate and coordinate effectively with related programs that share similar goals and objectives?			
	5. Are independent and quality evaluations of sufficient scope conducted on a regular basis or as needed to fill gaps in performance information to support program improvements and evaluate effectiveness?			
	6. Is the program budget aligned with the program goals in such a way that the impact of funding, policy, and legislative changes on performance is readily known?			
	7. Has the program taken meaningful steps to address its strategic planning deficiencies?			

Table 9.3 *(Continued)*

Section	Questions	Answer		
		Yes	No	N/A
Section III: Program Management	1. Does the agency regularly collect timely and credible performance information, including information from key program partners, and use it to manage the program and improve performance? 2. Are federal managers and program partners (grantees, sub grantees, contractors, etc.) held accountable for cost, schedule and performance results? 3. Are all funds (Federal and partners') obligated in a timely manner and spent for the intended purpose? 4. Does the program have incentives and procedures (e.g., competitive sourcing/cost comparisons, IT improvements) to measure and achieve efficiencies and cost effectiveness in program execution? 5. Does the agency estimate the budget for the full annual costs of operating the program (including all administrative costs and allocated overhead) so that program performance changes are identified with changes in funding levels? 6. Does the program use strong financial management practices? 7. Has the program taken meaningful steps to address its management deficiencies?			

Section	Questions	Answer		
		Yes, Large extent	Small extent	No
Section IV: Program Results	1. Has the program demonstrated adequate progress in achieving its long-term outcome goal(s)? 2. Does the program (including program partners) achieve its annual performance goals? 3. Does the program demonstrate improved efficiencies and cost effectiveness in achieving program goals each year?			

Table 9.3 *(Continued)*

Section	Questions	Answer		
		Yes, Large extent	Small extent	No
	4. Does the performance of this program compare favourably to other programs with similar purpose and goals? 5. Do independent and quality evaluations of this program indicate that the program is effective and achieving results?			

Figure: 2004 PART (general questions only)

goals of programmes is conceived within the PART assessment as being a hierarchical one. Consequently, the strategic goals in the strategic plans should be achieved if the programme outcome goals are achieved. More mundanely, this means that federal agencies should be using their strategic plan documents to complete Section II of the PART. OMB also indicated that changes in performance measures resulting from PART assessments should trigger consultation of stakeholders (OMB 2007: 8):

> Because of the importance of performance measures, OMB and agencies must agree on appropriate measures early to allow for review with relevant stakeholders if needed. If the agency intends to revise its strategic goals as the result of a PART assessment, the GPRA requires that relevant stakeholders be consulted during the strategic plan review.

In these ways PART assessments have formal links to the strategic plans created under GPRA, and, as the OMB suggests, it is possible that the PART assessments may lead to changes in strategic goals and stakeholder consultation. It is not clear from the examination of the PART, or the guidance issued by OMB, what long-term impact PART assessments have on the nature of strategic planning by federal agencies, but because of the use of PART assessments for budgeting by the US government, it can be said that they provide a way of connecting strategic planning to budgeting.

SCORECARDS

In some situations it may be civil services leaders or senior public managers who own performance measurement and reporting, and elected politicians who see these as

203

mainly a managerial matter of little direct interest to them. In such cases, the balanced scorecard (which we looked at briefly in an earlier chapter) may appear to offer a useful approach that might be seen as very different from the process of working from legal mandates to mission statements to performance indicators and targets. One argument for its use is that the balanced scorecard causes civil servants or public managers to consider a more diverse range of performance indicators, including indicators of relevance to service users, than they otherwise might. In other words, a balanced scorecard may encourage performance measurement to be less bureaucratic in nature and more 'customer-centric'.

So what is a balanced scorecard? It is a way of organizing performance data so that managers and staff at various organizational levels can monitor and discuss performance. The concept of a balanced scorecard is essentially very simple. It prompts organizations to formulate performance goals and measures using four perspectives. It has been considered for possible use in public services organizations for many years since its popularization in the early 1990s. For example, Boyle (no date: 8) suggested that it might be applied to the Irish civil service. In the case of the Irish civil service, as Boyle pointed out, the performance measurement system had to be linked to strategy since all government departments were working to a statement of strategy and mission, following the launch of the Strategic Management Initiative in 1994, and the passing of the Public Service Management Act of 1997:

> It is possible to see the ideas behind the balanced scorecard being adapted for use in the Irish civil service. Its focus on different stakeholders and their needs, on strategic management, and on presenting a balanced picture of key performance measures and indicators, is attractive for those concerned with performance measurement in the civil service.

The four perspectives of the balanced scorecard are the customer perspective, the financial perspective, the internal business perspective, and the innovation and learning perspective. Its value in any sector – public, private, or voluntary – is that it encourages organizations to use a basket of goals and measures and not to rely simply on, say, a financial measure of performance.

We will briefly look at all four perspectives, taking note of possible examples and mentioning one or two considerations. First, there is the customer perspective, which has become more important as a perspective in recent years. Boyle stresses the importance of the views of service users (i.e. the customer perspective). He says (no date: 9):

> Ultimately, most services are provided for the benefits of users, and their views on performance are important in determining how well or badly a service is provided. Defining users can be difficult at times in the civil service (Boyle 1996: 40), but a user perspective is important in judging performance.

This perspective might be reflected in a goal addressing the satisfaction of the public with the services they use, which may be assessed using surveys. Another option in measuring satisfaction levels is to monitor the number of complaints received from service users.

Second, there is the financial perspective, which might be reflected in a goal about containing spending within agreed limits or even making savings. Another financial goal may be earning revenue from user fees. It is worth considering how this goal may be seen as an aspect of modernization and reform. For example, public services have been exhorted to earn as well as spend (Osborne and Gaebler 1992). So as well as receiving funding from government, organizations may set goals in terms of income from charging fees. Osborne and Gaebler (1992) directly challenge the traditional attitude of reliance on 'tax and spend' thinking:

> We can no longer afford this attitude, in an age of fierce resistance to taxes. This is not to say that most public services should be sold for profit – most shouldn't. But think of all the public services that benefit individuals: the golf courses, the tennis courts, the marinas. Typically, the taxpayers subsidize those services. Average working people subsidize the affluent to play golf and tennis or moor their boats. Why not turn such services into profit centres?
>
> (Osborne and Gaebler 1992: 199)

If such services are profitable, affluent service users can be charged so as to subsidize the public services which are necessary for the average citizen.

The internal business perspective is the third perspective. It relates to how well the organization is functioning. One goal in this area might be improved service quality, which might be measured in a benefits agency, for example, by how many correct benefits assessments are made.

Finally, the fourth perspective is an innovation and learning perspective, which is concerned with goals focused on improvements and developments. An organization might measure these in various ways, for example, the speed of process innovations (e.g. e-government) or spend on staff development.

Boyle suggested the use of what he called an integrated performance measurement framework focusing on three groups of stakeholders, rather than the four perspectives of the balanced scorecard. These are, first, service users and policy makers (the parliament, the cabinet, and government ministers); second, resource controllers; and, third, staff and management. He claimed the first group is interested in results; the second is interested in financial management; and the third group is interested in human resource management (see Table 9.4).

Whether a public service organization uses some version of the balanced scorecard or an adaptation of it (such as Boyle's), the performance measures need to be linked to the mission statement and strategy. Figure 9.2 shows a layout for displaying the

205

Table 9.4 *Stakeholders and their interests*

Stakeholders	Service Users Parliament, Cabinet and Government Ministers	Resource Controllers	Staff and Management
Stakeholders' Interests	Results	Financial Management	Human Resource Management

```
                    ┌──────────────┐
                    │   Mission    │
                    │   Strategy   │
                    └──────────────┘
        ┌──────────────────┼──────────────────┐
┌───────────────┐  ┌───────────────┐  ┌───────────────┐
│ Stakeholder   │  │ Stakeholder   │  │ Stakeholder   │
│ Group:        │  │ Group:        │  │ Group:        │
│               │  │               │  │               │
│ Stakeholder   │  │ Stakeholder   │  │ Stakeholder   │
│ Interest:     │  │ Interest:     │  │ Interest:     │
│               │  │               │  │               │
│ Goals:        │  │ Goals:        │  │ Goals:        │
│               │  │               │  │               │
│ Key Tasks/    │  │ Key Tasks/    │  │ Key Tasks/    │
│ Targets:      │  │ Targets:      │  │ Targets:      │
│               │  │               │  │               │
│ Key           │  │ Key           │  │ Key           │
│ Measurements: │  │ Measurements: │  │ Measurements: │
└───────────────┘  └───────────────┘  └───────────────┘
```

Figure 9.2 *Displaying performance measures*

linkages from mission and strategy through to performance measurement, which is more or less as suggested by Boyle (with some minor changes).

The display may be completed as follows:

1 The mission statement and strategy of an organization are written into the mission and strategy box at the top
2 The key groups of stakeholders are identified and their interests clarified. These are summarized in the appropriate places in the performance measures boxes
3 The goals rows in the performance measures boxes are completed by identifying what has to be accomplished if the mission and strategy are to be successful

4 Key tasks/targets are time bound (have to be done by a specific date) and are 'operationalized' (i.e. more concrete) versions of the goals

5 Finally, the key measurements are the actual performance indicators used.

The balanced scorecard cannot make up for poor quality financial and performance data, and even with good quality data, performance assessment still requires strategic leaders willing to devote time and effort to understanding the implications of the data and then willing to take tough decisions on the basis of it.

DEALING WITH FUTURE UNCERTAINTY

In order to complete a performance plan some judgement has to be made about the trajectory of performance improvement over, say, a five-year period. Because of uncertainty about the future, it is unlikely that it will be possible to predict the exact trajectory of performance improvement for each strategic goal, and the performance plan will have to be based on some guesswork.

Public managers sometimes find it difficult to think through guesses about the future annual performance targets in a performance plan. They sometimes just do not know how to start, especially if extrapolation from past trends is inappropriate or not possible. One way to get the thinking started is to ask public managers to choose one of three types of performance trajectory. The first type is that that there will be a steady increase in performance over the five years. Type two envisages that progress in improving performance will be initially rapid and then slow down. Type three is that performance will actually deteriorate as the organization changes over to a new process and employees and managers are trained in new methods, but then in the last part of the plan period progress is rapid. These three types of trajectory can be represented on a graph (see Figure 9.3). Such graphs – showing three trajectories – can be used in strategic planning workshops to facilitate discussions by management teams, and to prompt them to think about the actions needed to implement strategic measures.

- Which trajectory seems most likely to apply to a specific strategic measure?
- Why will performance improvement follow this trajectory?
- What implementation actions will be taken, and when, to achieve this performance trajectory?

It is remarkable how this simple device can be used to prompt questions and cue thinking that enables management teams to confront the challenge of planning implementation. It is possible that public managers draw on tacit knowledge when they choose a trajectory and, having made the choice, they then surface their judgements about why the trajectory will be of that type.

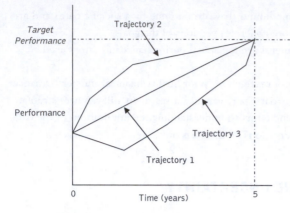

Figure 9.3 *Performance trajectory*

ACCEPTABILITY

Performance targets in UK public services have been very controversial. One group that has often complained about targets are public services professionals. This can be illustrated by the response of the medical profession to the publication of performance information by the English NHS in the summer of 1999. This was published on the Internet. The information had taken nearly two years to assemble, and included data on mortality rates after surgery, detection and survival of cancer, teenage pregnancies, and access to NHS dentistry. What was the response from the medical profession? One spokesman warned that it would put hospital consultants under pressure, and also raised a concern that doctors might refuse treatment because of the adverse effect on performance indicators of going ahead with treatment.

The justification for the exercise was that the statistics would be used by managers in the NHS to improve health services and reveal variations in results. However, the English Health Secretary warned that this was the first time that information had been published in this form and so there would be some data quality issues. He also warned that the data required careful interpretation. He was quoted as saying (Revill 1999: 2):

> These indicators are not league tables – to use them that way would be misleading. There will often be very good reasons why one organisation appears to be performing differently from others.

While public service professionals in many sectors complained that performance measurement was creating wasteful bureaucracy and distorting behaviour, the counter arguments were that performance information was needed to improve the responsiveness of services to the public and should be used pragmatically to improve the public services even if some of the data was far from perfectly accurate.

It is not just professionals who were uncomfortable with the use of performance targets. Managers in public services have also often been uncomfortable either with the idea of performance targets, or with their use in practice. First, many managers dislike performance management systems – they are uncomfortable for the individual managers. This is because individual managers may be held to account for performance that is less than satisfactory. Second, there may be problems over the selection of performance targets. Managers may regard the performance targets they have been given responsibility for as crude and not suitable for judging the success of the services they manage. Third, the data collected against these performance indicators may be of poor quality. Fourth, the managers may not be provided with performance information they need on a timely or frequent basis.

But targets are useful (whether quantitative or qualitative) so government can decide if its actions have been successful. The real issue, therefore, should be how to set targets as effectively and sensibly as possible.

But how can strategic leaders deal with the objections that may be put in the way of setting performance targets? First, what about the argument that performance targets were creating wasteful bureaucracy? While it is probably a good idea to be on guard against an excessive bureaucracy developing around performance targets, in the end governments need some priorities and performance targets to ensure the focus and persistence needed to achieve success.

Second, what about the view that performance measurement is disliked because it distorts performance or has unintended effects? Barber (2007: 80–1) appeared not be impressed by these arguments on the basis of his experience of heading up the UK Prime Minister's Delivery Unit:

> Here the debate is confused. If one purpose of a target is to enhance the priority of the focus area, it follows inescapably that some other areas will not be so prioritised and may suffer relatively . . . Unintended consequences are another sort of risk. I found that whenever a new target or goal is set, those who defend the status quo instantly explain all the unintended consequences that will ensue. With the focus on literacy and numeracy, such people predicted that the science results would go down. (They didn't – they went up . . .) When we focused on reducing street crime in 2002, senior police predicted that, as street crime fell, burglary and car crime would inevitably rise. (They didn't – they continued to fall . . .) So in the Delivery Unit, our reaction to all these dire predictions was not to accept them at face value since they so often proved to be urban myths, but always to agree we would check. Then, if the fear proved unfounded, the urban myth would be exploded; and if it proved justified, a political choice could be made about whether it was a price worth paying.

209

CASE STUDY

Department of Agriculture and Rural Development (DARD) of Northern Ireland

The example that follows is arguably a hybrid of a strategic plan undertaken voluntarily by managers as a way to improve their effectiveness and one that wraps around a performance budgeting framework. This is because, on one hand, the strategic plan contains vision, goals, and actions, but on the other it has a set of targets and linked to them a budget allocation. This strategic plan is a five-year plan for the Department of Agriculture and Rural Development (DARD) of Northern Ireland, which covers the period 2006–11. The diagram at Figure 9.4 provides a summary of the strategic vision, aims, and strategic goals. If we assume that the aim is a mission statement, it is not obvious that it should follow from the vision, though it might be expected that the strategic vision would be influenced by the mission (aim). Furthermore, while the strategic goals seem plausible in the light of the strategic vision, it is not clear that the strategic goals follow on from the aim. It may be that this diagram, which is based on an overview taken from the department's web site, shows the process sequence rather than logical links.

For each of the strategic goals there was a set of strategic objectives and a set of key actions. For example,

Strategic goal: To improve performance in the market place

Strategic Objectives:

1 Farm-gate sales and ancillary land based industries to be competitive in a reformed market

2 A more competitive food processing industry

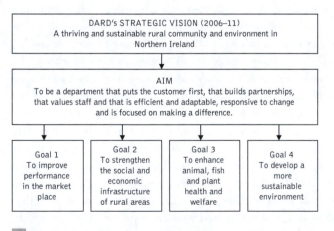

Figure 9.4 *Department of Agriculture and Rural Development (DARD) of Northern Ireland (2006–11)*

3　A more competitive fishing industry

4　A more competitive forestry industry.

Key actions:

1　Deliver a targeted strategy for life-long learning

2　Deliver a targeted strategy for R&D and technology transfer

3　Implement the NI fit for Market food strategy

4　Deliver sectoral strategic plans and support in line with industry needs

5　Deliver the Single Farm Payment.

The department presented this five-year strategic plan as influencing its Public Service Agreements (PSA) (which are focused on performance targets and budget), an efficiency plan and the departmental reform plan, all of which were framed on an annual basis. The strategic plan also influenced the corporate scorecard which included the key performance targets of the department. The PSA also influenced the corporate scorecard. All this was then cascaded down the organization on an annual basis through the scorecard and business plan for groups and agencies, and then down to divisional branch level, and even down to individual personal performance agreements. So the intention was that, through this system, you could trace a formal link between the personal performance agreement with an individual all the way through to the department's overall five-year strategic plan (see Figure 9.5).

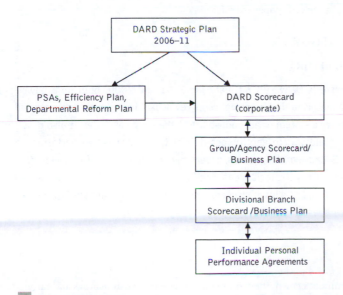

Figure 9.5 *Linkages*

The published DARD strategic plan contained the PSA as an appendix. The PSA showed that the objectives were to promote sustainable development of the agri-food industry and the countryside and stimulate the economic and social revitalization of disadvantaged rural areas; reduce the risk to life and property from flooding; promote sustainable development of the sea fishing industry; and maintain, protect, and expand forests in a sustainable way. The PSA stated the current expenditure levels and investment levels in terms of millions of pounds for 2006/07 and for 2007/08. The PSA also attempted to indicate the planned outcome for citizens. In this case, it was stated that one result of the PSA was there would be a competitive agri-food industry and improved animal health. The PSA included a number of targets. One example was a target which was stated as: Create conditions for the agricultural industry to achieve a 10.5 per cent improvement in total factor productivity between calendar year 2001 and 2008. Another example of a target was: Create conditions to increase value added per full-time employee equivalent in the Northern Ireland Food and Drinks processing sector from £22,400 (1999/2001 average) to £33,100 by 2008.

It is possible that such a strategic plan is really based on the department's understanding of its mission (especially in terms of who were the intended beneficiaries and what the benefits should be), its strategic vision, and its strategic situation. Alternatively, the strategic plan could be merely a 'gloss' put on plans chiefly aimed at meeting performance targets set in the PSA, and thus important for securing budget allocations. In the former case, the PSA is absorbed into the work of a strategically led public service; in the latter case the PSA drives and determines the activity of the department and the strategic plan is in danger of being a waste of time or a paper exercise.

MINI CASE STUDY

The Delivery Unit (UK)

The Prime Minister's Delivery Unit, between 2001 and 2005, built up a powerful process of monitoring the performance of key departments against targets and ensuring an effective system of accountability to the Prime Minister. It also developed a system for field work to identify specific initiatives to bring about performance improvements. Because of this, the UK government became more effective in managing performance in key strategic areas. The Prime Minister's Strategy Unit carried out a strategic audit in 2004 in which performance on the Prime Minister's priorities was reviewed. The results were very impressive (see Table 9.5).

SUMMARY

One choice for governments is whether to develop performance indicators and targets from political manifestos and surveys of public concerns, or whether to use a balanced

Table 9.5 Strategic audit of performance in 2004 (UK)

Goal	Direction	Ahead of 1997?
Health:		
nurse numbers	positive	ahead
doctor numbers	positive	ahead
heart disease mortality	positive	ahead
cancer mortality	positive	ahead
waiting list	positive	ahead
waiting times	positive	ahead
accident and emergency	positive	ahead
primary care access	positive	ahead
Education:		
teacher numbers	positive	ahead
teacher recruitment	positive	ahead
11-year-old's literacy	flat	ahead
11-year-old's numeracy	flat	ahead
14-year-old's English	positive	ahead
14-year-old's maths	positive	ahead
five A–C GCSEs	positive	ahead
specialist schools	positive	ahead
truancy	flat	equal to
Home Office:		
police numbers	positive	ahead
overall crime	positive	ahead
burglary	positive	ahead
vehicle crime	positive	ahead
robbery	positive	worse
violent crime	positive	ahead
gun crime	negative	worse
antisocial behaviour	positive	worse
likelihood of being a victim	positive	ahead
asylum applications	positive	ahead
Transport:		
rail patronage	positive	ahead
rail punctuality	positive	worse

scorecard approach. The balanced scorecard approach may be more suitable where there is little political leadership of strategic change and ministers have not developed the strategies or feel much sense of ownership of the strategies. In this case, the balanced scorecard is a useful framework for civil servants because it helps to broaden their work in monitoring and discussing performance. Critically, the balanced scorecard approach steers civil servants towards thinking about formulating performance goals and measures in ways that benefits users of public services. Boyle's (1996) view that a user perspective is important in judging performance may be noted here. But it is worth repeating that where there is strong and coherent political leadership, the performance measures may be more usefully – and more legitimately – directly drawn from manifestos and from public opinion polling.

When developed as part of strategic planning reforms, monitoring through performance measurement and management can be used to empower civil servants within an accountability framework. This has important implications for the relationship between politicians and top civil servants, but these implications may also be influenced significantly by the decision to use output measures or outcome measures in setting performance goals for government departments and public services. In the past, there has been a view that it is technically difficult to focus on outcome measures and much easier to collect data and report on output measures. There is evidence showing that a government which persists in trying to base performance measurement on the basis of outcome measures can be successful in establishing their use.

We also looked briefly at the development in the US of the PART, which takes federal agency strategic plans as the basis of programme outcome goals, and which enables programme results to be assessed and taken into consideration when the budget setting work is being done. It is recognized that the PART process can lead to changes in strategic goals, but it is not clear from the official guidance issued how else the nature of strategic planning might be affected by this development.

We looked at how performance plans may be drawn up on the basis of strategic goals, and we noted that public services managers are faced by problems of uncertainty when producing annual performance plans for, say, five years ahead. Finding ways to help managers to develop an understanding of the possible trajectories of annual performance targets that will lead to the accomplishment of strategic goals is important.

There are a number of technical and other issues in performance measurement and management. There are technical issues about the selection of performance indicators and problems of poor data availability and quality. The former problem will probably always be a source of argument, but data availability and data quality can be significantly improved if there is the will to do so, as was shown by the UK experience when the Prime Minister's Delivery Unit was established in 2001 (Barber 2007).

In this chapter we have also briefly considered why performance measurement is resisted, and how those responsible for measuring and managing performance in government may respond to doubts and criticisms of performance targets. Behind the resistance may be issues that are not so much technical as ones of acceptability to those affected by performance measurement. They threaten individual professionals and managers, and make them feel uncomfortable. Such systems not only make their results more transparent, but can also expose them to criticism if the performance of the organization they are managing falls short of political or public expectations.

214

Work-based assignment: mission statements and performance measures

The work-based assignments in this book are for civil servants and other public services staff who have four or more years of management experience.

Reflect on your organization's mission statement. Can you identify three or four key performance indicators based on this mission statement that could be used to evaluate the strategic effectiveness of the organization?

If this assignment is reviewed in class, present your conclusions on a flip chart and discuss with others. Compare performance indicators in a plenary discussion and identify the best ones. Discuss the basis for selecting the best ones – that is, what criteria were used for selecting the best ones?

Work-based assignment: balanced scorecard

Use the balanced scorecard to classify the performance indicators you developed in the previous assignment. Reflect on the results of this. Did you have a performance indicator for each of the four perspectives, or were their gaps in your coverage of the balanced scorecard?

DISCUSSION QUESTIONS

1   Which type of performance measures should public services use – output or outcome measures?
2   How helpful in exploring the idea of monitoring is the concept of the control cycle? Has it any disadvantages as a way of representing monitoring?
3   Should programme assessment be used to change strategic goals? How does programme assessment affect strategic management if it is carried out by ministry of finance officials and they are primarily focused on budget setting?
4   Is a scorecard approach the best approach to performance monitoring?
5   How do vested interests affect discussions of the value of performance targets?

FURTHER READING

Barber, M. (2007) *Instruction to Deliver*. London: Politico's.

Chapter 10

Evaluating strategic plans

> **LEARNING OBJECTIVES**
>
> - To clarify the nature of the evaluation process
> - To look at approaches to evaluation
> - To explore some evaluation tools

INTRODUCTION

Evaluation can be undertaken at the end of implementation and obviously this suggests that it is not the same as monitoring (see Concept Box 10.1).

It is difficult to find much attention paid to the deliberate and organized evaluation of a strategic plan or the results of implementing a strategy in most public services organizations. This is despite the fact that the question to be answered is simple enough to state: was the cost and effort of designing and implementing a strategy worthwhile? As York (1982: 140) put it, 'evaluation is basically a judgement of worth or an appraisal of value'. This could be taken to mean that evaluators of a strategy need to identify all the costs and all the benefits of undertaking strategy formulation and implementation, and appraise them to calculate the net benefit.

But evaluators of a strategy will normally want to answer other questions as well. For example, if strategic goals had been set as part of the strategy process, were all of them achieved? If the strategic goals were achieved, what can be learnt about the causes of success? If some goals were not achieved, what can be learnt about the causes of failure? If answers can be found to these questions then evaluation is important for strategic leaders so they can learn how to be more successful in the future.

CONCEPT BOX 10.1   MONITORING AND EVALUATION DISTINGUISHED

Monitoring can be defined as an assessment process that helps to keep strategic leaders informed of what is happening, and whether implementation of a

---

strategic plan is on track, and it helps those managing implementation to make necessary adjustments in good time when implementation is not as successful as it should be.

Evaluation can be defined as a process of making judgements, usually at the end of implementation (although it might occur part way through), to judge the worth of the strategic planning effort.

Both monitoring and evaluation may involve learning lessons.

In this chapter we will be looking at what is evaluated, approaches to evaluation, and some tools for carrying out evaluation.

WHAT IS EVALUATED?

Strategic leaders can ask the questions: was the effort to create and deliver the strategic plan worthwhile? How valuable was it? The strategic planning cycle can include setting priorities, formulating missions and goals, writing a strategic plan, implementing it, and then producing outcomes. All of this can be covered in evaluation.

It is quite possible for political leaders to judge at the end of a planning period that results were not significant enough and that plans and action should have been bolder. They can do this even though a strategic plan was successfully implemented and measured outcomes were in line with expectations. The politicians may belatedly realize that although desired outcomes were completely achieved, they simply did not produce the degree of public satisfaction or appreciation that had been expected. The politician could say the outcomes were achieved, but so what?

Politicians may also judge that the outcomes delivered were much more modest than hoped for. The evaluation might then look for a mistaken strategy or poor execution of the strategy. Did we have the right strategy, but implementation was poor? Or was implementation done well, but the strategy was wrong? Politicians may decide the strategy needs changing even if the mission and strategic goals remain appropriate. We can illustrate this by a quote from a speech of David Cameron, the UK's prime minister, who, like the previous Blair administration, made public services reform and modernization a high priority. In early 2011, he said:

So we are determined to modernize our public services and make them better for everyone . . . If we have learnt anything about public service reform in the past few decades, it's that simply setting standards and issuing diktats from Whitehall doesn't mean they actually happen. We do need structural changes – not just edicts about standards.

(Source: http://www.number10.gov.uk/news/speeches-and-transcripts/
2011/01/prime-ministers-speech-on-modern-public-service-58858;
accessed 3 February 2011)

217

APPROACHES AND BASIC POINTS

There are there are different approaches to strategy evaluation. One approach we might call a goals-based model, and this is where the view is taken that strategic goals were clearly defined at the beginning and strategic options were evaluated before strategic choices were made, and so any strategic action that is successful must, by definition, have been worthwhile. In this model of evaluation, the process is about checking that desired outcomes have materialized (see Concept Box 10.2). A stakeholder-based model may also assume that strategy formulation and implementation started with the definition of clear strategic goals, but assumes that the consequences of the process are not fully anticipated and that the valuing of the consequences can be appreciated from a variety of perspectives. There may have been important costs and benefits experienced by stakeholders that were not foreseen by the architects of the strategy. In a strategic planning process trying to put the public first it may be useful to use a third approach, which we will call the satisfaction-audit model, and find out if citizens and service users actually were left feeling satisfied. A fourth evaluation model could be defined as assessing strategic processes from a normative point of view – was the strategic plan developed according to some rules or standards about how these things should be done? This is called here a normative model of evaluation.

CONCEPT BOX 10.2   GOALS-BASED EVALUATION

The simplest form of impact evaluation is what is sometimes called a 'goals-based evaluation' (Patton 2002), in which policy makers want to know whether a desired outcome, target or goal has been achieved. This is a fairly straightforward issue of defining a desired outcome at the outset of a policy initiative and checking at some agreed future time whether this outcome has or has not been achieved . . . One limitation of goals-based evaluations is that they may not also consider the unanticipated outcomes or consequences of a policy initiative and, consequently, may give a partial, if not biased, view of the policy's outcomes.

(Davies 2004: 3)

We can make some more points briefly about strategy evaluation. First, while the aims of monitoring and evaluation are different, superficially some of the activities to carry them out may seem similar.

Second, evaluation is unlikely to be a purely analytical process. For a start, leadership credibility might be at stake as a result of the evaluation – a strategy that is evaluated as a failure and as a costly mistake is unlikely to be welcomed by strategic leaders responsible for its design and implementation. Evaluation may result in the allocation of praise and blame, and this will matter to incumbent strategic leaders as well as their rivals. Then there is another political dimension, in terms of factions and cliques within an organization that may be arguing about the strategy to be evaluated, with, for example, one management faction wishing to stick with the existing strategy (to whom it may seem highly important that the evaluation shows the strategy has been very successful and very worthwhile), and another management faction favouring a new strategy and wishing to see a strategy discredited. Obviously it is difficult to imagine a situation where there is no political rivalry, or even no open conflict at all, but some situations can be ones where the level of internal conflict and wrangling has become very dysfunctional and is preventing the existence of a cohesive and confident strategic leadership within the organization. When this is the case, the determination of who will carry out the evaluation, the terms of reference of the evaluation, the forum that will discuss and act on the evaluation, the public visibility of the evaluation process, etc., will become contested.

Third, it seems obvious that evaluation should piggyback on a performance measurement and performance management system as much as possible, but this will only be easily achieved if the strategic plan has been used to specify the performance data used in the performance management system. In some cases it will not be possible because the strategy and the performance management system are disconnected. The evaluation process might need to involve interviews and other data collection methods with a range of stakeholders of the strategy – including elected politicians, managers, professionals, and members of the public.

Fourth, an organization should be prepared to commit the necessary time and effort to collecting and analysing data for strategy evaluation, and probably ought to piggyback on existing performance management systems where possible. The organization may also want relatively subjective data obtained through interviews and questionnaires. For example, evaluation data might be collected by carrying out an on-line survey of an organization's managers in which they are asked to rate the impact of the strategy on the services they manage and the satisfaction of the public that use the services.

Fifth, as well as making comparisons of goals and outcomes, organizations should consider using time trend analysis in which pre-strategy and post-strategy data is compared. The use of time trend analysis to carry out an evaluation is not without its complexities, but it is a very useful complement to evaluations that compare target results and actual outcomes. In Figure 10.1, the time trend analysis appears to show that a new strategy has been successful because the results do not follow the past trend in a straight line, but show a steeper upward movement in performance.

219

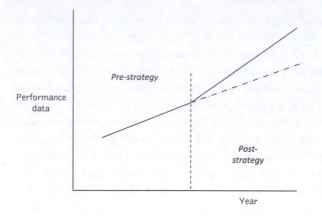

Performance data

Pre-strategy

Post-strategy

Year

Figure 10.1 *Time Trend Analysis*

NORMATIVE EVALUATIONS OF STRATEGIC PLANNING PROCESSES

An interesting approach to evaluating planning processes was developed as part of the implementation of the United States Government Performance and Results Act of 1993 (GPRA). The act was aimed at improving the focus of federal activities and at better measurement of results. The key requirements were that federal agencies produced strategic plans and annual performance plans. The strategic plans enabled better focusing of activities by getting agencies to rethink and clarify their missions, and the annual performance plans were the basis of performance measurement that allowed progress to be evaluated and also provided important information for budgeting purposes. The performance plans were intended to deliver the strategic plans, which were required to cover five fiscal years in the future. The strategic plans and performance plans were to be submitted to the American Congress for the first time in late 1997.

In the summer of 1996, the Office of Management and Budget carried out a review of the strategic plans of federal agencies (including those that were under development). This produced four concerns:

1 The annual performance goals were not adequately linked to the general goals in the strategic plans
2 There was a lack of interagency coordination to ensure consistent goals
3 Where the leadership of a federal agency was not involved in the preparation of the strategic plan, the plan was poorer
4 There were few signs of extensive consultation with stakeholders in the preparation of strategic plans.

220

These concerns were clearly reflected in an evaluation worksheet which was developed for use by the United States Congress to evaluate the strategic plans of federal agencies. The evaluation was concerned with compliance with the GPRA. In late 1997 this worksheet had ten evaluation factors:

1. mission statement
2. general (strategic) goals and objectives
3. strategies to achieve general goals and objectives
4. relationship between general goals and annual performance goals
5. external factors
6. programme evaluations
7. treatment/coordination of cross-cutting functions
8. data capacity
9. treatment of major management problems/high-risk areas
10. congressional and stakeholder consultations.

Each strategic plan was to be scored on all these factors, and a strategic plan could get awarded a total of one hundred points (ten points for each factor). In fact, there were five bonus points given for the inclusion of realistic performance measures.

The scoring of each factor involved assessing a number of items and each of these had varying maximum scores. For example, the mission statement factor had four items, two of which were worth a maximum of three points and two worth a maximum of two points. A mission statement that covered the federal agency's major functions and operations could score up to three points; if it reflected the agency's statutory authority it could score up to another three points; if it was results-oriented it could get two more points; and if the mission statement made it clear why the agency existed and what it did, it could score another two points. Thus the maximum score of ten points could be achieved on this factor by scoring the maximum number of points on each of the four items.

The 20-item worksheet, at Table 10.1, to evaluate strategic planning aimed at performance improvement is inspired by the Congress worksheet. Some of the Congress items are paraphrased or combined together, but some new items have also been introduced.

This is what might be termed a 'normative' evaluation. A strategic plan that scores highly using the worksheet is demonstrating conformance to a set of ideas about what would be a good process for producing a strategic plan and is not being judged in terms of the consequences of the strategic plan. Since the 1993 legislation was using strategic planning as an essential framework for results-oriented government, the evaluation worksheet concentrated on the features of the strategic planning process crucial to that agenda. Obviously, if the law had been aiming at the development of federal agency strategic planning for different purposes, the construction of the evaluation worksheet would have been significantly different.

221

Table 10.1 *Evaluation worksheet – for strategic planning aimed at performance improvement*

Worksheet	Item	Score
Factor 1: Mission Statement	1 Does the mission statement make it clear who are the intended beneficiaries of the activities of the organization?	Maximum 10
	2 What benefits are intended as outcomes?	
	3 Does the mission statement identify the main activities of the organization?	
	4 Does the mission statement explain what the organization does and why in terms of its legal mandates?	
Factor 2: Strategic Goals	5 Are strategic goals logically related to the organization's mission?	Maximum 10
	6 Are strategic goals results-oriented and measurable?	
Factor 3: Strategies	7 Do strategies logically realign or develop programmes and services to achieve the organization's strategic goals?	Maximum 10
	8 Do strategies logically realign or develop the capabilities of the organization to achieve the organization's strategic goals?	
	9 Do strategies logically realign or develop the alliances and co-operative activities of the organization (e.g. with other public service organizations)?	
Factor 4: Relationship between Strategic Goals and Annual Performance Goals	10 Are annual performance goals logically linked to strategic goals?	Maximum 10
Factor 5: Situational Analysis	11 Does the strategic plan identify and take external factors into account as threats and opportunities?	Maximum 10
Factor 6: Performance and Programme evaluation	12 Does the strategic plan explain what performance and programme evaluations were used?	Maximum 10

Table 10.1 *(Continued)*

Worksheet	Item	Score
Factor 7: Partnership Working	13 Does the strategic plan provide evidence of discussion and planning with other public services organizations that have similar functions/programmes/services?	Maximum 10
Factor: 8 Public Consultation and Involvement	14 Did the organization consult or survey the public as part of the strategic planning process?	Maximum 10
	15 Did it consult the public on the strategic plan in an open-minded, constructive, and good faith manner?	
	16 Was the organization responsive to the views and suggestions of the public in finalizing the strategic plan?	
Factor 9: Performance Measurement and Reporting Systems	17 Does the strategic plan contain baseline data relating to all the strategic and annual performance goals?	Maximum 10
	18 Does the organization have the capacity to collect and report reasonably accurate data in relation to all the strategic and annual performance goals?	
Factor 10: Feasibility Assessment and Risk Analysis	19 Were the strategies contained in the strategic plan subjected to rigorous assessments of feasibility before being approved or authorized?	Maximum 10
	20 Was a risk analysis of proposed courses of action (strategies) part of the strategic decision making process?	

AN ACADEMIC FRAMEWORK FOR EVALUATING A STRATEGIC PLAN (HEYMANN 1987)

Heymann's (1987) model of strategy in which the plan is used to align organizational capacity and external support with desirable strategic goals to meet social needs offers another approach to assessing a strategic plan (see Figure 10.2).

Consider, for example, the following evaluation questions suggested by Heymann's framework:

1 Do the organization's strategic goals still correspond to current social needs, or have the goals lagged behind changes in social needs?
2 Did the strategic plan bring the following into a consistent alignment: desirable strategic goals linked to the political objectives of elected politicians and

223

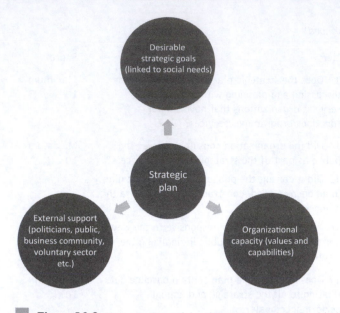

Figure 10.2 *Heymann's model – the strategic plan should align goals, support and capacity*

public and social needs; external support from politicians, the public and other external stakeholders; and organizational capacity?

3   Was the strategic plan developed through a process that created the support of partner organizations?

CONCEPT BOX 10.3   A PRACTITIONER'S VIEWS ON EVALUATION

By Adrienne Roberts, who has held senior positions in local and central government and now works independently in the public sector as an adviser and interim executive from her company Guy Harlings Consultancy.

On the face of it, the answer is simple. Against the objectives, assess the delivery and put either a tick or a cross in the box. There are occasions when this is what happens, but there are lots of considerations and challenges that can get in the way.

What is the big picture for your strategy? How clear are you about the overall landscape in which your strategy is intended to be implemented? Are all the levers and connectivities mapped and understood? Do we see which are the short cycle processes and systems, and which are the long-term intergenerational cycles?

A whole systems approach gives us a mechanism for assessing these questions, but it is rare, in my experience, that much effort is put into that meta level strategic appraisal. There is a job to be done and we want to get on with it! The challenge, however, is there may well be unintended and long-term consequences of the strategy that never get evaluated.

In the 1980s, local government was under severe pressure to reduce cost, reduce size, and reduce overheads. The strategy was to open services up to the market, and the theory was that market forces would create an equilibrium that would give value and more efficient service. Schools sold their playing fields, the meals they produced for our children were done at the lowest possible cost, public transport was deregulated, and our parks and open spaces were contracted out. How was that strategy evaluated? Costs were reduced and new markets were developed, but what of the total impact on our public realm, on children and young people – their ability to exercise and eat well? Those long-term effects are possibly only now coming to the fore and causing great concern.

Who is doing the evaluating? Best practice would say that independent evaluation is best. It brings a degree of rigour and objectivity that those who were involved from the start would be hard put to achieve. For statistical, demographic, and scientific evaluations that is probably right – but what about the passion, the experience, the relationships, and the arrangements that went with the delivery and the achievements or failures? There is often real learning and culture change that comes about through new ways of working and problem solving that is felt and understood most strongly by those who were involved. This 'naturalistic' approach is, of course, potentially dangerous for the objectivity of the evaluation, but it might make one think that in setting any strategy the 'how' as well as the 'what' are worth evaluating for benefits and learning. Relationships can be tested and strengthened, new means of communicating and sharing information evolve, an appreciation of differing perspectives and histories can grow, all of which have a qualitative impact on delivery, but may not necessarily get evaluated.

There are other pros and cons to the issue of who does the evaluation around the ability of the strategy sponsors to hear and see the messages coming from the evaluation. This stems not so much from the rigour of the exercise, but the positioning and communicating of the evaluation.

Internal evaluation feels different to recipients. It is 'evaluation of us' not 'evaluation for us' and it can feel part of an on-going narrative rather than a real opportunity to stand back and reflect. The organization just gobbles it up, digests it, and moves on; and the formalities or starkness of an external evaluation are not there to create any uncomfortable feelings in the stomach! So there is a real chance that the lessons are not heard or learnt. It is possible that the regime is such that the evaluation produced provides only acceptable messages and some of the trickier issues go unremarked.

On the other hand, external evaluation is sometimes hard to place, especially when it has had a long-term perspective, reviewing activity and outcomes over a long period. Life has moved on, the original protagonists are long gone, who is there to hear the message? Equally, in a society where today's news is everything, the short term drives our decision making. What processes do we have at our disposal to look back over a generation and project forward over a generation to plan what next?

Really hearing the conclusions of an external evaluation of a long-term strategy takes some doing. Making decisions on a new strategy as a consequence takes even more effort because it is like turning an oil tanker.

A strategy may have been in place for some time, possibly years. It is now part of the infrastructure and fabric of partnerships, job design, and resource allocation. In other words it has become a way of life and the evaluation may mean a fundamental redesign. How often do we properly plan for this stage that may not fit neatly with our strategic planning processes and will require a programme of work in its own right in order to reconfigure or refocus the strategy and subsequent implementation?

How specific is the implementation? How real is it to attribute outcomes to the actions taken? Sometimes good things happen; sometimes bad things happen. It is not uncommon for things to be attributed to the plan when, in fact, it is sheer accident or serendipity. There are occasions when the public commitment to a strategy, and the sheer force of energy behind it, make it too sensitive or embarrassing to be able to make rational assessments of practical consequences. The force of an individual's experience, in any event, outweighs their willingness to be swayed by a subsequent dispassionate analysis of outcomes. The chain of events that may be triggered can, in real life, lead in all sorts of interesting directions, and create tensions and dynamics that were not planned or required by the strategy. Programme management is a good tool and, used well, helps keep a project on track, but real people, their energies, and conversations and actions exist outside the standard proforma given to them to return to the project manager!

Who is listening? Solutions are what we want. We can see the problems and often leaders may feel they just know the solution and that is the right thing to do. Evaluation and reflection is not on their radar and, anyway, the type of work envisaged in the solution sits comfortably with their view of life. This is a linked point to the issue of 'how big the picture is', but it can also be an emotional tussle. Sometimes, we just do not want to give up our pet theories. We are emotionally, if not intellectually, wedded to them and believe that if we just work hard enough, put in enough resource, go that extra mile, it is bound to work!

Who needs evaluation? There is a darker aspect to this problem. Evaluating a strategy in the environment I have described can be quite dangerous to the evaluator, particularly if it is an internal person. Objective assessment of the benefits and disadvantages may be heard as disloyalty and lack of commitment to the programme. In that case, it is worth planning the manner in which the evaluation is fed back, and playing a longer game. There may be some credible stakeholders who can play a role and are less likely to be seen as partisan. Creating a context and environment where the messages are being fed in gradually can be a more productive way of getting the key players to listen. Evidence, facts and figures, and national and international trends, may assist in putting the evaluation on a non-emotional footing and provide an opportunity to be open and honest in the challenges. But beware! In the public sector whether in executive or non-executive roles, passion and emotion lie not far below the surface in us all. Sometimes none of us are listening – we just want it to work.

SUMMARY

In this chapter we noted the possibility of different approaches to strategy evaluation, which is concerned with judging whether a strategy has been worthwhile or not. We distinguished evaluation from monitoring activity, which is used during implementation and for the realization and maintenance of the strategy.

We presented four models to indicate some of the choices strategic leaders have in designing practical evaluations of strategy.

- Goals-based model: evaluation is about checking that desired outcomes have materialized
- Stakeholder-based model: evaluation is based on appreciating that the valuing of the consequences can be from a variety of perspectives
- Satisfaction-audit model: evaluation researches the satisfaction of citizens and service users
- Normative model: evaluation checks if the strategic plan was developed according to some rules or standards about how these things should be done.

This chapter included a brief note on the use of trend data for evaluation rather than just data comparing intended outcomes and actual outcomes.

This chapter also included the contribution of a practitioner who drew attention to the meaning and impact of evaluation for managers and professionals. She provides an alternative perspective on evaluation – quite different from cool and analytical guidance on how to do evaluation as if it is just a matter of data, evidence, and analysis. She also stressed that it is not easy for those who have a stake in a strategy evaluation to really hear the conclusions of an evaluation.

Work-based assignment: evaluating your own organization's strategic plan

The work-based assignments in this book are for civil servants and other public services staff who have four or more years of management experience.

Does your own public service organization have a strategic plan produced in the last five years? If it does, review the evaluation worksheet with 10 factors and 20 items presented in this chapter (which was based on the draft of a US Congress evaluation tool). Prepare your own version of this evaluation worksheet, changing any items you think need to be changed and work out a detailed scoring system (so that the maximum score on each item is clarified). Then use it to evaluate the strategic planning effort in your own public services organization. You may need to collect information and study strategic documents to carry out this evaluation. Based on your evaluation, identify any shortfalls in the way the strategic planning process was carried out in your own organization.

DISCUSSION QUESTIONS

1   Is there really a difference between monitoring and evaluation as suggested at the outset of this chapter? Would it be better to combine monitoring and evaluation as a single activity? What are the advantages, if any, of keeping monitoring and evaluation as separate activities?

2   Is there a best model for evaluating strategy?

3   Do elected politicians learn lessons from studying the previous government's mistakes? What factors make it difficult for a new government to learn from what the previous government did?

4   Who should do evaluations of strategy? Should organizations pay outsiders to come in and do evaluations?

5   Is it dangerous for your career to be an internal evaluator of an existing strategy? Why?

FURTHER READING

Patrizi, P. A. and Patton, M. Q. (eds) (2011) *Evaluating Strategy*. San Francisco, Jossey-Bass.

Chapter 11

Issues and Challenges in Practice

INTRODUCTION

Much of what we have covered in preceding chapters has been concerned with concepts and techniques. In this chapter we explore the issues and challenges of strategic leadership, starting with the introduction of strategic planning as a specific type of innovation. The chapter also looks at some evidence about the benefits of strategic planning innovations in government, alignment of intentions and plans between the political and civil service worlds, tensions between different parts or branches of central government, whole of government ideas, issues of civil servants working with politicians, community strategies and partnership working, and competitive situations in the public services. This chapter looks at both the national level and the local level of government. It serves to highlight the complexity and difficulty facing strategic leadership in the public services.

BRINGING IN STRATEGIC PLANNING AT NATIONAL LEVEL AND CHANGE MANAGEMENT

Strategic planning not only brings about innovation – it can itself be an innovation in how public services are managed. The introduction of strategic planning at national level can be at the instigation of different parties and can be for different reasons. In the UK during the last decade there has been sustained pressure to improve public services, and top politicians saw the possibility of the public services using strategic plans to advance modernization. The idea of strategic planning may have been brought to the Prime Minister's attention by a special adviser (Lord Birt). The context for this was political openness to applying business ideas to the public services. Significantly, therefore, the idea of using strategic planning to encourage step change and innovation came from the political leadership in government. In these circumstances, the issue of developing strategic planning in government becomes one of the receptiveness of senior civil servants to moving away from traditional administrative habits and their ability to respond quickly with a 'can do' attitude.

It is interesting to compare and contrast the UK with the case of Ireland's much earlier experimentation with strategic management from 1994 onwards (Collins 2007). It seems that in Ireland the process did not begin with politicians but was an initiative of the senior levels of civil servants in Dublin (see Research Box 11.1).

RESEARCH BOX 11.1   THE BIRTH OF THE STRATEGIC MANAGEMENT INITIATIVE IN IRELAND

Neil Collins (2007) reported that the Civil Service Training Centre created networks of senior civil servants in the 1980s. One of these networks – the Assistant Secretary Network – came to the conclusion that there was a need to improve civil service management. The Strategic Management Initiative (SMI) of 1994 appears to have come out of this (Collins 2007: 37):

> Papers and proposals written by the Network were distributed across the management structure of the civil service. The government supported this reform drive and formally announced the SMI in February 1994. A Coordinating Group of Secretaries-General – the most senior officers of each department – was established to facilitate and develop reform efforts and to broaden them across the whole public service.

> Meanwhile a group of eleven Assistant Secretaries drafted from across the civil service produced a dissertation entitled *Strategic Management in the Irish Civil Service: A Review Drawing on Experience in New Zealand and Australia,* written as part of a M.Sc. degree undertaken by the group at Trinity College, Dublin... The full report (Byrne *et al.* 1994) was 'fed into the Co-ordinating Group of Secretaries charged with responsibility for the initial development of the SMI' (O'Dowd 1995: 51). The report concluded:

> There is a need for a process of reform [in Ireland] which is sustained, systematic, comprehensive and participative. It should be based on the same underlying approach as in Australia and New Zealand.
>
> (Byrne *et al.* 1994: 5)

In the UK, the focus was on the public services systems and the function of strategic planning was perceived as bringing about change in these systems. There was a political climate (at the top) of interest in importing private sector ideas (such as strategic planning) and a key voice in support of strategic planning was from a person who was a special adviser to the Prime Minister. In contrast, in Ireland the focus was improving the management of the civil service, and strategic management was equated with better management. The climate that mattered (initially anyway) was among the civil servants, and this was positive about reforming management in the civil service. Civil servant networks were at the heart of developing ideas on management reform. A key group in support of the reform was the top levels of the civil service. We should also note the very important facilitative role in the development of the SMI of university education (Trinity College, Dublin) and the Civil Service Training Centre. This does not seem to have a clear or convincing parallel in the UK case. In contrast with the UK case, however, strategic planning reforms that are strongly owned by civil servants depend upon the support of the elected politicians, and this support needs to be whole-hearted if the civil service leaders are to embark on significant strategic change. If the politicians are really just acquiescing in developments, and rubber-stamp rather than really support the strategic plans, the leaders in the civil service may use the strategic plans to make modest improvements rather than risk transformational change because political support is not certain.

Sometimes the drive for strategic planning and modernization generally has been fuelled by political values and public pressure (doing more with less). In some countries, the reforms of public management (including the introduction of financial management reforms and strategic planning) may be motivated by other causes, such as in the case of Turkey where it was partly explicable in terms of recent challenges to the financial stability of government (2001), and partly a desire to achieve EU accession.

Civil servants charged with bringing in strategic management find the change management aspects of this very challenging. The process of implementation of a strategic management system for central government can be designed in a professional way, but there will often be major issues of institutional inertia to be overcome.

One example of an actual model used for bringing in strategic planning was the Trinidad and Tobago Government 1993 initiative on strategic planning (see Concept Box 11.1). Concern about the ownership of the strategic planning process probably explains why change teams or steering groups were composed of representatives of all levels in the ministries. The analytical steps were opened up to wider involvement

231

through workshops, think tanks, and brainstorming groups. The importance of maintaining political support was presumably the reason why ministers were kept informed about, and included in, the process of producing the plans. There was, finally, attention to communication to a wider audience – again presumably to ensure wider ownership of the resultant strategies.

CONCEPT BOX 11.1   TRINIDAD AND TOBAGO GOVERNMENT INITIATIVE ON STRATEGIC PLANNING 1993

The key features of the process used to deliver the requirement to produce five year strategic plans in 1993 were:

1 Permanent Secretaries in all ministries were given responsibility for the development of the strategic plans.
2 Change teams or steering groups were set up – these were representative of all levels of the individual ministries.
3 Workshops, think tanks, and brainstorming groups were used to carry out the analytical steps leading up to, and including, the development of strategies.
4 Planning teams were then set up – these were sometimes the same as the change team created earlier in the process.
5 Government ministers were kept informed and were included in the process.
6 The process provided for the identification of people responsible for implementation of strategy.
7 Evaluation of strategy implementation was explicitly planned to be part of the overall process.
8 Efforts and results of the strategic planning were communicated more widely.

Source: Commonwealth Secretariat 2002; pp. 156–7.

IS THE EFFORT TO BRING IN STRATEGIC PLANNING WORTHWHILE AT A NATIONAL LEVEL?

In some countries at least, strategic planning appears to have developed more quickly at sub-national levels. This would appear to be the case in the US, in Germany, and the UK. For example, if you date the first explicit strategic plans in the UK as 2004–5, it is clear that corporate strategic plans were being developed in UK local government in the 1990s.

Why did strategic planning develop more slowly at national or federal level than at sub-national level in these countries? Perhaps it is caused by the different backgrounds, education, and training of those in leadership positions in the civil service at national or federal level and in, say, local government; and perhaps reflecting differences in the hold on the organization of traditional administrative culture. Or perhaps it is an assessment of the applicability of strategic planning, with its benefits assessed as being less pronounced at a national or federal level than at sub-national levels. So, in the light of the latter possibility, do evaluations of the impact of strategic planning and management at national and federal levels show there are positive impacts for the effectiveness of government?

There is some evidence from the US, which evaluates the impact of the GPRA of 1993 that brought in strategic plans for federal agencies in the US in order to improve the effectiveness of federal programmes and public accountability. The aim was to achieve an improved focus on results, quality, and customer satisfaction. As an Executive Guide on the legislation put it (GAO 1996: preface): 'GPRA forces a shift in the focus of federal agencies – away from such traditional concerns as staffing and activity levels and toward a single overriding issue: results.'

Did the 1993 Act make federal government actually perform better? The GAO Federal Managers Survey data showed only about a quarter reporting that the extent of improvement caused by the efforts to implement GPRA 1993 had been 'moderate', 'great', or 'very great'. On balance, it appears the evaluation is positive – with more reporting an improvement than no improvement, but many managers reported not feeling able to give a judgement about impact (see Table 11.1). This might indicate that there were improvements, but there were a number of possible factors, or it

Table 11.1 *Impact of GPRA 1993*

Extent of improvement	Program(s)/operation(s)/ project(s) in which you are involved %	Program(s)/operation(s)/ project(s) of your agency %
To a very great extent	2.9	2.3
To a great extent	5.2	6.2
To a moderate extent	14.7	17.0
To a small extent	16.2	16.3
To no extent	10.0	8.7
No answer	2.4	1.5
I have not been sufficiently involved in GPRA to have an opinion	48.7	47.9

Note: Data from GAO Federal Managers Survey of 2003 (*n* = 503). The question asked was 'To what extent, if at all, do you believe that efforts to implement GPRA to date have improved...'

might indicate that in half the cases the implementation of the strategic planning was ineffective (for whatever reason).

Turning now to the Irish experience of recent years, Government departments were requested under Ireland's SMI of 1994 to produce strategy statements and business plans. The first strategic plans appeared in the same year (1994) and by the end of it nearly all Irish government departments had met the requirement to produce a strategic statement and action plan. The second round of strategic planning took place in the period 1998–2000 as a requirement of the Public Service Management Act 1997. And there was a third round of strategy statements and business plans in the period 2001 to 2003/4. Support for the process was given to the departments in 1998 in the form of guidelines.

What benefits were formally sought from the initiative? There were three key results areas: contribution to national development, excellent service to the public, and effectiveness in the use of resources (Boyle 1995a: 26). The Irish SMI was also intended to produce a more joined-up approach – this was to be achieved through a co-ordinating group of civil servants who would recommend changes to department strategies.

In 2002, a management consultancy firm, PA Consulting Group, produced a report evaluating the SMI and a follow up programme, Delivering Better Government (DGB). The report contained a reference to some criticisms about the early days of strategic planning (2002: 25):

> The initial Statements of Strategy prepared by the civil service came in for criticism in some quarters. Much of this early criticism suggested that the statements were somewhat stylised and academic in tone, and more importantly, that they were insufficiently attentive to scanning the organisational environment.

But the report (2002: 25) identified progress in the quality of strategic planning:

> The most recent round of Strategy Statements produced across the civil service provide evidence of a sophisticated capacity to consider, analyse, and present the strategic context within which Departments/Offices find themselves. Almost all these documents contain common core elements-statement of mission and values, high level goals, strategies, objectives, and performance indicators. Equally all these statements present – in one form or another – an analysis of the business environment and of the key factors which are likely to influence that environment over the next three years.

The overall finding of the PA Consulting Group was that the Irish civil service in 2002 was a more effective organization than it was ten years earlier, and that this improvement was in part due to the SMI launched in 1994. It may be significant that

234

the SMI emerged as an idea from the civil service and was approved by the politicians, suggesting that the ownership of the innovation was at least partly located in the top ranks of the civil service.

INTEGRATION ISSUES

Anne Drumaux's detailed exploration of strategic plans in the Belgian Government warn us that politics and policies are not always aligned, that plans are not necessarily integrated with budgetary resources, and, in the end, she seems to suggest that strategic planning is not necessarily a strong system or framework for action because of the effects of emergent developments, but that strategic planning may play a part in clarifying ideas and influencing conditions in which action takes place (see Research Box 11.2).

RESEARCH BOX 11.2   STRATEGIC MANAGEMENT AS A REFORM IN THE BELGIAN FEDERAL ADMINISTRATION

By Anne Drumaux, Solvay Business School, Université Libre de Bruxelles, Belgium

Strategic management was introduced in 2000 into the Belgian Federal Administration within the framework of a larger reform, called the 'Copernicus Reform'. The federal reform aimed[1] at introducing new dynamics into administration by a redefinition of the status, selection, and role of top civil servants. Enrolled through a new assessment with a term mandate of six years, so called 'top-managers' were asked to define administration strategy into true management plans. In this vision, strategic plans were key elements in order to elaborate and to implement public action priorities as well to evaluate top civil servants actions. Nowadays, even if the Copernicus Reform is not sustained anymore at the political level, strategic plans still exist, as well as the 'virtual' matrix organization introduced by the reform.

Intentions cartography

Using a typology proposed by Poister and Streib (1999), three models[2] characterize the intentional strategic management in the Belgian Federal Administration (Drumaux and Goethals 2007) (see also Figure 11.1):

■   The first is a strategic management turned outwards: a high relative proportion of objectives focus on external relations, and programmes and services, to be delivered to external customers. This model is found in the horizontal ministries[3] (ICT, Personnel & Organization, Budget & Control), which is logical due to their role turned towards the development of programmes and services for the use of the vertical ones. The same tendency can be seen both in the Economy and the Scientific Policy plans, which is related to their prompting role

■ The second model is a strategic management turned inwards. Human relations and internal management system represent, proportionally, the highest concerns in this management plan; the Defence plan belongs to this category, while the Finances and the Public Health plans are also strongly polarized towards the internal management system

■ The third model is a strategic model equally polarized towards all four dimensions (external relations, programmes & services, human resources, internal management system); the Justice, Foreign Affairs, Mobility, and the Social Integration plans belong to it; the Home Affairs plan is polarized towards three dimensions and, to a lesser extent, towards human relations.

Strategic plans processes
Strategic management is not only a question of intentions; the processes through which actions are decided and implemented are equally important (Mintzberg 1978). How are politics and policies related? Do we find top-down hierarchy, or eventually bottom-up relations between objectives, activities, and projects? How are strategic management plans and operational plans coordinated? A detailed analysis (Drumaux and Goethals 2007b) allows several conclusions:

■ First, as presented in Figure 11.2, there is not always a clear top-down hierarchy between the view of the minister (politics level) and the design of policies (policy level). This is shown, for example, by the unbundling between the orientation note of the Minister of Justice based, even in operational details, on a bottom-up approach, and the justice management plan prepared by the Ministry President with the help of consultants. Both documents were prepared in 2003.

■ Second, regarding the internal hierarchy between plans, the relationship might be top-down between the top manager's strategic plan and the departments' strategic plans, but becomes nonexistent between those and operational plans on the core business of the ministry. This is illustrated by an example from the Mobility Ministry (see Figure 11.3). The President's management plans focus on functional objectives (Personnel &

Organization) instead of core activities (Mobility), and the chain is broken at the level of operational plans.

Similarities and differences with other experiences
Largely inspired by the 'New Public Management' thinking, the Belgian Federal experience has been focusing merely on accountability at the level of top managers. From this perspective, strategic management is more a by-product of the reform than an aim in itself. Using Joyce's typology (1999), the strategic plans of the federal administration are in fact a kind of hybrid between an unfinished 'traditional/classic' model and a formal 'business-like' model:

- They are partially top-down in their conception from mission definition to operational objectives, nevertheless with some process irregularities as previously shown. Moreover, the plans have not been really and systematically connected to results or to resources and budget process.
- They rely on a formal autonomy of top managers that are responsible for the elaboration of plans, but the autonomy is not systematic due to unclear relations between politics and policies levels.

What factors influence the specific forms of strategic management?
Different factors might influence models of strategic management. Some are obviously of an institutional nature: (non)involvement of parliament in performance assessment, respective roles of budget authority and ministries in policies definition, role of cabinets versus top civil servants, and (in)sufficient stability of political intent. Others are cultural, or, at least, more organizational: elite selection modes for top civil servants, effective empowerment, and accountability culture.

What are the potential benefits of strategic management for top civil servants and politicians?
A survey among top managers of the Federal Belgian Administration (Drumaux and Goethals 2007) confirms the existence of some 'effective behaviours' of public top managers, during the strategic process, that have already been documented by Ring and Perry (1985) in another context. Indeed public decision makers are burdened by the specific constraints of the political, institutional, and administrative system. To be effective, their behaviour has to be incremental and adaptive, allowing flexibility, searching and binding in multiple stakeholders' interests, and be based on influence rather than authority. In this perspective, strategic plans allow top civil servants to clarify constraints, but, despite the plans, effectiveness forces them to stay open to emergent

strategies because of their position. At least, this is the condition to make the best out of them. From the politicians' point of view, strategic management has the advantage to seem compatible with the primacy of intention over action, that is, the dominant paradigm in the ideas sphere, and in their professional practice. Provided that one remains aware that this a heuristic short-cut, intentional strategy may contribute to clarify strategic and operational objectives, and create conditions for action since the sole rhetoric on intentions would not be sufficient from the citizens' point of view.

Has strategic management a future in federal administration?

Since the Copernicus Reform is not sustained any more at political level, the risk is high that strategic plans lose their main quality of being an interactive management tool between political and administrative levels, and join the 'club' of forgotten past reforms. Finally, it is difficult to predict the future of strategic management in federal administration since the existence of a federal state, and obviously those of the administration itself, are nowadays in question. It seems clear that strategic management cannot develop without any political vision.

In a number of countries, the spending by government ministries is subject to a final decision made in Cabinet (see Table 11.2). Two exceptions to this are the UK, where it is the Treasury (in effect, a Ministry of Finance), and the US, where it is the President who makes the final decision. It is interesting, therefore, that the development of strategic planning at the central level of government has, at times, been in some tension with the planning of public spending in both the US and the UK.

In the case of the US, the tension between the planning of public spending and strategic planning of federal agencies came to light through a programme assessment process. As we noted in an earlier chapter on monitoring, the OMB set up a task force to create a tool called the PART. In 2002, the OMB made assessments of programmes in federal agencies, and these informed the President's budget for 2004. Although Section II of the PART focused on strategic planning, when the US GAO carried out an evaluation of PART in 2004, it expressed concern about the linkage between strategic plans carried out under GPRA 1993 and the programme assessment carried out using PART (US General Accounting Office January 2004a (January): 27):

The PART was designed for and is used in the executive branch budget preparation and review process; as such, the goals and measures used in the PART must meet OMB's needs. However, GPRA – the current statutory framework for strategic planning and reporting – is a broader process involving the development of strategic and performance goals and objectives to be reported in strategic and annual plans. OMB's desire to collect performance data that better align with

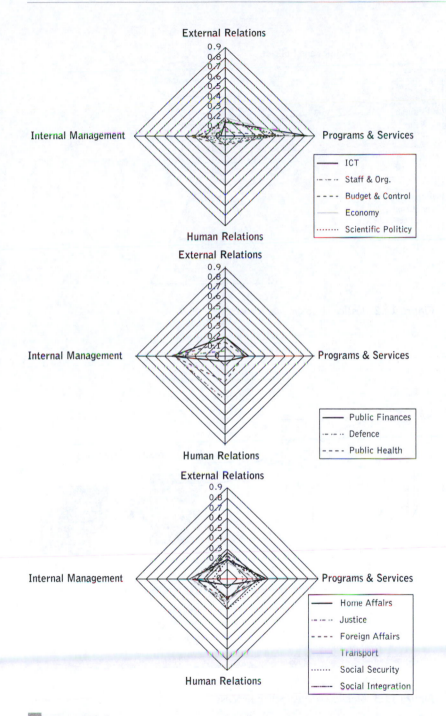

Figure 11.1 *Intents mapping of federal strategic plans*

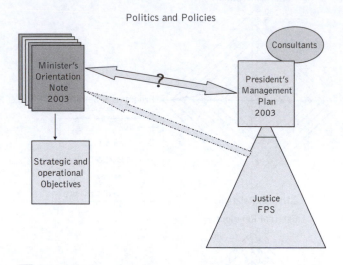

Figure 11.2 *Justice strategic plan process*

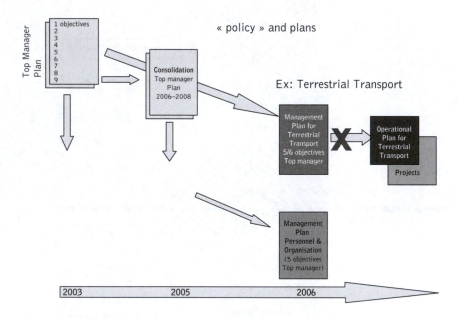

Figure 11.3 *Mobility strategic plan process*

Table 11.2 *Public spending system*

Country	Basis of setting spending limits for ministries	Final decision on ministries' spending	Arrangement in congress to establish total budget before individual item
Sweden	Medium-Term Expenditure Framework	Prime Minister	Yes
UK	Medium-Term Expenditure Framework	HM Treasury	No
Australia	Medium-Term Expenditure Framework	Cabinet	No
New Zealand	Medium-Term Expenditure Framework	Cabinet	No
Netherlands	Medium-Term Expenditure Framework	Cabinet	Yes
Norway	N/A	Cabinet	Yes
USA	Suggestion only	President	Yes

Source: Presentation in Istanbul at World Bank supported symposium in 2005 by Doy-oung Min, The World Bank, "Introduction to MEF in Korea" – citing OECD-World Bank Budget Practices and Procedures Database as original source

budget decision units means that the fiscal year 2004 PART process was a parallel competing structure to the GPRA framework. Although OMB acknowledges that GPRA was the starting point for the PART . . . the emphasis is shifting such that over time the performance measures developed for the PART and used in the budget process may come to drive agencies' strategic planning processes.

Why would this be a problem if strategy was driven by budget? The GAO argued that performance information should reflect a consensus on goals. It also argued that GPRA goals and measures were based on a wide range of stakeholder interests (i.e. a consensus). Consequently, OMB was substituting its judgement on key performance goals for those contained in a much more widely based and consensual judgement on goals and measures.

In some ways the challenges for US government of linking strategy and budget processes in 2002–03 (the 2004 PART process) paralleled the challenges that faced the UK government in integrating the 5-year strategies and the Comprehensive Spending Review (CSR) decisions and Public Service Agreements (PSA) in the period 2003–04.

In the case of the UK, HM Treasury (a ministry of finance) was in charge of CSR, which set the departmental expenditure limits and allocated resources. The first was 1998. It was repeated in 2000, 2002, and 2004. PSAs, accompanied the CSR, and were national targets agreed by departments and the HM Treasury. The aim of the

241

national targets was to make sure that measurable outcomes were delivered in return for resources. The Chancellor had a lot of control of policy through the CSR and PSAs. In 2004, the Chancellor (the minister in charge of the Treasury) presented the 2004 CSR to the House of Commons on 12 July.

Also in 2004, the Cabinet, led by the Prime Minister, produced 5-year strategies that were created by all departments and were largely shaped or set by the Prime Minister and his Number 10, Downing Street organization. Ministers played a key role in the formulation of the strategies – most particularly the Prime Minister. Therefore, we can say that the Cabinet 'owned' them.

In 2004, there was bound to be potential for disagreement between the Prime Minister, who had shaped the 5-year strategies of the three main areas (health, education, and home office), and the Chancellor, who presided over the separate process of the CSR and PSAs. Would the strategies and the CSR and PSAs dovetail, having been done separately? The slightly later release of the Home Office 5-year plan may have reflected this tension. On 10 and 11 July, the Treasury came up with several hundred million pounds sterling extra for the Home Office. (Health and Education spending were already planned.) A top civil servant involved in delivering the Prime Minister's priorities remarked:

> A process which had begun in September 2003 and which was at first not taken seriously in several departments had resulted in an agenda for the public services [the five year strategies] which would dominate the next parliament . . . It was a personal achievement for him [the Prime Minister], and one was left to wonder how much more he might have achieved had we put in place a coherently organised centre of government and developed an approach to strategy which was better integrated with the Treasury.
>
> (Barber 2007: 217)

Barber (2007) clearly thought this integration problem at the heart of government was so serious that he proposed organizational changes to address it (see Figure 11.4).

In both the US and the UK cases, there was an issue of cohesiveness between two parts of the government. In the UK this was the Prime Minister and Cabinet on one hand and the Treasury on the other; in the US it was between the Congress and the Executive. In the US, the PART was being used by the Executive to prepare and formulate the President's fiscal year 2004 budget (see Figure 11.5). The congressional interest in the GPRA is implied in the following statement (US General Accounting Office 2004a: 2):

> GPRA requires not only a connection to the structures used in congressional budget presentations but also consultation between the executive and legislative branches on agency strategic plans, which gives Congress an oversight stake in GPRA's success.

242

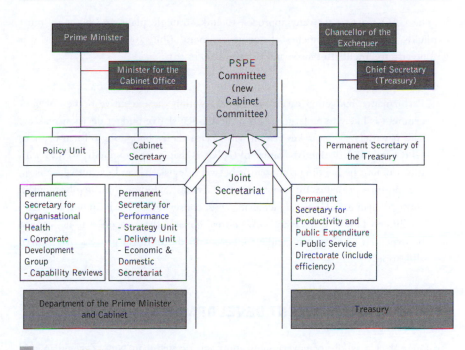

Figure 11.4 *Barber's (2007) proposed structural changes*
Adapted from Barber (2007), p. 319.

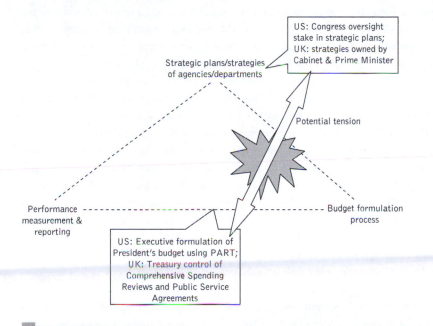

Figure 11.5 *Cohesiveness in government*

The GAO warned that any approach to link strategic plans and budgets 'must explicitly involve both branches of our government' (ibid 2004: 2). The issue was getting an agreement (Robinson and Brumby 2005: 28):

> Performance budgeting carried out solely within the executive branch of government is likely to be largely disregarded in legislative budget decision-making. This is widely seen as a key reason why performance budgeting reform prior to GPRA failed. A distinctive feature of GPRA is that it aims explicitly to deal with this problem by building a consensus between legislative and executive arms on expenditure priorities by participatory processes including joint involvement in strategic planning. However, achieving such consensus is clearly an extraordinarily difficult task – since, as the GAO notes, consultative processes alone 'cannot be expected to eliminate conflicts inherent in the political process of resource allocation'.

WHOLE OF GOVERNMENT DEVELOPMENTS

An attempt at a whole of government approach occurred in New Zealand in mid 1993. The New Zealand Government published a strategic document for the whole of government, called *Path to 2010*. Interestingly, this document was developed by the political adviser to the prime minister and was published just a few months before the election (Osborne and Plastrik 1997: 87). This reverses the orthodox assumption that politicians win elections, and then, in government, set government policies, and then, finally, these are delivered through strategic planning by civil servants. In this case, the strategic planning came first and then there was the election. Something similar happened in the UK when strategic planning by the prime minister and the cabinet produced strategic plans that became the basis of the election campaign in 2005, and was then implemented following electoral success for the Labour Party.

This document was a 35 page vision and strategy paper. In it, 41 departments and ministries were given outcome goals based on a time horizon of three to five years. These goals were known as strategic result areas. Again, just as in the case of the American initiative with the GPRA, this document was strongly focused on getting better results. Government departments were to realign their activities accordingly, and it was hoped that this would lead to better co-ordination across government. Government managers were reported as liking the reforms (Osborne and Plastrik 1997: 90): 'Agency executives say their organizations have a sharper focus and clearer missions, and that they must grapple with much less conflict over objectives.' In fact, a judgement made subsequently was that objectives were still problematic, and that this attempt at strategic planning for the whole of government suffered from a disconnection between politicians and public sector chief executives, with the former focused

244

on outcomes, and the latter held to account for outputs (Schick 2001). This point is examined again below.

The application of the idea of strategic planning to the whole of government received a strong endorsement in an official report of the US General Accounting Office (GAO 2004b). In this report to certain members of the United States Senate and the House of Representatives, the GAO recommended that the OMB develop a government-wide performance plan, and that the President develop a government-wide strategic plan. The strategic plan for the whole of government was justified by saying that such a plan could better achieve the integration of government activities and, thus, better achieve national goals. The GAO noted that the OMB considered that the President's budget could serve as a government-wide strategic plan and an annual plan, but was of the opinion that the President's budget was not appropriate for this purpose because it did not provide a long-term perspective; nor did it provide an integrated perspective on the federal government's performance. It recommended that Congress should amend the GPRA of 1993 to require the President develop a government-wide strategic plan.

WORKING WITH POLITICIANS

One of the most important issues in central and local government is how cohesive leadership can be developed across the political management interface between politicians on one side and civil servants and top managers on the other. This issue can be seen as an aspect of the concern highlighted by PA Consulting Group when evaluating the Irish experience of strategic management in government departments – the concern being about how politicians and managers worked together to align policy making and strategy.

Schick's writing about experiments in reform in New Zealand highlighted concerns about the relationship between chief executives and ministers in terms of outcomes and outputs, with the suggestion that the politicians want the outcomes, and yet the focus in accountability arrangements is on outputs. Much depends in this situation on the effective linkage of outputs and outcomes.

Schick's (2001: 5) lecture at the New Zealand Treasury discussed the difficulty of progress on policy and strategy in the New Zealand case:

> The problem goes beyond communication and role definition to the use of power and resources of government to promote change. The problem is not one of measurement, but of focus. The State Sector and Public Finance Acts make chief executives responsible for the details of operation; this legislative framework does not bar them from considering outcomes and policy linkages, but it nevertheless gives them an operational role that weakens their connection to ministers. While managers focus on the minutiae of internal operations, ministers

245

are interested in how to shape New Zealand's future. The connection between the political and managerial world is impaired if each side remains absorbed in its own narrow concerns and the two do not share enough in common to make for a satisfying relationship.

Schick also argued that operational management became, in effect, a constraint on the strategic management of government. Whereas Strategic Results Areas (SRAs) and Key Result Areas (KRAs), which were introduced in the 1990s, could have been useful in implementing the government's strategic vision, he suggests that, instead, they became justifications for activities and for additional resources.

In fact, once they were embedded in performance agreements, the KRAs became the checklists by which managers ran their operations to show they were producing the expected results. The government had good cause for abolishing the SRA/KRA system, but doing so left it without a systematic means for deploying budget allocations in the service of its strategic priorities.

(Schick 2001: 5–6)

The issue of managers working with elected politicians is also a challenge in local government. Some interesting perceptions of this are presented by a former chief executive of a county council (see case study).

CASE STUDY

Who sets a strategic vision: the elected politician or the manager? Are chief executives the local authorities' strategic leaders – and should they be?

By Roger Latham, former Chief Executive of Nottinghamshire County Council and currently Visiting Fellow of NTU Business School

The old nostrum that it is the politicians that set the political direction for an authority, and it is the officers who implement it, is nonsense. The development of policy through the direction of any local authority is the result of a complex interplay between elected politicians acting in their roles as community leaders, 'scrutineers', and executive decision makers; and the roles of officers as advisers and communicators of strategic direction. One of the current difficulties that exist within local government is the fact that strategic plans in many local authorities are made up of local deliveries of what are, effectively, the national strategic plans determined by central government without any significant local government input. Officers are often placed in a position where they need to advise local members of the imperative of including this or that national strategic element in the local delivery plan, which may not accord with local political decisions, or even community wishes, but which nevertheless has to play its part in what is essentially a 'command and control' hierarchical structure.

The complexity of the relationship between members and officers is made more difficult if the members themselves cannot find a consensus statement of vision or 'place of the future', or have no such view as part of their manifesto commitments. In these cases they can often end up by substituting the professional view of the future based on information that is a very managerialist strategic plan, which overcomes and replaces the politicians' legitimate vision.

An additional form of weak political leadership comes, paradoxically, from the problem of strong political factional infighting between members of a control-ling group. Switches in control in leadership, the gaining of the upper hand by one faction, or another, can result in considerable uncertainty about the direc-tion of policy, and often sudden considerable switches to one policy direction or another. In such circumstances, managerialist solutions for significant issues are often paralysed. Day to day work continues, but there is no strategic direction and, effectively, strategic planning goes out of the window.

An alternative case where there can be no clear political leadership comes if there is no overall control of the council, and particularly if this is an unusual situation resulting from loss of control by a strong controlling group with a long history of control. Very often in such circumstances the chief executive is left to pull together the various parties following an election and to see if a compromise solution can be reached. In some circumstances, this can be achieved by formal or informal coali-tion, but, where this cannot be achieved, then the situation can result in considerable strategic drift over a period of time, and again, although the day to day work will often be delivered, the drift will become apparent as there is no capacity for taking key prioritization decisions that form part of any strategic plan.

A different, but equally calamitous, scenario for joint relationships between members and officers in the progression of a strategic plan comes if the members have a very clearly defined view of something that is either at odds with the reality of the situation on the ground, or is thoroughly impractical in terms of capacity or funds to deliver. Central government, who is the provider of almost 85 per cent of all local government expenditure, will inevitably have the major say in what is delivered locally. If it is antagonistic to them, the local strategic plan becomes impossible.

In both the too weak and too strong scenarios, relationships between members and officers in achieving a strategic plan can be very testy indeed, and it needs careful management to avoid difficulties.

The best strategic plans develop when there is a clear understanding of role between member and officer, and a recognition that they have equal parts to play in developing the strategic plan that members can own and sell within their communities, and which officers have confidence in implementing and planning for managerially over a sufficient length of time. Strategic planning can often be badly damaged by frequent and disruptive changes of administration, and the best plans are those in which the vision is owned and accepted across the authority instead of just solely by the controlling group.

Assuming, though, that there is a good balance between political and managerial leadership that makes a strategic plan possible, it is necessary for both members and managers to have a good respectful working relationship. There needs to be lots of contact, but it needs to be on a professional basis and avoid the dangers of over socializing. Local authority officers serve all the council, unlike civil servants, and need to remember that factual advice needs to be given impartially. They cannot say one thing to one group and a different thing to another. This can often lead to a grey area around the role of advice and, under council policy, council officers cannot give advice that would be contrary to an authority's policy, acknowledging the fact that the policy will often be set by the controlling group. Any controlling group will, therefore, inevitably gain a larger slice of time from an authority's officers since they are critical in determining the policy that then sets the tone of advice for the whole organization.

However, it is very clear that, from time to time, the relationship can break down and often the key point of that relationship would be a breakdown between the leader and the chief executive. In such circumstances there are two alternatives:

1 Political parties may act to replace a dysfunctional political leadership, but have a tendency to be reluctant to do so unless the situation becomes particularly bad.

2 More commonly, the task is to replace a senior management leadership, which can often be achieved much more straightforwardly.

When there is a real breakdown, with dysfunctionality at both managerial and political level, then it is often necessary to bring in an outsider, but they have to have executive authority and it is rare for independent consultants to have that. Very often, the outsider has to be imposed on the authority, with grudging acceptance, in order to do their job. The outsider has to have the 'walk away' option, and the consequences of walking away have to be significant for the organization and the dysfunctional individuals within it. These situations can often be intractable. 'Basket case' authorities can often go on for a long time, especially if both managerial and political levels are dysfunctional. Repeated interventions may be needed, but there can be a real danger that these simply exacerbate the chaos. However, if improvement can come then there may be need for repeated support once things start to go on the mend.

Interventions that are based on legalistic codes of conduct or governance, and their adoption by an organization, rarely work. They are an expression of good practice, but they cannot drive it. Codes imposed on an organization by others are often resented by people who feel that they are an unnecessary imposition on their way of practice, or an unnecessary slur to their integrity.

COMMUNITY STRATEGY AND PARTNERSHIP WORKING

Roger Latham points to the increased attention given to discovering and addressing the problems facing communities and the development of partnerships:

> Many of the problems facing communities which local government seeks to address are complex, multi-service and, indeed, multi-agency issues. Increasingly, individual local government departments cannot meet the needs of service users on their own and have to operate on an increasingly corporate basis. Over the last decade there has been a burgeoning use of partnerships, including both formal and informal, to draw together individual agencies in recognition of the fact that the complexity of modern social problems in today's society cannot be met even by a single local authority operating within its own area.

In the UK, since the early 1990s at least, local government has investigated the views and concerns of their communities using a range of methods including surveys, neighbourhood forums, citizen juries, focus groups, service user panels, and on-line channels (e-democracy). Sometimes, these attempts at engagement have been linked to community leadership and strategic planning. Some examples from the 1990s include the work of North East Lincolnshire Council, at the time a newly formed English local council, which committed itself to being a strategic organization that was forward thinking. It set up a strategy review process. In each policy area this process entailed the council first carrying out a review with the involvement of community representatives (lasting between three months and a year), and then producing a 3–5 year strategy, which was agreed with partners. East Ayrshire Council, in Scotland, consulted its citizens and used this to establish a vision based on core values (quality, equality, access, and partnership), which then framed the planning of service delivery. Epsom and Ewell Borough Council, just south west of London, used surveys of citizens to find out their opinions in relation to its strategic framework document. Harrogate Borough Council, in Yorkshire, involved external organizations in strategic planning and development by forming the Ripon Consortium to address city regeneration needs and to bid for external funding. All these UK examples from the 1990s show not only the use of strategic management and strategies by local public services organizations, but also the interest of local councils in experiments in engaging with citizens and with local partners.

These developments in community leadership and partnership working, initially begun on a voluntary basis, were underpinned by legal changes. A new performance management regime was introduced into local government by the Local Government Act 1999, which brought in a duty on individual councils to provide best value. In broad terms, this duty entailed not only looking for performance improvements, but also greater accountability to local communities. So, the legislation underpinned both

249

top-down enforcement of performance planning and improvement, and greater local accountability to the public. The best value circular issued by the DETR (Department of the Environment, Transport and the Regions) talked about the community leadership role of local government, involving the development of a community strategy and a vision for the community, and the mobilization of strategic partners in the interests of the social, economic and environmental well-being of their areas. According to the circular, the community strategy should be the first step in creating best value. It would shape the individual council's strategic objectives and priorities. The Local Government Act (2000) embedded in law the government's view that community leadership was at the core of what modern local government does. It gave the responsibility of creating local community strategies to Local Strategic Partnerships (LSPs). Over the next two years there was widespread activity throughout England forming LSPs or turning existing partnership bodies into LSPs. These developments united again the idea of leadership – in this case community leadership – and strategy – in this case a strategy for a community rather than an organization. The idea that local government should provide leadership to their communities and ensure there is a strategic vision for their area – their 'place' – could be seen as the essence of what was called the 'place-shaping agenda'.

There has often been an appreciation of the value of strategic planning for community leadership and partnership working. For example:

> According to commentators such as Wilson and Charlton (1997), Boyle (1989), and Mattessich and Monsey (1992), developing a strategy or mission for the partnership is essential as it shapes the development of the initiative in the early stages, defines the scope of activity, and provides a constant reminder to everyone of the aims and objectives of the partnership.
>
> (Greer 2001: 43)

Local councils have attempted to link their corporate strategic plans to their community strategy. This approach is represented in the diagram at Figure 11.6, which is based on one prepared by the London Borough of Lewisham.

There have been issues in how community leadership worked in England. One has been how this is managed in the context of relationships between central and local government. Chief among these has been the constraints (perceived or real) on local autonomy. If central government uses its funding power and top-down performance management too strenuously, local politicians and managers may feel that they can only operate in compliance mode. As a former chief executive of a county council, Roger Latham, expresses it:

> If strategies are simply local action plans then there is no pressure to do any better than to comply with what is required at minimum cost. There needs to be

250

freedom to move resources outside the minimum levels if priorities established in a strategy are to be given impact through additional resource.

The biggest challenge in providing community leadership, and doing this through community strategies, has not changed noticeably over this period – how can the public be meaningfully engaged with the process of formulating strategic plans? Can the vision for the community be genuinely informed by local people? Can the priorities reflect local people's priorities? If headway is made on this, undoubtedly there will be challenges (and even conflicts) caused by differences between the representation of the community's priorities through these involvement channels, and the elected politicians' views of these priorities based on their involvement in traditional democratic representative structures.

PUBLIC SERVICE COMPETITION

Consideration of the use of competition in the public services to increase efficiency and bring about improvements could be based on a contrast between a traditional situation, characterized as an absence of competition, and post-reform situations, in which competition is present. But competitive situations vary.

One variation in competitive situations is created by who the competitors are. Take the case of public services commissioned by government and paid for out of taxes. In this case, the government may set up a situation in which there is competition between public service providers. There can also be situations in which the competition for government contracts is restricted to private sector organizations, and then takes the form of contracting out services to the private sector. Yet another option is where government creates competition between public and private sector organizations to win contracts to deliver public services. The UK's local government provides examples of this last situation in the 1980s. In-house service organizations competed with private organizations to win contracts in a wide range of service areas.

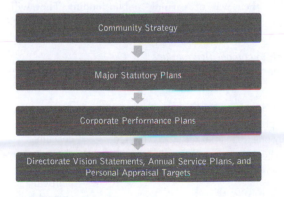

Figure 11.6 *Hierarchy of strategy and planning*

Another variation in competitive situations can be summed up in the contrast between situations in which there is competition for contracts, and other situations where there is actually competition for the choices of service users. The situation in which there is competition between providers combined with public service consumers being able to choose between providers is arguably the situation where the competitive pressures on organizations will be at their greatest.

An example of the latter case can be found in Osborne and Gaebler's (1992) presentation of a case study of public education reform in Minnesota (United States). They described how a new delivery system was created based on giving students and their parents a choice of schools, forcing schools to compete, and state funding allocations then being based on the choices made. They argued that this 'choice system' created a revolution in public education that could not be achieved by other measures such as public services leaders exhorting schools to improve, or legislation ordering improvement. The introduction of the system took place incrementally, beginning in 1984 and with the final stage commencing in 1988. Critically, it was not just a matter of schools competing to be chosen by students and parents; the schools were also thereby competing for funding. While this could be seen as a top-down reform, Osborne and Gaebler noted the existence of evidence showing that public support grew with experience of the choice system in Minnesota.

Common and his colleagues (1992) attempt to distinguish six competitive situations, which they place in a spectrum they describe as stretching from the least competitive to the most competitive. Part of their analysis concerns the number of providers and the number of purchasers of public services, which they use to characterize competitive situations at the least competitive end of the spectrum (see Table 11.3).

It may be that the introduction of more competition between providers of public services will trigger a convergence of leadership and strategic management between the public and private sectors. If so, we expect some organizations will seek to compete by improving their services and innovating to increase the effectiveness of the services they provide. This will be their way of 'earning' public funding. They will

Table 11.3 *Monopoly through to competitive markets*

1	2	3	4	5	6
Monopoly/ Monopsony (one provider and one purchaser)	Monopoly/ More than one purchaser	More than one provider/ Only one purchaser	Competitive internal market	Competitive market with limited consumer choice	Competitive market with consumer choice but still some political control

carry out research into what it is the public wants, and work hard at understanding the requirements of commissioners of public services. In relation to their organizational capacity, they will make strategic plans and will work at getting a cohesive response in adapting to a more competitive situation. In relation to external support, they will develop their communication strategies to ensure the public are informed about the strengths and achievements of their organizations, and they will seek to get closer to political oversight bodies.

There are likely to be other organizations that will concentrate on operational management, and will strive to cut service delivery costs to ensure they maintain financial stability in the face of intensifying pressures created by competition. They will look to effective operational management skills.

What is the evidence based on what has actually happened when competitive pressures have been introduced? A review of the application of competition to UK public services in the 1980s and early 1990s suggests that competition strategy tended to be essentially cost-cutting in order to lower the price of services (Common *et al.* 1992: 41).

SUMMARY

Bringing in strategic plans is a public management innovation. The issues faced in delivering strategic plans may well depend on the circumstances in which strategic planning is introduced, who instigates its introduction, and the motives for the innovation.

There is some evidence that shows strategic planning innovations in government have made things better, but the evidence base is still meagre. The US evidence suggests that very many federal managers do not know enough, or feel confident enough about what they know, to offer an opinion on the impact of strategic planning by federal agencies. There is obviously a need for much more evaluation of strategic leadership and strategic management in government.

Detailed studies of strategic planning in government do indicate that there are problems of integration, and that, in practice, there are many imperfections and misalignments in how strategic planning is executed. This indicates that either more work is needed on effective implementation, or that reality is always more complicated than the designs we put on paper. There may also be an indication here that the plans as implemented will always be to some extent contested, negotiated, and emergent.

There have been some attempts at whole of government strategic leadership and planning (e.g. in New Zealand), and the ideas of government-wide strategic planning have been argued as an essential development (e.g. in the US). In addition there is an increasing appreciation that government needs to focus on key outcomes and find ways of using these to direct the work of civil servants working with politicians.

Finally, in this chapter we looked very briefly at the 'break' from an organizational focus in strategic leadership with the growth of community strategies and partnership working, and we noted the possibility of some convergence (at least in provider bodies) with private sector practices because of the emergence of more and more competitive situations in the public services.

This chapter showed that, however simple are some of the current ideas of strategic leadership, they have to measure up to a world of practice that is full of complexity and difficulty.

Work-based assignment: integration mapping

The work-based assignments in this book are for civil servants and other public services staff who have four or more years of management experience.

This assignment is inspired by Anne Drumaux's work on federal strategic planning in Belgium. Please get hold of as many of the following documents as possible for your own organization:

Policy documents (reflecting or containing the outcomes the politicians want)
Corporate strategic plan
Departmental strategic plans
Operational plans
Annual budget document

Analyse the content of the documents you obtain and consider three questions:

1 Are the contents of the various documents aligned?
2 Are any of the documents clearly not integrated with the rest?
3 Do you get the impression that these documents were created by processes of planning that are top-down, or bottom-up, or something else?

DISCUSSION QUESTIONS

1 Can civil service leaders ever use strategic plans to bring about transformational change in cases where politicians are not interested in strategic planning and see plans simply as management tools?
2 Is the evidence for the benefits of strategic planning at national or federal level of government convincing? If you think it is not, what evidence would be needed to test the case for strategic planning?
3 Are budgetary processes always in tension with strategic processes?
4 Should there be whole of government strategic plans?
5 How should public services models of strategic management be changed to suit (a) community leadership responsibilities, and (b) increased levels of competition between public service providers?

254

FURTHER READING

Mulgan, G. (2009) *The Art of Public Strategy*. Oxford: Oxford University Press.
OECD (2005) *Modernising Government: The Way Forward*. Paris: OECD.

NOTES

1   Besides a re-engineering of the structure of Federal Administration into a matrix of vertical and horizontal ministries (for example, Finance for the first type, and Personnel & Organization for the second type) and a proposition to suppress ministry cabinets

2   Based on the proportion of plan's objectives in each of the following categories: internal or external stakeholders, internal management and process, programmes, and services

3   Relabelled Federal Public Service (FPS) by the reform

Chapter 12

Reform, Leadership, and Strategy

LEARNING OBJECTIVES

■ To develop an appreciation of the overall nature of public services reform over the last twenty years
■ To explore the concept of the strategic state
■ To underline the contributions of leadership and strategic planning to reform and modernization

INTRODUCTION

It is possible to imagine the modernization and reform of the public services and the civil service proceeding in a number of different directions (and possibly all at the same time). At the present time, it can be argued that three dimensions of the modernization process could be around the degree of focus on the performance of the public services, the relationship with the public that the public services serve, and the relative sizes of the state and civil society. Using the first two dimensions, we can imagine four future scenarios — not as predictions, but as possible futures (see Table 12.1). These are labelled:

1 Professional and authoritative
2 Professional and responsive
3 Streamlined and efficient
4 Strategic and enabling.

This chapter is mainly concerned with the emergence of the fourth of these scenarios, strategic and enabling. During the 1980s, the use of strategic planning began to spread at sub-national levels of government. During the 1990s, strategic management

Table 12.1 *Four scenarios of the future of public services and civil service (imagined futures)*

Professional and authoritative	Professional and Responsive	Streamlined and Efficient	Strategic and Enabling
Public Services —Belief that a responsible and professional civil service is the key to both flexibility and the quality of public services —Professionals are trusted to know best; emphasis is on responsibility rather than accountability —Professionals must be supervised by others in same profession —Interest in developing evidence-based policy making —Codes of professional conduct	Public Services —Professionals consult public and service users to find out their preferences (surveys, focus groups, etc.) —Use of quality and customer care programmes —The use of quality circles —The development of complaints procedures —Planning systems in which budgets are allocated after careful assessments of needs —Ombudsman systems developed as a back up to internal complaints procedures	Public Services —Line management, clear objectives, and competent civil servants are seen as key to efficient public services —Outsourcing and compulsory competitive tendering to the private sector is used as a cost reduction measure —Use of performance management systems and performance indicators —Development of resource management initiatives, management information systems, and performance budgeting —Organizations subject to inspection systems, audits, and special measures for failing organizations	Public Services —Strategic planning and community planning and innovation are used to identify and pursue priorities of the public —Ministries headquarters are slimmed down —Government seeks to empower the public (as citizens, as members of the community, and as users of public services e.g. user choice of provider) —Interest in development of strategic commissioning systems —Financial systems designed to empower service users

Table 12.1 *(continued)*

Civil Service	Civil Service	Civil Service	Civil Service
—Modern strategies on HR, workforce planning, recruitment, reward and retention —Commitment to merit based HR systems —A professional infrastructure is developed for all civil servants	—Professional education modified to encourage listening to clients and their preferences —Customer care training programmes and development of expertise in quality management	—Training budgets are focused on developing competency so that individuals work in line with roles and standards —Incentive payment systems are favoured but there may be concerns about capability of managers to operate properly	—Leadership development is a priority —Talent management systems —Strategic thinking skills and can-do attitude fostered among senior civil service grades

eventually came to be seen as a defining feature of modernization of government in the sense that governments were urged to be more strategic and less focused on service delivery. This is very important. Strategic management is a formal management process, but there was a growing judgement that government should be seen essentially as a strategic actor. In fact, the aim of creating the state as a strategic actor – the 'Strategic State' – came to be important for some leading politicians.

Measures to reduce the size of the state sector have occurred in various countries from the 1980s onwards. Privatization programmes were one instrument for reducing public sector spending and employment. Civil service and public employment numbers have also been cut through downsizing and other measures. In the 1990s, for example, central or federal employment numbers fell in a number of countries including Australia, Germany, Spain, Sweden, United States, and Canada (OECD 2005). There may be ideological reasons for such changes, but fiscal and political conditions may also be factors. OECD research indicated that cutbacks in public employment are linked to periods of political crisis, and it has been suggested 'that some cutbacks were made without strategic forethought' (OECD 2005: 163). Later in this chapter we return to this topic of cutbacks to consider the impacts of the 2007–9 financial crisis.

DEVELOPING THE STRATEGIC STATE

Osborne and Gaebler (1992) argued for the move away from an old model of the public services as a monopoly supplier. They suggested that this old mode, bureaucratic government, involved both policy making and service delivery being carried out within a single-organization departmental structure. They recommended the splitting up of departmental organizations into organizations focused on policy making, and organizations focused on service delivery. This type of restructuring they termed separating 'steering' and 'rowing'. This restructuring then permitted government to operate in two new ways. First, as a catalysing government, it could encourage private, voluntary, and public organizations to engage in problem solving for society or for a community. Second, government could also make use of competitive forces in the delivery of public services. This they termed competitive government (see Figure 12.1).

The UK example of restructuring government departments by creating Next Steps agencies (starting in the late 1980s), was probably an important influence on Osborne and Gaebler's idea that governments needed to split steering (policy making) and rowing (service delivery). The Next Steps initiative was a structural change of the UK civil service. The Next Steps report by Jenkins and others in 1988 recommended the separation of policy support to ministers from executive work, which included service delivery, regulation, tax collection, etc. This Next Steps reform meant a change from the old organizational form, in which a permanent secretary headed up a hierarchical civil service, and each and every department was responsible both for policy support and execution. In this new model, the minister linked directly to the permanent secretary of the department. Following the development of Next Steps agencies, there was no longer a simple hierarchical civil service in each government department. The minister now related to the permanent secretary who headed up the remainder of the department – in fact the department centre – which provided policy support, and

Bureaucratic Government
- Monopoly
- Control located in bureaucracy
- Focus on inputs
- Rules and Regulations
- Public treated as clients
- Develop and deliver services to deal with problems
- Spend money on providing public services
- Centralized authority within the bureaucracy
- Bureaucratic mechanisms
- Provider of public services

Entreprenurial Government
- Competition between service providers
- Citizen empowerment – control pushed into the community
- Goal driven organizations – missions are important
- Public treated as customers and offered choices between providers
- Prevent problems before they emerge
- Earn as well as spend money
- Decentralized authority – participatory management
- Market mechanisms
- Catalyser of action by all sectors to solve community problems

Figure 12.1 *Osborne and Gaebler's reinvention of government (from bureaucratic to entrepreneurial)*

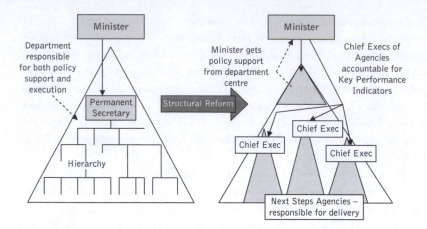

Figure 12.2 *Creating Next Steps Agencies from bureaucracy*

also related to one or more chief executives, each of whom headed up Next Steps agencies, and who were responsible for the delivery aspect of the civil service. The chief executives of these agencies were accountable to the minister for key performance indicators for their agencies. By 1998, agencies were the main service delivery arm of the civil service. Over three-quarters of the people in the civil service were in agencies or in departments operating on Next Steps lines (see Figure 12.2).

Did the Next Steps agencies improve the performance of government? Because of changes in the key performance indicators from year to year, the trend in performance has to be judged on the basis of cases where year to year comparisons can be made. According to a government report on the Next Steps agencies in 1998, performance improved compared to 1997 in 52 per cent of the cases where the comparison could be made.

In 1998, the UK government was keen to stress the political ownership of the Next Steps agencies. The following quote is taken from the Next Steps report of that year:

> Last year's Next Steps report, included, for the first time, reports by individual ministers on the performance of their agencies. This demonstrated the government's determination to ensure that the structure of accountability for the work done by agencies was clearly understood, i.e. that ministers remained fully accountable for the performance of their agencies. The public service agreements (PSAs) demonstrate the willingness of the government to impose on ministers the disciplines which had contributed to the success of agencies – the setting of clear, stretching performance targets is a key part of the philosophy underpinning Next Steps.

Returning to the Osborne and Gaebler proposals, as we have noted, they were keen on the separation of steering from rowing functions for a number of reasons,

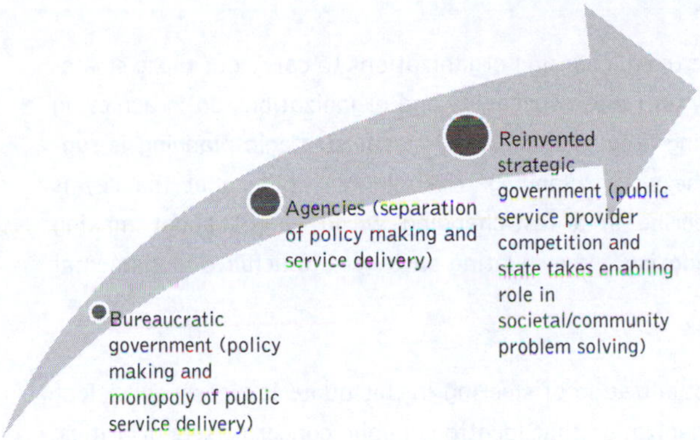

Figure 12.3 *Steps in the reinvention process*

including the possibility that a government that concentrated on steering could make use of competition between service providers to improve public services. They also supported the idea of government catalysing solutions and mobilizing support of voluntary and private sector organizations. They criticized the tendency of government always to solve problems by resorting to taxation, and then setting up new public services to address the problems. Important in this book is the point that their arguments were essentially a call for governments to concentrate on steering, which meant, in effect, saying the top priority for government was its strategic function and not its delivery function. The diagram in Figure 12.3 summarizes the steps in the reinvention process based on Osborne and Gaebler's proposals.

Why did they call the strategic function 'steering'? It is possible that the word steering was used by Osborne and Gaebler, and Osborne and Plastrik, in preference to the phrase strategic planning because in the 1980s there were persuasive voices that rejected strategic planning as a bureaucratic process (for example, see the work of Peters and Waterman in their book *In Search of Excellence*). So they may have used the word 'steering' rather than strategic planning, but also offered the definition of it as policy making (see Concept Box 12.1).

CONCEPT BOX 12.1   STEERING AND STRATEGY

Osborne and Plastrik (1997: 106–7) attempted to explain the difference between steering and strategic planning:

Some people classify tools such as the Oregon Benchmarks and Sunnyvale's budget system under the umbrella of 'strategic planning'. We have deliberately stayed away from that label, because what we are talking about is better described as steering than planning. Steering is about setting goals, choosing strategies to achieve them, choosing organizations to carry out those strategies, measuring how well those strategies and organizations do in achieving the goals, and making adjustments. This is what strategic planning is supposed to do, but the word 'planning' mistakenly implies that the key is creating plans. Steering in a fast-changing world is not about making plans; it is about choosing and evaluating strategies to achieve fundamental goals.

Comment: The conceptualization of steering in this quote is clearly consistent with a government organization that identifies public concerns, sets priorities, and develops strategic goals, and then commissions other organizations to provide services, or enables other organizations and stakeholders to engage in problem solving. Maybe, the reluctance of Osborne and Plastrik to use the phrase 'strategic planning' is less justified in these times of increased appreciation of the importance of implementing and delivering strategic plans. The phrase 'strategic planning' does not have to be interpreted as assuming that plans are the key. For many years, now, governments have been aware that implementation and delivery are the acid test of strategic planning. It is the strategy as implemented (the strategy in action) that counts, not the intended strategy (as contained in a strategic planning document).

Osborne and Gaebler constantly referred to leaders in their proposals about reinventing government, and they warned that continuity in leadership was a key factor: 'When leaders come and go it is impossible to create fundamental change' (Osborne and Gaebler 1992: 326). It is a reasonable conclusion that they were implying good leadership was needed for the success of reinvention, but they made few detailed observations about the work or the skills of leadership.

In 1999, an OECD symposium, looking at the future shape of government reform, made the following suggestion about the significance of reforms taking place in many countries (OECD 2000: 11):

The purpose of reform is to make government more responsive to society's needs. People want government that does more and costs less. Much of current public reform is an effort to meet society's needs by providing better, faster and more services from government.

The OECD symposium advocated strategic reform, which was public services reform that was led by a vision that enabled strategies to be developed according to a 'guideline'. The report argued that government alone had the 'global perspective and the analytical resources to do the strategic planning necessary for internal reform' (OECD 2000: 41), but warned government not to think that the 'critical duty of strategic planning makes the reform agenda any less the property of citizens' (ibid 2000: 42). Governments need to achieve service outcomes wanted by the public (see Concept Box 12.2).

CONCEPT BOX 12.2   STRATEGIC REFORM

Strategic reform involves developing a clear vision, building a constituency, planning tactics to achieve outcomes and communicating the vision and anticipated outcomes to stakeholders and the public at large.

A common vision serves to unify political leaders, senior officials, front-line workers and the general public. It also provides guidelines for choosing goals, for developing strategies to achieve those goals and for measuring results. In order to articulate a common vision, government should learn to consult with stakeholders and bring together their many, varied visions.

(OECD 2000: 13)

The OECD symposium of 1999, on the future of government reform, not only framed much of the analysis and conclusions in terms of being strategic, it also endorsed the role of leadership in reform. Leaders, the symposium report said, were important for the reform process.

Leaders within government are key to bridging the gap between the development and the implementation of reform. OECD countries have used leaders at many different levels of government as drivers of reform.

(OECD 2000: 15)

Governments involved in reform and modernization were not only recommended to deal with reform as strategic reform, but also to make use of leaders acting as change agents 'to help their colleagues understand the strategy and values underlying reform efforts' (OECD 2000: 76). In effect, the OECD report's ideas were built around seeing relationships between reform, strategy, and leadership (see Figure 12.4).

Individual countries could be found echoing these OECD views of modernizing government. We can note the following quote from a Foreword to a 2006 report outlining the findings of capability reviews of UK civil service departments, which argued along similar lines about the need for government to be strategic:

To meet these challenges the state must provide the same level of customer service as the public have come to expect in every other aspect of their lives. To achieve

263

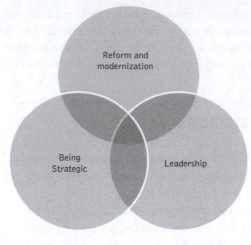

Figure 12.4 *Reform, leadership and strategy*

this, the role of the state is not to control, but to enable. Making modern public services the cornerstone of the enabling state – where the state provides strategic direction not micromanagement – requires a transformation of how we deliver our services. (Tony Blair, Prime Minister, in Foreword, Capability Reviews: the findings of the first four reviews. Prime Minister's Delivery Unit, 2006)

This concept of the strategic state implies the need to develop the capabilities of politicians, civil servants, and public services managers. There is a need for strategic policy making skills, meaning better capabilities for thinking about the future when preparing policy, and for more rigorous planning of the delivery of policy. There is a need for better skills in strategic planning and strategic management in ministries and public service organizations generally.

Michael Barber, a highly successful civil servant in the UK, conceptualized what we will call the strategic state as based on a core of strategic direction and performance management with appropriate capability, capacity, and culture, and operating using a variety of structures (command and control, devolution and transparency, and quasi-markets) (see Figure 12.5). This is clearly a variant of the Osborne and Gaebler ideas of reinventing government.

It may be useful here to emphasise three key points about the strategic state. First, the strategic state probably requires capability to be developed in both strategic thinking and performance management at the centre of government, and also in individual government departments. Second, the effectiveness of political and civil service leadership through the development of a strategic state will depend on the coherence and integration that can be achieved. Third, strategic planning will be an important public management tool used in the strategic state for service innovation and transformation.

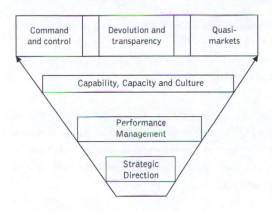

Figure 12.5 *Barber's concept of the modern state (2007)*

CAPABILITIES

Special units can be one way of creating capability within government for the new strategic state. These special units may be needed permanently, but they are probably most needed during the transition to a strategic state. The leaders of special units in government probably need to be people with clout (authority) and good interpersonal skills, and who are respected by the key interest groups (Beckhard and Harris 1987: 75).

The UK government set up a number of specialist units as it moved towards the creation of a strategic state, including the Prime Minister's Strategy Unit, to address long-term developments, and the Delivery Unit, which was a performance management unit focused on the delivery of the Prime Minister's priorities. The Prime Minister's Strategy Unit, based in the Cabinet Office, only came into existence in 2002, a year after the Delivery Unit. It was previously the Forward Strategy Unit, which had been set up to do blue skies policy thinking for the Prime Minister. The numbers of people working in the Prime Minister's Strategy Unit fluctuated as people brought in from outside came and went. Some of those who were brought in actually came from outside the civil service.

The Prime Minister's Strategy Unit also provided support to the strategy units in individual government departments. An appreciation of the Unit's work in supporting strategy work in individual departments was provided by the Director of Strategy in the Department for Environment, Food and Rural Affairs (DEFRA) when giving evidence to the Public Administration Select Committee. She said: 'I think it was a good idea to create the Prime Minister's Strategy Unit and it has done some very useful work for DEFRA which has informed decision making . . . the net benefits report looking at the future of the fishing industry, where PMSU, working with DEFRA, spent a year throwing quite a lot of people at quite an intractable problem and came

265

up with interesting and different solutions, which DEFRA on its own would not have generated, was a very useful process' (Rutter 2007).

Michael Barber, who headed up the Delivery Unit until he resigned in 2005, emphasized the critical importance of building trust of others in the units.

> I've often conceptualized my job as managing the frontiers – making sure that in No. 10, the Treasury, the Cabinet Office and generally among the political classes we are trusted so that everyone in the unit can get on with their job. As trust in and respect for the brand increases, each member of staff is quite literally able to add more value because departments are more receptive.
>
> (Barber 2007: 66)

The Prime Minister told the Delivery Unit staff in 2005 that 'the Delivery Unit was the most successful change he made to the machinery of government . . . He said he . . . appreciated the fact that they didn't just monitor performance but pitched in and helped. He told them that departments liked the way the Delivery Unit related to them' (Barber 2007: 259).

The Delivery Unit particularly needed skill and sound judgement to build an effective working relationship with the Treasury. This was because the Treasury was a very powerful centre in the government, and also already had its own agenda on delivery through the introduction of PSAs.

> . . . departments might see the Delivery Unit as alternative means of lobbying for extra public money – they might argue, for example, that any given prime ministerial priority could not be achieved with the funds the Treasury had allocated to them . . . I quickly quashed the Treasury's fears . . . [The Delivery Unit worked on] . . . the assumption, however unreasonable it might have sometimes appeared, that the allocated funds were always sufficient. If a department disagreed, we sent them to the Treasury.
>
> (Barber 2007: 56)

Sir Michael Bichard, speaking from his own personal experience of working as a civil servant at the top level of government, told the Public Administration Select Committee that in the end specialist units were not enough and that it was necessary to change the government organization itself:

> I do not believe that you can change government by setting up central units. You change the behaviour of different departments by focusing on how they are valued, structured and behave. What you have at the centre are what I will call centres of excellence which are stimulating, supporting, sometimes challenging . . . if you want to get departments focused on results and outcomes, you have

to change the way in which you train, develop civil servants, the way they are rewarded and recognised and all the rest of it. You do not do it from the centre.

(Bichard 2007)

Mulgan, another ex-high ranking civil servant, argued, in 2005, that the centre of government had to retain a strategic capability even if it did not keep specialist centres. Government could not operate on the basis that all of its strategic capability was located in government departments.

. . . in my view the central government, Number 10, Cabinet Office and Treasury, certainly does need some people who are taking an overview of strategic direction, management of money, IT, communications and the limited number of functions you have to have in the central government . . . You do not necessarily need those to be organized in units.

(Mulgan 2007)

During 2006–7, the UK civil service carried out Capability Reviews that assessed departmental capability in three areas: leadership, strategy, and delivery. Its objectives were to:

- Bring about a step change in the capability of departments for future delivery.
- Improve the capability of the civil service to be ready for the challenges of tomorrow as well as to meet today's delivery challenges.
- Assure ministers that departments' civil service leadership is suitably equipped to develop and execute ministerial strategies.

We can note in the last objective of the programme that there was a clear conception of strategy being politically owned; and it is clear that the role of the civil service leadership is to develop and execute the politically owned strategies.

The review process, formally speaking, was intended to address questions such as:

- Do departments have the right strategic and leadership capabilities?
- Do they know how well they are performing, and do they have the tools to fix the problems when they underachieve?
- Do their people have the right skills to meet both current and future challenges?
- Do they engage effectively with their key stakeholders, partners, and the public?

The reviews found many variations between departments in terms of capability. An interim conclusion, based on 12 reviews, was that government departments were relatively strong in respect of strategy, but there was a weakness in terms of delivery. More specifically, there was a poor record of turning outcome-focused strategy into

267

delivery. The intention was to address the weaknesses found through plans to improve the capability of the departments.

COHERENCE AND INTEGRATION

Central units, providing they are led skilfully, can provide a quick fix to the problem of a lack of strategic management capability in the heart of government. They can also be very useful for creating more integrated, more corporate ways of working, in the face of strong departmentalism. These integrated more corporate ways of working are, of course, essential for the cohesion that is a prime requirement of strategic management aimed at bringing about strategic change. Mulgan, again in evidence to the Public Administration Select Committee, said:

> Many of the machineries we are talking about here like strategy units . . . are attempts to counteract that [problem of departmental silos] and to get government to think more corporately.
>
> (Mulgan 2007)

Barber, previously the civil servant heading up the UK government's Delivery Unit, was interested in the practical implications of modernizing government for the functioning of the centre of government, and produced ideas on how strategic direction, funding, and performance management could all be made more cohesive in the UK government (see Figure 12.6).

STRATEGIC PLANNING AS A REFORM AND MODERNIZATION TOOL

Whatever they are named, a strategic state that is also heavily involved in modernization and reform will be using plans to bring about changes in public services systems. In the UK, the Blair Government produced five-year strategies in 2004–5 that contained proposed changes to public services – notably in health, education, and criminal justice systems. These strategies shared a similar set of assumptions about the benefits that had been achieved by top-down performance management by the government, and about the importance of changing to other models for reform and modernization. These assumptions were reflected in the following judgement in a discussion paper by the Prime Ministers' Strategy Unit on the UK government's approach to public service reform (2006: 8–9):

Top-down performance management has limitations however and the Government has taken steps to design the system in a way that maximizes performance improvements.

Evidence suggests that top-down approaches may sometimes:

- Increase bureaucracy, where it is possible that the work in achieving targets or undergoing inspection may make information and other demands on services take up disproportionate amounts of time that might be used more productively;
- Stifle innovation and disempower staff, by restricting the ability of professionals to react to local and user needs and preference; and
- Create perverse incentives, distorting professionals' behaviour away from addressing user needs and preferences.

The discussion paper also included a model of a self-improvement system that delivered continuous improvement, and only one of the 'pressures' was identified with performance management. An examination of the components of this model shows that strategic planning did not feature in the headlines of reform, but it might be

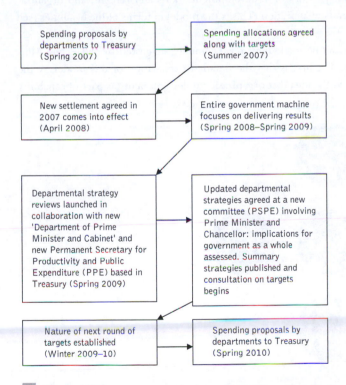

Figure 12.6 *Barber's Single, Integrated, Three Year Cycle*

inferred as contained in a concern for the building up of the capability of the civil service. Essentially, the Strategy Unit was suggesting that better services for all, the end result of public services reform, was produced by the interplay of pressures for change and enhanced capability and capacity. The pressures for reform originated from top-down pressures from the centre of government, quasi-market arrangements, and from service users. The top-down pressures from the centre of government were pressures to improve performance: stretching outcome targets, regulation and standards setting, performance assessment (including inspection), and direct intervention. The quasi-market pressures were created by competition and contestability, and by commissioning services. Pressures from service users (described in the model as users shaping the services from below) were formed by giving users a choice of provider, personalization of services, and engaging users through voice and coproduction. A final pressure from the users was defined as created by funding following users' choices. The use of funding in this way could arguably be seen as a quasi-market pressure, but obviously funding following users' choices theoretically should empower users, in other words magnify the pressure for reform by users. As well as these various pressures, the model portrayed reform as being assisted by the growth of capability and capacity in the civil service. In the model, capability and capacity is seen as a function of three factors: leadership; workforce development, skills and reform; and organizational development and collaboration. This is the model in terms of the headlines (see Figure 12.7).

Three comments can be made here on the model suggested by the Prime Minister's Strategy Unit. The first is that the detailed explanation of this model by the Strategy Unit included the idea that organizational development (as part of capability

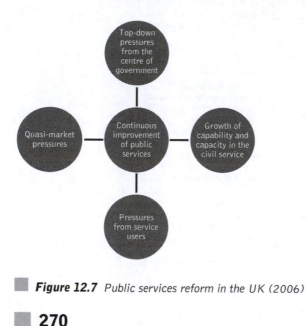

Figure 12.7 *Public services reform in the UK (2006)*

and capacity development) involves 'making central government more strategic with Departments focusing on defining outcomes they want from the public services they are responsible for, designing the system needed to achieve them, and commissioning services from a wider range of providers than in the past' (Prime Minister's Strategy Unit 2006: 12).

We noted above that the UK government had carried out a comprehensive review of capability for all the main government departments in 2006 and 2007. And it was also noted that these reviews probed the capability of departments in relation to strategy as well as in relation to leadership and delivery. So, in recent years the UK government attempted to institutionalize strategy as an organizational capability within the UK civil service.

Second, in the Strategy Unit's model, partnership working appears under the label of organizational collaboration and is seen as an aspect of the building of capability and capacity in the civil service. Arguably, it might have been expected that strategic level partnership working would have been more prominent in the setting out of the model. This point should not be exaggerated because organizational collaboration is identified as an element in capability and in capacity development. Third, and finally, we can make the observation that it is interesting that a group of civil servants working under the umbrella of the Prime Minister's Strategy Unit should be concerning themselves with describing, explaining, and possibly popularizing the reform model of the UK government. This simple fact surely supports the idea that, in recent years, the UK government closely associated strategy with public service reform, even if the model itself seems to indicate no great importance attached to strategic planning or strategic plans.

RESEARCH BOX 12.1 STRATEGIC MANAGEMENT IN FRENCH GOVERNMENT ORGANIZATIONS AND PUBLIC SERVICES

By Robert Fouchet and Emil Turc, Institute of Public Management, Paul Cezanne University, France

Over the last twenty years, the key word for enforcing strategic management processes in the French public sector has been 'modernization'. This stays as a token to the French government's commitment to adopt new management approaches and tools within a preserved 'dirigiste' framework. Created by General de Gaulle, the General Committee for the National Plan was the main tool for adjusting the annual focus of state budgeting and bringing up to date the national infrastructures and equipments. Four-year plans and parallel eight-year economic projections were the main framework of national policies. These were implemented in turn by government representatives (prefects), and the state administrations and agencies through a top-down approach. Public service provision was essentially entrusted to public administrations, agencies, and firms (although, since the nineteenth century, alternative approaches were widely used for local public services, such as delegation to private companies through competitive tendering).

In reaction to the pressure of economic globalization, public opinion, and, to some extent, of European law, successive governments since 1981 have initiated and supported the devolution of state competencies to autonomous local governments (*decentralization*). Administratively, the initiatives focused on the renewal of public services through private sector methods (*modernization*), and the decentralization of implementation decisions to local echelons of public administration (*déconcentration*).

Modernization and *déconcentration* reforms focused on improving the structure and performance management of the central state's services and institutions. Public policies and decisions devised at the centre were transmitted to local agencies alongside tools and solutions for implementation. The public managers received wider autonomy and more feedback was sent up the line, whereas responsibilities gained greater clarity with the creation of 'accountability centres' in each public organization. A flurry of department mission statements (*projets de service*) were defined in the wake of PM Rocard's thrust for 'renewed' public services (1989). Eventually, prefects acquired greater freedom to adapt public services to local demand, functioning as co-ordinators and controllers of local state organizations.

Major progress for strategic management at all government levels came with the implementation of the new philosophy of state budgeting (*LOLF*) as of 1 January 2006. Inspired by the American GPRA, the budget laws institutionalized the cycle of strategic planning, performance budgeting, implementation, performance management, and budgetary adjustments. The public managers' obligation to produce performance data, connected to greater influence on spending processes, and clearer management responsibilities, have started to shift the focus of control from budget allocations to outputs and outcomes. Stronger accountability affects both administrative and political leaders. Public managers are responsible to the prefects and ministerial programme managers, and programme managers are, in turn, accountable for their public policies towards their hierarchy, and along with the ministers, in front of parliament.

Although the new structures and management processes have empowered local public managers, the steering role of government was not diminished (Meny 2008). Public managers in ministry departments and public administrations may yield and display a strong administrative leadership on condition that it is supported by, and does not overshadow, the political leadership of the elected officials. Enforced party discipline and role ritualization enhance the legitimacy of authority lines. Nothing is decided in a ministry without approval from the 'functional equivalents' in the ministers' cabinets (including the Prime Minister's), who are themselves connected to their opposite numbers in the Elysée. Illustrating this mechanism, the General Review of Public Policies (GRPP) was launched in June 2007 by the French government and under the direct patronage of the French presidency. A major thrust for the modernization trend, the GRPP is destined to bring more legibility to the state's policies and interventions, to reduce the complexity of the state apparatus, and diminish its size and expenses. Based on input from the ministries' audit teams, the reform produced visible outcomes over the last four years: new policy foci, creation of one-stop shops for the unemployed, taxpayers, or businesses, simplification of administrative procedures, reduction of waiting times, merger of local agencies, the decrease of 10 per cent of public senior managers, etc. A significant support to GRPP implementation was the performance data made available by the information-intensive *LOLF* budget processes of the state apparatus.

A main priority of the renewal and modernizing efforts is to increase the responsiveness and quality of public services. However, the French approach contrasts with the UK's view of service quality as the result of service providers competing in quasi-markets. Neither is it the result of systematic benchmarking, since the various attempts to implement a 'barometer' of public services since 2003 have not produced significant results (Trosa 2009). Instead, the governments initiated a long succession of top-down quality projects. PM Rocard's circular on the 'Renewal of public services', the founding act of recent modernization efforts, mentioned, in 1989, the need to improve public services through the enrichment of service information for users on all available supports, the adaptation of opening hours; better access for disabled persons, seniors, or foreigners; enhanced interactions between users and civil servants; and facilitated administrative procedures. PM Juppé's 1995 circular on the reform of the state and public services followed suit. More recently, one of the first objectives set for the GRPP (July 2007) was the greater quality of public service delivery (one-stop shops, shorter delays for administrative solutions, improved treatment of complaints, and the development of e-administration). Curiously, as the first national results, published in March 2011, corroborated the successful top-down implementation of these programmes, it is the citizens that seem unaware of the progress achieved. This may be explained by lack of external communication and citizen involvement. More successful appears to be the design and experimentation of public service charters such as 'Marianne' (the symbolic figure of the French Revolution), inspired by the UK Cabinet's 'Charter Mark'. Generalized in all state services since 3 January 2005, this list of commitments for service quality may soon become a quality label, like its British counterpart.

While the status of the citizen-client has been enforced in British administrations through 'choice and voice', the feedback from, and roles of, French citizens seem to have evolved within restricted limits. On a general basis, the enforcement of public service responsiveness, either as adaptations to specific needs, or as citizen capacity to influence the design of service offers, is dismissed as a non-issue within the ideological framework of French public services. Indeed, the definition of public services includes the 'mutability' condition, that is, their capacity to evolve in response to the evolutions of French society. However, some declarative attempts appeared as soon as 1989, with PM Rocard's circular, 'we must associate users to the improvement of public services [. . .] The user must become a partner who contributes with suggestions and proposals'. In reality, most efforts were made to improve the treatment of citizen complaints (52 per cent of citizens were satisfied with the solutions provided as of March 2011). The GRPP specifically addresses the management of complaints, notably in the field of social services (health insurance, family support, unemployment benefits, etc.). The Ombudsman institution is enforced (le *Médiateur de la République*), becoming an independent authority in 1989, and receiving increased means to inquire into the citizens' problems as of 2005.

The citizens were promised more influence over administrations in the field of local government. Starting in 1983, local democracy was gradually enriched with participative approaches such as public enquiries (1983), municipal requests for advice (*consultation*) and people's initiatives (1992, 1995), the set up of district councils for cities with populations exceeding 80,000 (2002), and local decision referenda (2003). In practice however, the only device to articulate effectively participation and decision making is the referendum, as it has the capacity to block the projects of local governments. Then again, its effectiveness is greatly limited by thresholds set at 50 per cent of electoral participation and the majority rule (Lefebvre 2009). Participative democracy is incipient still.

Discussion questions:

1 In your opinion, how did the *déconcentration* reforms and, respectively, the budgeting reforms (*LOLF*), impact administrative leadership in state institutions and public services, and political leadership in state institutions and public services?

2 The UK government's Prime Ministers' Strategy Unit presented a model in 2006 describing the UK government's approach to public service reform. It identified four mobilized forces: Market incentives, Users, Capacity building, and Top-down performance management. Which approaches are represented (or under-represented) in the French approach to public sector modernization?

3 How would you characterize the French state's use of strategic management and tools?

4 Which are the main differences between the French and the British citizens' input for shaping and delivering public services?

STRATEGIC LEADERSHIP AND PUBLIC SERVICE REFORM

The OECD symposium on the future of government firmly connected leadership and reform (OECD 2000: 74):

> Leadership plays an important role in the implementation of reform because it involves two of the most important aspects of reform: change and people. While leadership and management skills are both important for any organization, the need for leadership is determined, in part, by the amount of change an organization expects or wants to undergo. Leadership is an important tool for promoting and managing change. It is therefore increasingly important for countries undergoing public sector reform.

The report saw the need for leadership as varying directly with the amount of reform being undertaken. 'The deeper and more widespread the reform, however, the more need there is for leaders' (OECD 2000: 76). As we have seen in early chapters of this book, leaders have to manage in pluralistic situations where there are different interest groups, and they have to be skilled in creating coalitions for change from stakeholders. This is true for reform as well as for other change situations. The OECD symposium drew attention to the fact that there can be issues for leadership that are specific to the context of reform, such as governments losing the trust of citizens and being seen as out of touch. It also drew attention to variations in government organizations such as the degree of centralization that would affect the structure of leadership needed. In the symposium discussions, there tended to be an assumption that leaders needed to be dispersed throughout an organization to further the process of reform.

Leadership does matter in terms of the effectiveness of public services organizations in responding to reform pressures (see Research Box 12.2 with details of the study carried out by Martin (1999)). But leaders do not find the role they play easy.

275

They have to worry about the support they get from politicians and the conflict that is inherent in change. The challenges of leadership in a reform context are, however, personal challenges and can result in the personal development of those who accept the responsibilities and difficulties of leadership (see Concept Box 12.3 by Nahit Bingöl).

RESEARCH BOX 12.2   LOCAL GOVERNMENT REFORM AND LEADERSHIP IN AUSTRALIA

Martin (1999) carried out interviews and a questionnaire survey in a representative sample of 26 local councils in Victoria, Australia, during 1997. The questionnaire survey data was provided by 214 responses. Based on his research, he concluded that leadership, planning, and performance management were important in the way the councils responded to reforms. He also found that some of the councils were evolving from a traditional culture of compliance to an outcomes-oriented approach.

Martin interviewed chief executives and directors, and a representative group of staff in each council. He used a questionnaire survey to get staff perceptions of the managerial organization and culture in their council. The reforms originated from the Australian federal government and from the Victorian state government. The state government had instigated various reforms in the 1990s, including reforms centred on boundary restructuring (council amalgamations) and compulsory competitive tendering. Martin reports that compulsory competitive tendering was the reform that was widely regarded having had the most impact. The councils were also being affected by spending cuts and rate capping leading to downsizing. The overall climate engineered by these reforms and developments was that of pressure on the councils to cut costs.

Findings

His interviews of local government managers showed that they were primarily concerned to comply with the state's requirements in respect of compulsory competitive tendering to achieve a specified 'percentage of operating expenditure to be subject to competitive tender with a minimal dislocation to the organization' (Martin 1999: 28). In a similar vein, Martin remarked (ibid 1999: 28): 'Much of their concern was about the administration of contracts, at the expense of thinking about the strategic choices before the council in the way in which works and services were tendered out such that the process enhanced local governance.' In other words, Martin's research showed that the management response to the reform was administrative compliance and not a strategic or entrepreneurial response. He summed up the managerial response as follows (ibid 1999: 29): 'While popular conceptions of the new public management, as found in Osborne and Gaebler's (1992) *Reinventing Government*, are commonplace in local government professional journals there was little evidence that this way of thinking and acting was occurring across local government organizations.' Martin commented that performance management was not sufficiently strategic, and that many of the managers in the local councils could not articulate the strategic choices that were available. He linked this weakness to the persistence of 'an administrative, regulatory mindset of local government' (ibid 1999: 34).

Martin's analysis of the questionnaire data revealed strong correlations between three factors: leadership and planning (correlation coefficient = 0.707), leadership and job performance (correlation coefficient = 0.669), and job performance and planning (correlation coefficient = 0.667).

Leadership items in the questionnaire were: senior management show by their actions they are putting clients first; management keeps the organization on course; leaders demonstrate their commitment to what the organization is trying to accomplish; there are leaders who symbolize its values and beliefs; and management set precedent for others.

Planning items were: we strive to follow organization's plans; organization has very clear goals; participation in strategic planning is encouraged; progress towards planned objectives is regularly reviewed; and this organization has a defined plan to meet its goals.

Job performance items were: individual rewards are based on performance; we accept people who do not fit in providing they produce results; emphasis is on achieving results; there is a clear way of measuring performance in this organization; and members care about and strive for excellent performance.

Martin's discussion of his findings includes the following characterization of leadership (ibid. 1999: 32):

From the discussions with managers and from the profile responses it is clear that effective local government leaders have a broader view and are aware of the major issues facing their organizations. They do not deny conflict and uncertainty during this transition period. They use the energy that drives conflict to create new ways of working. They are certainly focused on the task, which is clearly defined – and they present a consistent message to staff who are engaged in learning new ways of working in Victorian local government.

He stressed the importance of leaders having a constant focus on the key things, saying that this helps with getting through organizational change successfully.

CONCEPT BOX 12.3   STRATEGIC LEADERSHIP IN THE PUBLIC SERVICES OF TURKEY

By Nahit Bingöl, Director General, Regional Development and Structural Adjustment, State Planning Organization, Turkey

Gaining momentum after the middle of the last decade, Turkey has embarked upon a comprehensive and ambitious set of public sector reforms. Several domestic and external dynamics led to change efforts. Among them were the substantial change in the political establishment due in part to the severe financial crisis in 2001 and the aftermath, the EU Accession process, and the tacit societal demand that is manifest especially in urbanization. Major reform processes addressed, among others, Public Management, Public Financial Management, Personnel Regime, Social Security, and Health. The proliferation of these initiatives called for effective leadership at all fronts, and provided a fertile ground for those who have the ability to take responsibility.

Change in the public sector and any *strategic* ingredient of it have operated at two levels in Turkey. Design and management of public sector reforms make up the macro level, whereas those at a given public organization correspond to the micro level, the critical factor being the interplay between them. Experience in Turkey confirms that strategic leadership is a concomitant prerequisite. Strategic management, for instance, could apply to both levels, one may talk about strategic management *in* reform in the public sector at large, while it may be possible to refer to strategic management *as* reform for a particular agency. Change efforts required effective leaders both in the management of reforms and in individual organizations to realize them as intended.

Political leadership is the foremost prerequisite as rubber-stamped initiatives have not got rooted. As political and administrative realms operate on different rationalities, striking an effective balance between them is a preferred state. Bureaucratically led reform proposals have not worked unless political buy-in takes place, though political ambitions have also encountered resistance unless bureaucratic consultation is carried out.

Studies and practice concur that the attributes of strategic leadership in the public sector could be summed up in three characteristics: a visionary attitude, an ability to create and sustain motivation for self and others, and a demonstrated belief and practice in collectivism. Design and management of reforms in Turkey have required, in addition to these qualifications, the ability to adapt universal experience to domestic structures. Leadership is instrumental in creatively blending universally accepted merits with those of the domestic requirements to be able to convince and steer the change resistant milieu. Context-blind adoption of change tools have always been faced with ineffective implementation of change initiatives. Many pragmatic adjustments are needed for a meticulously crafted change and risk management plan. People have expected quick results, yet the results required time. It has, therefore, proved critical to manage the trade-off. Ultimately, if leaders of change are successful in creating a critical mass of people and discourse that will, in turn, create its own momentum for sustained change, change takes place.

Experience in Turkey has vindicated the validity of universal principles of change, yet it also confirmed that cultural background and conditions matter equally. Visioning and passion, having in-depth knowledge of legislation and public organizations, and creating a team of good calibre have been essential components and qualifications. The first is critical because, in the absence of it, the change movement becomes erratic. The second proves that, without this knowledge, the movement will not be authoritative enough to overcome resistance. Without the third the movement will not be put into action effectively.

It might be relevant to frame the lessons learnt in the Turkish experience by way of questions that follow:

What is the orientation of strategic leaders to change? In Turkey it was a wholehearted answer to the needs of a vibrant society that has been going through modernization and urbanization.

What strategic management tools, if any, should they use? Political and public sector leaders should definitely make use of change management knowledge and practice, and be competent in risk management as many unprecedented details hinder implementation along the way.

What strategic leverage points can leaders use for bringing about modernization and innovation? Design and management of reforms cascade from political leaders through front-line employees. Establishing a network of change champions at all levels, and being able to create a network among them, would certainly be useful in building channels to facilitate the flow of passion. Professional consultation services in public relations and communication is *sine qua non* as public officials may not be versatile enough to administer this very critical aspect of reform management. However, any abilities that the digital world offers should be accepted.

What are the costs and benefits of being a strategic leader in today's public services in Turkey? Change is a challenge to power and interest groups. It poses political and personal risks of rapid elimination. If not carefully administered and effectively communicated, it may backfire. It is a real test of stress and passion. The most rewarding benefit is self-discovery.

REFORM AND CUTBACKS

The 2007–9 financial crisis triggered another episode of cutbacks in some countries as governments responded to the debts by reducing government budgets. This pressure for cutbacks was very serious in some countries, and yet negligible or virtually non-existent in other countries – it is important to note that not all countries were afflicted by the crisis to the degree that, say, the United States, the UK, Greece, and elsewhere were. According to Kaletsky (2010) the central paradox for countries in the wake of the financial crisis is this: 'a bigger role for government in macroeconomic management and financial regulation will have to be combined with a generally smaller and less costly government' (Kaletsky 2010: 274). He was convinced that countries would have to choose 'between higher taxes and cutbacks in social entitlements or big reductions in all other discretionary public activities, including the core responsibilities of government, ranging from defense and law enforcement to support for scientific research and national culture' (ibid 2010: 274). In the UK, the coalition government elected in 2010 sought to handle this paradox by reducing public activities and supporting the concept of the 'big society', (see Concept Box 12.4), with an idea of a more powerful civil society. This could be consistent with the idea of a move towards smaller government, but it would also be compatible with a further development of public services reforms towards a strategic, enabling state that had begun to emerge in the UK in the previous decade.

CONCEPT BOX 12.4   THE BIG SOCIETY

David Cameron, the UK Prime Minister, made a speech in Liverpool in July 2010 outlining his idea of the Big Society:

But before I get into the details, let me briefly explain what the Big Society is and why it is such a powerful idea.

You can call it liberalism. You can call it empowerment. You can call it freedom. You can call it responsibility. I call it the Big Society.

The Big Society is about a huge culture change . . .

. . . where people, in their everyday lives, in their homes, in their neighbourhoods, in their workplace . . .

. . . don't always turn to officials, local authorities or central government for answers to the problems they face . . .

. . . but instead feel both free and powerful enough to help themselves and their own communities.

It's about people setting up great new schools. Businesses helping people getting trained for work. Charities working to rehabilitate offenders.

It's about liberation – the biggest, most dramatic redistribution of power from elites in Whitehall to the man and woman on the street.

And this is such a powerful idea for blindingly obvious reasons.

For years, there was the basic assumption at the heart of government that the way to improve things in society was to micromanage from the centre, from Westminster.

But this just doesn't work.

We've got the biggest budget deficit in the G20.

And over the past decade, many of our most pressing social problems got worse, not better.

It's time for something different, something bold – something that doesn't just pour money down the throat of wasteful, top-down government schemes.

The Big Society is that something different and bold.

It's about saying if we want real change for the long-term, we need people to come together and work together – because we're all in this together.

Source: http://www.number10.gov.uk/news/speeches-and-transcripts/2010/07/big-society-speech-53572; Accessed 15 August 2010

Earlier in this chapter we noted the conclusions of some OECD research suggesting that cutbacks have sometimes been made without strategic forethought (OECD 2005). This problem seems to be implied in a warning given by Kettl (1996) in testimony to a Joint Hearing of the Committee on Government Reform and Oversight, US House of Representatives, and Committee on Governmental Affairs, US Senate. He warned that citizens might be angry if the services on which they relied were poor and unreliable:

That is not an inevitable outcome. But it is a likely result unless government's policy makers realize that shrinking the government's size is not one problem but two: first, eliminating what can and should be cut; and second, ensuring that what is left – what policy makers determine is the core that government can and should manage – works well. So far, public debate has focused on the first problem. Sooner or later, we will have to turn to the second. And unless we solve it, public anger at government, its institutions, and its elected officials is likely to grow even bigger.

(Kettl 1996)

SUMMARY

In this chapter, the ideas of Osborne and Gaebler were quoted extensively to highlight how reform and modernization of public services is based on the idea of the government's strategic function becoming more important. They also said that the public had to be treated like customers and not (passive and deferential) clients. The public will resent being offered standardized services by the public sector, when they experience more individualized treatment by the best of the private sector businesses. If this is not heeded, they warn, the public will desert public services.

Their views on how to change public services were summarized as being that the providers have to listen more to what the public wants, and the public must be offered a choice of public service providers. Osborne and Gaebler wanted to see funding following the choices made by customers. This means that the adaptation of public services takes place through competition between service providers. It is not about turning public services into private services.

Looking back over the last 30 years we can say that the idea of strategy went from being a management tool voluntarily borrowed from the private sector by some managers and chief executives in the public sector, to becoming an idea that was hegemonic in the public sector. The strategic state, as we have said, was embraced by some political leaders. The fiscal crisis of 2007–9 (which impacted on countries very differently) may, in some countries, serve to reduce the size of the public sector, but the downsizing of public services may also accompany the continued movement towards the strategic state. The idea has spread that senior civil servants should be reinvented as strategic thinkers. Various public sector experts have argued that reforms of public services should be carried through as strategic changes. And there have been experiments in using written strategic plans specifically as tools to reform public services systems.

In this chapter, we have also seen that reform and modernization have not only been connected to the idea of being strategic, but also to the idea of leadership.

Work-based assignment: Does leadership and strategic planning enable effective responses to reform pressures?

The work-based assignments in this book are for civil servants and other public services staff who have four or more years of management experience.

Hold a meeting with your direct reports and ask them what they see as the management response in your organization to pressures for reform and innovation. Discuss this response with them, and probe their judgements and experiences of the nature of leadership and strategy in your organization using the items in the questionnaire survey carried out by Martin (1999) in a sample of Australian local councils (see above). Use this discussion to write a report evaluating the contribution of leadership and strategic planning to successful adaptation to reform pressures.

DISCUSSION QUESTIONS

1   How would you define the 'strategic state'? Is this idea found in Osborne and
    Gaebler's proposals – or are they advocating something else?
2   What are the conditions or factors that are important for the success of the
    strategic state?
3   Does the research by Martin (1999) show that it is important to look at the
    purpose of reform and modernization (e.g. to cut costs, to improve services, to give
    more choice to the public, etc.) when looking at the leadership and strategy issues?
4   What is the biggest issue for strategic leaders in a reform and modernization
    context? Is this evident in the Concept box by Nahit Bingol?
5   Was Kaletsky right that in future 'a bigger role for government in macroeconomic
    management and financial regulation will have to be combined with a generally
    smaller and less costly government' (Kaletsky 2010: 274)?
6   How can governments' ensure there is sufficient strategic forethought when
    making large scale cutbacks?

FURTHER READING

OECD (2000) *Government of the Future.* Paris: OECD.
Osborne, D. and Gaebler, T. (1992) *Reinventing Government: How the Entrepreneurial
    Spirit is Transforming the Public Sector.* Reading, Massachusetts: Addison Wesley
    publishing company.

Chapter 13

Reflections on strategic leadership

LEARNING OBJECTIVES

■ To develop a brief appreciation of the circumstances, relationships, characteristics and challenges of strategic leadership in the public services
■ To consider the idea that strategic leaders have had a critical role to play in the modernisation of state and society as well as the improvement and transformation of individual public services

This book has reviewed a wide range of ideas about strategic leadership and strategic management, and it has made use of actual cases and research findings. It has generally taken a very positive view of the contribution of strategic leadership in the public services, while at the same time acknowledging the difficulties and challenges of being a strategic leader. This book has been written (probably instinctively) with the hope of offering a balanced and realistic view of strategic leadership, whilst not being keen on either an unrealistic view of leadership as heroic and all-conquering, nor on a 'critical view' that is mainly concerned to debunk the pretensions of strategic leadership.

In this last and very brief chapter, we will be generalizing based on all the preceding chapters. A key generalization to begin with is that strategic leadership in the public services is sometimes successful and is sometimes a failure. It depends on the skill of the leader, on the circumstances, and probably many other things.

The ideas of leadership and strategic planning have been spreading through government organizations at all levels, from local through to national, and they have mingled with the ideas of policy making and law making, and the habits of bureaucratic decision making. Sometimes leadership and strategic planning combine with policy making – leading to attempts to define a synthesis, which may be termed strategic policy making. Of course, strategic leadership is not to be found everywhere in the public services and nor is the practice of it completely uniform in terms of intentions, processes, and techniques.

The innovators of leadership and strategic planning in public services, from the 1980s onwards, have been working to make government services better. They have wanted to see greater clarity about missions and more logical linking of goals, activities, and resources. They have wanted strategic planning as a vehicle for greater attention to stakeholders, and as a process that is open to them through consultation and even joint planning. They have wanted strategic management as a framework for public financial management; for setting goals and linking performance measures, activities and budgets; and for providing new accountability mechanisms. They have aspired to steady improvements through strategic management, and they have wanted to see public services systems radically transformed through strategic plans and management.

You may think there is a convincing case for leaders to create and implement strategic plans, but it is also the case that successful implementation of strategy is a challenging task. We have, at times, emphasized in this book the issues and challenges, as a corrective to the idea that leadership and strategy are easy. They are not. Some of the biggest strategic leadership challenges get little attention in most books on strategic management in the public services. These include:

1   Using strategic management to support the realization of outcomes desired by politicians
2   Making sound strategic decisions even though there are conflicts of interest and inertia to be managed in all strategic management processes
3   How to involve the public and be accountable to them when they lack interest in strategic management processes – presumably because they want good services and their concerns and problems addressed without having to spend time getting involved in public meetings and other processes of engagement
4   Making sure management systems ensure strategic plans are implemented
5   How to give attention to the introduction and maintenance of strategic management in the midst of a range of public services reforms which compete for attention.

This book has drawn attention to these things, but it cannot be claimed that answers – or simple answers – have been provided.

This book has reviewed research into leadership in the public services that has suggested leaders need to be honest and have integrity – keeping their promises and practising what they preach. They need other personal qualities as well. They need, for example, to be diplomatic and skilled in handling conflicts; they need to be good at seeing patterns in data about the situation of their organization and its activities; they need to be good not only at analysing a situation, but also seeing the means and opportunities for moving the organization on; they need to be patient and resolute in seeing the implementation of strategic decisions though to realization over a number of years; and they need to be good at understanding and working with political pressures.

Perhaps, above all, a leader in the public services needs to exhibit confidence in the future of the public services. They need to have a vision of the future of public services. This is important for their credibility as a leader. This does not mean, however, that leaders should be expected to have mysterious or unexplainable intuitions about the future, or should lay claim to certainty about the future based on forecasts. The leader should, however, have confidence that desirable futures can be worked towards and made more likely to occur (Nutt and Backoff 1992). Anticipating the future in this case means a pragmatic pursuit of better or ideal futures. This requires of leaders a personal outlook on life not of blind faith, but of hope (Milner and Joyce 2005).

Leaders in the public services probably ought to have a public service ethos. This means that a leader of public services should believe in the importance of public services serving the public and doing this in a way that is for the good of society, with society defined as the public, or the community, or citizens. The public service organization is not an end in itself. Consequently good public service leaders will work at understanding what elected politicians are requiring on behalf of society and, at the same time, they will consult and listen to citizens and service users. Helping public service organizations to be responsive to the public will be challenging for strategic leaders partly because the public can hold what seem contradictory attitudes (e.g. spending on services and funding this from more taxation). Strategic leaders will also find it challenging to develop this responsiveness of public services to the public in respect of sections of society and sections of communities that appear disengaged and even antagonistic (as was manifested in the English riots in 2011). Arguably, this specific challenge to strategic leaders is predictable from the theories of postmodernism advanced by Lyotard and Baudrillard with their highlighting of the possibility for surprising action by marginal groups in society (youth, black people, etc.) (see pages 33–5 in Chapter 2). Therefore, public services leadership cannot be exclusively concerned with the work of leading people who work for the public services organization, and cannot place the well-being of the people employed in the organization above all other considerations. They have to relate the needs and aspirations of those inside the organization to the requirements of politicians, and the needs and aspirations of the public – and then seek to integrate these in a workable combination.

A lot of space has been given in this book to a specific concept of leadership which is focused on encouraging and enabling public services to change and adapt by solving problems that are difficult to solve on the basis of expert knowledge alone. The leader has been defined throughout this book as the person who is the enemy of inertia, educates and mobilizes others, disturbs the status quo, and gets others to both learn and change their values and norms in line with necessary adaptations in the organization and its activities. This is enabling leadership that carries through adaptive work (Heifetz 1994). The challenges of this should not be underestimated in those public services organizations that employ large numbers of professionally minded employees where leaders encounter much resistance to the creation of services that put the public first – sometime called 'customer-centric' organizations.

This particular conception of leadership does not require the leader to make all the decisions, or even most of the decisions. The leader keeps on spreading responsibility for the success of the organization. Of course, strategic leaders will look for opportunities to use strategic decision making to spread responsibility.

Obviously, bringing more people into the strategic decision making process does not necessarily make it any easier for the leader to resolve the differences of attitude and interest that characterize each stakeholder. The leader still has to resolve conflicts and seek to integrate the varying purposes that are found naturally. Ideally, the leader is looking for win-win resolutions of conflict that create as much consensus as is possible around the strategic decision made (Osborne and Gaebler 1992). The key assumption here is not that consensus and harmony is a natural state of affairs, but rather that leaders in public services use strategic planning to move organizations, despite conflicting interests, to as much integration and consensus as they can manage.

Creating consensus may be made easier to achieve if the leader spends time communicating the mission, strategic vision, and values of the organization (or partnership) and convincing stakeholders that the leader holds to these as a matter of conviction, and that these are being implemented consistently and steadfastly. This is a key aspect of credible leadership in public services.

From the above description of leaders and adaptive work, it is obvious that this kind of leader is not an autocratic one, but may be a very challenging one. These leaders have to both encourage people to come out of their comfort zones and, at the same time, secure their co-operation. This emergence of co-operation may be assisted by some degree of general commitment to shared mission, vision, and values, but it also requires leadership work on integrating conflicting interests and attitudes. To the degree that co-operation is achieved, and responsibility is shared, it is likely to be because a leader has fostered leadership at all levels of the managerial hierarchy and created, thereby, a networked body of leaders (Osborne and Gaebler 1992, Joyce 2004).

Also we should stress the dynamic aspect of leadership through strategic management. The external circumstances, not least the pressures for change from the politicians, keep on changing. Leaders of public services, therefore, have to continue to monitor the circumstances to evaluate the need for strategic responses and adaptation (Heymann 1987, Moore 1995). The relation of leaders and politicians has to be considered as a part of this ongoing responsiveness to the circumstances. Should they be trying to convince the politicians that change should be delayed or resisted? Should they concentrate on negotiating additional resources to allow the organization to respond to political pressures for change? Should they argue for politicians to recognize that the pressures for change imply a change of mission and, thus, a switch in the deployment of resources? Should they respond to pressures for changes by promises to the politicians that public services systems can be transformed, or that more can be done with less?

The strategic leader is always thinking about not only the most obvious solution to a problem in the current situation, but also how decisions can be made so that they add to the likelihood of longer-term success. Strategic decisions, therefore, have to anticipate and help create the future situation of the public services.

We can say that the leader in public services can use strategic management to help his or her organization to cope with changing circumstances. While this is true, the phrase 'changing circumstances' is probably too bland to describe and to understand the work of strategic leadership in the public services in recent decades. Circumstances are always changing to some degree, but in recent years, right around the world, public services leaders have been asked to bring about public services and public management reforms. Indeed, a case can be made that strategic management has been a result of public management reforms (OECD 1999). However, strategic management has also been a tool for public services reforms. So, there has been a need to understand not only how leaders are using strategic management, but also how strategic management has been a highly important part of reforms in a number of countries. At times, there have been glimpses of government organizations acting as the leadership of society or their community, and doing so through the form of a 'strategic state'.

There is no doubting that leaders are expected to carry a heavy burden in keeping complex public services changing and evolving – often trying to catch up with rapid changes in society's structure and in the lifestyles of the people, families, and communities that make up society. Strategic leadership can be stressful and exhausting. At the same time, it can be incredibly self-actualizing as people develop their capacities by pursuing their values and commitments to the service of society and the communities that make it up.

DISCUSSION QUESTIONS

1   Should we always assume that the strategic leadership role is occupied by senior civil servants and top managers of government agencies? If elected politicians are the strategic leaders in public services, do all the generalizations in this final chapter still make sense?

2   What is your pen portrait of the ideal strategic leader in the public services?

3   How are the circumstances of strategic leadership in the public services likely to change in the next ten years? What developments in the practice of strategic leadership will be needed?

4   Will strategic leaders in the future need to be more radical and experimental in terms of innovation, or will they need to be more focused on strategic financial management? Or both?

5   How can strategic leaders in government develop strategic foresight about the next ten years?

FURTHER READING

Heifetz, R., Grashow, A., and Linsky, M. (2009) 'Leadership in a (Permanent) Crisis', *Harvard Business Review*, July–August 2009, pp. 62–9.

Corporate strategy workbook

This workbook is designed for public services managers and it is hoped will help elected politicians and managers capture their strategic thinking and planning for a new corporate plan to deliver the outcomes sought by elected politicians.

The workbook consists of a number of worksheets that support a process with seven main steps:

1 Identification of strategic goals from top policy outcomes and formation of strategic management groups
2 Stakeholder analysis
3 Situational analysis
4 Mapping context of strategic priorities, envisioning strategic success, and generating ideas for strategic action
5 Idea appraisal
6 Planning delivery of the corporate plan, information requirements and reporting systems
7 Integrating Corporate Planning processes with other management systems.

This process should deliver all the basic elements of a corporate planning process that incorporates a concern for issue management as well as performance management (see Figure A.1).

CONTENTS: PROCESS STEPS AND WORKSHEETS

Identification of strategic goals from top policy outcomes and formation of strategic management groups
Worksheet 1 – Listing of Strategic Goals
Worksheet 2 – Forming Strategic Management Groups (SMGs)

Stakeholder analysis
Worksheet 3 – Stakeholder Analysis

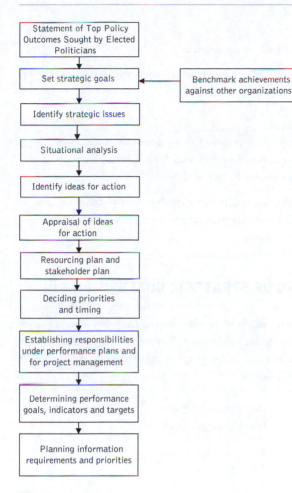

Figure A.1 *Strategic performance management with an issue management element*

Situational analysis
Worksheet 4 – Exploration of Public/Community Problems
Worksheet 5 – Opportunities and Constraints

Mapping context of strategic priorities, envisioning strategic success, and generating ideas for strategic action
Worksheet 6 – Trend Analysis
Worksheet 7 – Interpretive Structural Modelling (Strategic Goals)
Worksheet 8 – Vision of Success Statement
Worksheet 9 – Forming Strategic Issue Agendas
Worksheet 10 – Generating Ideas for Strategic Action

Idea appraisal
Worksheet 11 – Evaluating Ideas for Strategic Action

Planning delivery of the corporate plan, information requirements, and reporting systems
Worksheet 12 – Stakeholder Plan
Worksheet 13 – Resources Analysis
Worksheet 14 – Defining Strategic Performance Goals, Indicators, and Targets
Worksheet 15 – Identifying Information Requirements for Reporting Systems
Worksheet 16 – Allocating Management Responsibility

Integrating corporate planning processes with other management systems
Worksheet 17 – Developing a Calendar for Integration of Corporate Plan Processes
    with Budgetary and Other Processes

WORKSHEET 1: LISTING OF STRATEGIC GOALS

This worksheet is the foundation for the success of the whole process. The policy outcomes sought by elected politicians are written into the left hand column. Now formulate up to three strategic goals per policy outcome. For each strategic goal suggest how achievement of the goal can be measured – using what performance indicator?

Top Policy Outcomes Sought by Elected Politicians	Description of High Level Strategic Goals	Performance Indicator
	1	
	2	
	3	
	1	
	2	
	3	
	1	
	2	
	3	
	1	
	2	
	3	

WORKSHEET 2: FORMING STRATEGIC MANAGEMENT GROUPS (SMGS)

The initial assumption is that there should be a SMG for delivery of all the strategic goals, and who needs to be involved can be decided by looking at the top strategic goals and answering the three questions

Top strategic goals	What expertize or experience would be useful in respect of this strategic goal?	Who is best equipped to lead on this strategic goal?	Who needs to be involved in addressing this strategic goal? Suggest some possible names

WORKSHEET 3: STAKEHOLDER ANALYSIS

Stakeholders are anybody who is likely to be affected by the corporate plan or who can affect the corporate plan. Obvious stakeholders include the public, service users, employees, suppliers, other public services, businesses, the voluntary sector, etc.

To complete this worksheet, first, name all the key stakeholders of the organization.

Next, suggest the top two or three criteria used by each stakeholder to assess the effectiveness of the organization. For example, do service users care most about the level of customer care or quality or are they only interested in the reliability of a service? Is the tax they pay for public services in their top criteria?

The list of stakeholders may need to be reconsidered as you complete the worksheet. For example, it may be necessary to distinguish different groupings among service users or employees if they vary in the criteria they use to judge the organization or if they vary in their relative importance. For example, do people living on pensions have different criteria from other users of services?

Finally, assess the relative importance of each stakeholder. You could use a simple scoring system to rate importance:

1 = not important; 2 = slightly important; 3 = very important; 4 = most important.

293

Please note that you may need to define what you mean by 'important'. For example, does important mean powerful or does it mean a stakeholder whose needs or wants the organization intends to make a high priority?

Summarize the results of your analysis in the worksheet — include only the eight most important stakeholders.

Stakeholder	What criteria do stakeholders use to judge effectiveness of the organization?	Relative importance of each stakeholder
1	1 2 3	
2	1 2 3	
3	1 2 3	
4	1 2 3	
5	1 2 3	
6	1 2 3	
7	1 2 3	
8	1 2 3	

WORKSHEET 4: EXPLORATION OF PUBLIC/COMMUNITY PROBLEMS

This worksheet is designed to produce a 'problem brief'. This may be based on interviews with key people and key stakeholder groups as well as discussions in workshops. The brief provides a concise summary of the main public problems or community problems that the organization wants to solve (e.g. teenage pregnancies, community safety issues, anti-social behaviour). This is informed, where possible, by empirical data on the problems. The data may provide a baseline against which improvements can be measured. The data may describe in some way the nature of the problem and show its trend over the last 5 years. The worksheet may be copied and used for further problem briefs.

Public/Community problem brief 1   Date prepared: . . . .

1   Name of public/community problem:

2   Indicators of development of the problem (empirical data) and evaluation of future trend if no new action is instigated:

3   Impact of problem on public/community (empirical data):

4   Analysis (why is this problem difficult to solve?):

5   Current measures being taken by organization:

WORKSHEET 5: OPPORTUNITIES AND CONSTRAINTS

The data for this worksheet can be pooled from interview data and discussion groups in strategic workshops. If the data is being generated in a workshop, individuals should be asked to first silently brainstorm their perceptions of the opportunities and constraints for the corporate plan. This ensures that a wider range of opinions surface.

Definitions:

*An **opportunity** might be some external event or development that could be exploited to make the corporate plan more successful. For the purposes of this worksheet, an opportunity might also be some strength or resource that the organization could use to achieve more success through the corporate plan.*

*A **constraint** could be a weakness or a deficiency that might prevent or impede success in relation to the corporate plan. But it could also be something external – some event or a trend – that will make achieving a successful corporate plan more challenging.*

Both the opportunities and constraints should be ranked in order of importance and this ranking discussed with elected politicians and senior managers. Importance may need to be defined. For example, a specific opportunity or constraint might be rated as more important if there is a widespread consensus that it could impact in a big way on the hopes for a successful corporate plan.

The 8 top opportunities (ranked)	The 8 top constraints (ranked)
1	1
2	2
3	3
4	4
5	5
6	6
7	7
8	8

WORKSHEET 6: TREND ANALYSIS

This worksheet summarizes the trends affecting the whole of the organization over the last 4–5 years. Will these same trends continue impacting over the next 4–5 years?

Checklist: how is the public changing? How are lifestyles in the county/locality changing? Is the organization meeting different public needs now as against five years ago? If it is meeting different needs, are there any trends evident in this? Have there been any trends in the changes of who the users of services are? Are the services or service delivery processes the same now as five years ago? Are the key partners the same as five years ago? Have the organization's suppliers changed – and, if so, is there any trend in this? Have the organization's capabilities changed in any way over the last five years? Have management capabilities changed? Have IT capabilities changed? Are there any changes/trends in the organizational structure? Have there been any important trends in the availability of financial and other resources? Have the main types of interface with the public changed – is there any trend towards different patterns in how the public access services? Have there been any trends in changes in the workforce? And so on.

Trend no.	Description of trend over last 4–5 years and empirical evidence on the trend	Impact of trend on organization	Expectation of direction of trend over next five years
		Low/Medium/High	Continue/Reverse/Other
1			
2			
3			
4			
5			
6			
7			
8			

WORKSHEET 7: INTERPRETIVE STRUCTURAL MODELLING (STRATEGIC GOALS)

Interpretive structural modelling can be used in a variety of ways in a corporate planning process. It can be used to capture judgement about cause and effect relationships between strategic goals and/or strategic issues, which can be useful in deciding on the best points of leverage in bringing about change. It can be applied to explore causal linkages between multiple strategic actions, which can be useful when planning the implementation of a corporate plan. In this case, the intention is to use it to think about cause and effect relationships between strategic goals (see Worksheet 1).

The interpretive structural model in this worksheet depicts the cause and effects linkages between the main strategic goals. *This model could be presented in a narrative form, but there are important advantages in presenting it as a diagram — as shown in the box below.*

*Note: A diagram of a **model** consists of arrows and boxes. Each of the top strategic goals is represented as a box. Each arrow is taken to mean that obtaining results with one goal will also produce results in terms of another. So, if it is thought that making progress with one strategic goal will have positive consequences for another, then this is shown as an arrow between them (see Figure A.2).*

This worksheet is probably best based on discussions by the SMG (see Worksheet 2). The SMG should discuss possible 'patterns' of cause and effect between the strategic goals. This discussion may draw on evidence regarding cause and effect linkages, but it is to be expected that the SMG will have to use their experience and judgement and this will inevitably contain some subjectivity. This subjectivity is not a problem and is unavoidable. The SMG should diagram their model.

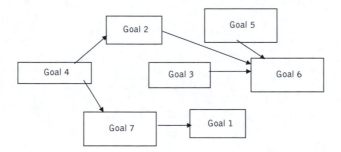

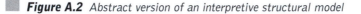
Figure A.2 *Abstract version of an interpretive structural model*

Model for set of strategic goals

Please draw your interpretive structural model in this box

WORKSHEET 8: VISION OF SUCCESS STATEMENT

This worksheet could be done by the SMG. Note: The vision of success statement is NOT a strategic vision statement in the usual sense. The usual vision statement acts as a challenge or target for strategic change. In this corporate planning process the strategic challenges have been set by the elected politicians as policy outcomes. Thus the vision of success statement provides managers with a narrative about what things will look like when the challenges have been met. The vision of success statement helps to imagine and create ideas for management action in order that the policy outcomes of politicians are realized.

The SMG should write this statement as an optimistic scenario of the future based on 'reasonable hope'. It is important that the SMG make explicit in the statement the chief benefits that the public or service users will enjoy (as a result of strategic action) in 5 years time. Also the statement might contain references to new activities and new 'interfaces' between the organization and the public/service users. Mention might also be made of any critical new capabilities the organization will have developed to deliver the benefits and any new partnership working that will be established. The SMG should write this positive scenario as a very short paragraph of 5–15 lines only.

_____

_____

_____

_____

_____

_____

_____

_____

_____

_____

_____

_____

_____

_____

_____

_____

_____

The SMG should also prepare a pessimistic scenario for 5 years time. This would spell out gaps or shortfalls in the chief benefits for the public and/or service users of the organization's activities, dysfunctions in the organization's main activities, and problems with the main interfaces between the organization and the public/service users. The SMG prepares this by making negative assumptions about what is achieved over the next five years. This should influence the SMG's planning in the sense that the SMG will be clearer about the kinds of developments the organization needs to avoid.

_____

_____

_____

_____

_____

_____

_____

_____

_____

_____

_____

_____

_____

_____

WORKSHEET 9: FORMING STRATEGIC ISSUE AGENDAS

This worksheet should be a summary of work done by the SMG.

The SMG is asked to look at its strategic goals and its associated performance indicators. For each strategic goal, the SMG asks: Why do we think it might be difficult to succeed with this specific goal? What might make achieving success with this goal difficult? In other words, what are the top strategic issues for this corporate plan? What evidence have we got, or could we get, to substantiate the existence of each issue? After checking on the evidence about the existence of the issues, the SMG should rank in order of importance the issues for each goal.

It would be good to have at least one top strategic issue identified for each strategic goal.

Policy Outcome	Strategic Goal	Issues: Why is it difficult to achieve success on this goal?	Evidence that difficulties (issues) really exist?
	1		
	2		
	3		
	1		
	2		
	3		
	1		
	2		
	3		
	1		
	2		
	3		
	1		
	2		
	3		
	1		
	2		
	3		

WORKSHEET 10: GENERATING IDEAS FOR STRATEGIC ACTION

Brainstorming Ideas

Very often managers are asked to simply brainstorm ideas for actions to achieve strategic goals. Sometimes they are asked to do this brainstorming on the basis of a SWOT (Strengths, Weaknesses, Opportunities, and Threats) analysis. In this corporate planning process we want to 'cue' the creativity of SMG by asking it to construct 'narratives' (Figure A.3) based on three contributory sources of ideas already generated by them (Nutt and Backoff 1992):

1 Vision of success statement
2 Ideas about opportunities and constraints, and
3 Ideas about the top strategic issues.

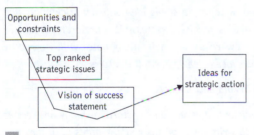

Figure A.3 Three contributory sources of ideas

A question to cue the brainstorming of ideas might be framed as follows:

How can the organization act to use an <u>opportunity</u> so that it will reduce or solve a <u>strategic issue</u> in such a way as to take us towards the <u>vision of success statement</u>?

Another question to cue the brainstorming could be:

How can the organization act to deal with a <u>constraint</u> so that it will reduce or solve a <u>strategic issue</u> in such a way as to take us towards the <u>vision of success statement</u>?

Ideas that are formed in such a way should be especially powerful – they should be strategic not only in the sense of bringing into being the future desired by the elected politicians, but also in the sense of being strategic because they 'lever' more change than other alternative actions would.

Note: brainstorming should be imaginative and creative and will therefore produce many poor ideas that need to be weeded out at a later stage through careful evaluation of the ideas. The SMG should be warned not to be discouraged by this. The SMG should be assured that if there is one really good idea in 20 poor ideas that this will be enough to make the difference.

Workshop 'Silent Planning' Exercise for SMG

This exercise exploits the use of nominal group technique to make planning a very inclusive process, but there is also a very interactive element. It needs to be facilitated.

The process is as follows:

Each member of the SMG is asked to review Worksheets 5, 8 and 9 and note the top opportunities, the top constraints, the benefits for the public/service users, and the top strategic issues. Each member of the SMG is given a pad of sticky notes and told that they should write only a single idea on each sticky note and that the idea should be expressed as concisely as possible – preferably in one or two words. They should also be warned that their sticky notes will be read by others so they should write their ideas clearly in capital letters.

The next steps are conducted in complete silence.

First, they are given four questions and asked to brainstorm as many answers as possible to each of them and to write these on their sticky notes until they can think of no more ideas. It would be good if each person comes up with at least eight ideas per question. The four questions are:

What are the key opportunities for achieving the strategic goals on which we are working?
What are the key constraints for achieving the strategic goals on which we are working?
What new or better benefits should we be offering the public/service users in five years time?

What key strategic issues do we need to solve?

Four charts are placed on a wall close to where the SMG is working. Each is headed by one of the four questions. Post-it notes are placed on the wall to the left of the relevant chart.

The SMG members queue up and visit each chart in turn; they take a sticky note blindly (without looking to see which of the sticky notes they have picked up). They place them on the flip chart. This involves them comparing the idea on the sticky notes with those already put on the chart. If a sticky note with a similar idea is already on the chart they place the new one to its immediate right. If there are no similar ones up already, they start a new line. They place only one sticky note on a chart before moving on to the next chart and repeating the process. The members of the SMG continue to do this until all the sticky notes are on the four flip charts. No one is allowed to move any sticky note already placed on a chart. Nor is anyone allowed to speak during all this. It is carried out silently.

The remainder of this exercise is carried out as a group discussion. First the SMG looks at each line of sticky notes and labels it with a short name. Then the SMG comments on the relative lengths of each line of sticky notes. The most interesting ones are possibly the longest lines. Then the SMG notes the longest lines on each of the four charts and begins to discuss how they might be woven together into a narrative about possible courses of action. The discussion should also identify which strategic goals are likely to be impacted and which goals have still not been addressed.

This may sound complicated but people usually get the hang of it pretty quickly. During the last stage you need people to be imaginative and open minded about the possibility of weaving together a story about courses of action. Groups can become quite engrossed in this exercise and find it very enjoyable. Sometimes there are individuals who feel it is childish. This can sometimes depend on the professional background of the individual.

Strategic Goal	Description of idea for strategic action under the Corporate Plan	Short name for idea	Check: how much impact on the strategic goal will this action have?
	1		
	2		
	3		
	4		
	5		
	6		
	7		
	8		
	9		
	10		
	1		
	2		
	3		
	4		
	5		
	6		
	7		
	8		
	9		
	10		
	1		
	2		
	3		
	4		
	5		
	6		
	7		
	8		
	9		
	10		

1
2
3
4
5
6
7
8
9
10

1
2
3
4
5
6
7
8
9
10

WORKSHEET 11: EVALUATING IDEAS FOR STRATEGIC ACTION

Each proposal — idea for strategic action — needs to be evaluated. (If the list of ideas for each strategic goal is too long, some screening criteria may be needed to bring the list down to a manageable length of, say, ten to twelve.) Suggestion: group together into programmes of action those ideas which seem to be related ideas for action.

The first step is to decide the criteria to be used in appraising each idea. The selection of criteria may be influenced by the need to devise a strategy to suit the specific situation, but commonly used criteria are:

- *Feasibility: Can the strategic action be delivered? Can it be made to happen?*
- *Suitability: Will the strategic action lead to the right results in terms of a strategic goal?*
- *Acceptability: Will the strategic action produce results that will be perceived as satisfactory by important stakeholders?*
- *Timeliness: Will the strategic action have its beneficial impact in the required timescale?*

307

Each idea for strategic action is appraised using selected criteria. This can be done using a table – see the table example below. The selected criteria are entered in the left hand column. A weighting is decided for each criterion: a weighting of 1–4 is used, with 4 being the highest weighting to indicate that the criterion is very important. Each proposal is scored on a scale of 1–10 for how well it meets each criterion. The scale is defined as follows: 1 = totally fails criterion, 4 = just meets criterion, 6 = meets it comfortably, and 10 = ideal. This is then multiplied by the weighting to give the weighted score on this criterion. In order to make comparisons, the same criteria, weightings and scales need to be retained for each evaluation.

A made up example of a possible set of criteria and scores for a fictitious proposal for strategic action is shown below. In this example there are eight criteria and the maximum total score is 50. But the number of criteria can be varied and the maximum score will vary depending on weightings used.

The total scores are meant to aid discussions by the SMG about the relative merits of different courses of action. The total score should be taken into account, but not seen as decisive in the discussion of the courses of action.

Proposal: 'Example'

Criteria		Weighting (1–4)	Raw Score (1–10)	Weighted score
1	Acceptability to the general public	2	4	8
2	Acceptability to other key stakeholders	1	7	7
3	Benefits to service users	2	6	12
4	Consistency with mission	1	6	6
5	Technical feasibility	1	5	5
6	Cost and financing	1	2	2
7	Cost effectiveness	1	8	8
8	Timeliness	1	2	2
			Total score =	50

Proposal 1: (name)

Criteria	Weighting	Raw Score	Weighted score
1			
2			
3			
4			
5			
6			
7			
8			
			Total score =

Proposal 2: (name)

Criteria	Weighting	Raw Score	Weighted score
1			
2			
3			
4			
5			
6			
7			
8			
			Total score =

Proposal 3: (name)

Criteria	Weighting	Raw Score	Weighted score
1			
2			
3			
4			
5			
6			
7			
8			
			Total score =

Proposal 4: (name)

Criteria	Weighting	Raw Score	Weighted score
1			
2			
3			
4			
5			
6			
7			
8			
			Total score =

Proposal 5: (name)

Criteria	Weighting	Raw Score	Weighted score
1			
2			
3			
4			
5			
6			
7			
8			
			Total score =

Proposal 6: (name)

Criteria	Weighting	Raw Score	Weighted score
1			
2			
3			
4			
5			
6			
7			
8			
			Total score =

WORKSHEET 12: STAKEHOLDER PLAN

When an organization has decided on a strategic action, it needs to decide how it will implement it. This should be informed by an analysis of the likely reactions of stakeholders to the implementation of the strategic action. This analysis involves identifying stakeholder groups in terms of their likely attitude to the chosen strategic action, and in terms of their power. Based on this analysis managers need to think about how they will communicate and promote the plans to carry out strategic actions. Managers may need to think about the timing of such actions and even think about revising the action itself to make it more acceptable to groups currently likely to be opposed to it.

Definition

Stakeholders: individuals, groups, or organizations who are likely to affect or be affected by the corporate plan and its associated strategic action.

The analysis:

1   *Stakeholders are listed for the strategic action (and note that the list may change for different strategic actions).*
2   *Then, for the specific strategic action, the stakeholders' likely reactions are rated on a scale of −5 to +5. Those who are likely to welcome or support the strategy are rated as +5, and those who are most likely to be strongly opposed are rated −5. When stakeholders are unlikely to react either positively or negatively, they are rated as 0.*
3   *Finally, rate the power of stakeholders. Using a scale of 1–10, rate them as 10 if they are extremely powerful; if they have little power rate them at 1 or thereabouts.*

Stakeholder	Attitude to proposed action (Rated on scale −5 to +5)	Power (Rated on scale 1–10)

The stakeholders can be mapped using these scores and this seems to help in various ways when thinking about a stakeholder plan for implementation, see Figure A.4.

The stakeholder plan may entail negotiations with stakeholders who are likely to oppose proposed strategic action. Supporters may be asked to help sell the idea to others who are less sure about the desirability of the action. Pilot projects may be used to win over those who are important but are not yet convinced that the idea for a strategic action is a good one. And so on.

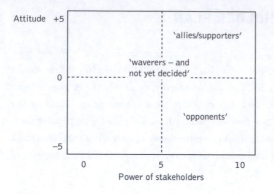

Figure A.4 *Stakeholder attitude and power relationships*

WORKSHEET 13: RESOURCES ANALYSIS

A resources analysis is useful in planning the implementation of action. A careful assessment needs to be made of the resources required for <u>each</u> strategic action and how they can be mobilised. The basic approach is to identify the required resources, who controls or owns those resources, their availability, and their criticality to the implementation of change.

The most obvious resources needed to implement strategic changes include money, skills, legitimacy, power, time, commitment, etc.

In the table below rate availability of each resource on a scale of 1–10. Resources with uncertain availability are 10. Resources that are definitely available are rated as 1. Rate the criticality of resources from 1–10 with 1 representing resources which are not important and 10 representing essential resources.

Required resource	Owner, supplier or controller of resource	Availability of resource (Scale 1–10)	Criticality of resource (Scale 1–10)

This table helps you to identify systematically which resources need most attention (i.e. those which are not available but are highly critical), and draws attention to where those resources are currently located. This is important information for planning strategy implementation.

WORKSHEET 14: DEFINING STRATEGIC PERFORMANCE GOALS, INDICATORS AND TARGETS

This worksheet needs to be completed for each strategic goal. You need to think about performance indicators and for each strategic goal you need a series of annual performance targets set for years 1–5. Target performances should be feasible but challenging.

To begin completing this worksheet, first identify the strategic goals which may be used to draw up a list of the performance goals. Then identify a performance indicator and a target performance (for the current year) for each of them. For example, a public services organization might have a performance goal to 'improve the way we deal with the public'; the performance indicator could be 'speed of answering the phone', and the target performance could be 'answering within six rings'.

To finish the process you need to set annual performance targets for the period of the corporate plan. The worksheet asks you to identify target performances for years 2, 3, 4, and 5. As before, try to set targets which are feasible but challenging.

Strategic performance goals and performance indicators	ANNUAL PERFORMANCE TARGETS (YEAR)				
	Year 1	Year 2	Year 3	Year 4	Year 5
1					
2					
3					
4					
5					
6					
7					
8					
9					
10					
11					
12					
13					
14					
15					
16					
17					
18					

WORKSHEET 15: IDENTIFYING INFORMATION REQUIREMENTS FOR REPORTING SYSTEMS

This worksheet also needs completing for each strategic goal. There has been considerable criticism that managers fail to monitor and evaluate the results of their organizations. One important barrier to monitoring and evaluation is the lack of information. This worksheet helps you to plan how to meet your information requirements.

The organization needs to set up reporting systems and organize at least an annual meeting to review actual performance against target performance. Ideally the reviews of performance should also look at performance trends over several years and there should be annual reports of strategic performance results to the public and employees. Academic research (Poister and Streib 2005) shows these two ideals are associated with better performance by local authorities.

Setting up reporting systems involves ensuring the supply of required information to scheduled meetings of management groups on a regular basis, to study reports and decide on corrective action, and report back to more senior management.

In terms of planning information requirements, the main thing here is to think through systematically what information you require in relation to each of the strategic goals you have established. The worksheet invites you to assess the availability of information required for evaluating achievement of the target performance, and rank the strategic goals in order of priority. After carrying out this assessment you should be clearer about what actions are needed to set up information systems and their relative importance based on the importance of the strategic goals.

Strategic Goal	Availability of information required to evaluate achievement (circle answer which applies)	Priority of strategic goal (show rank order of importance)
1	Available/Need to collect information	
2	Available/Need to collect information	
3	Available/Need to collect information	
4	Available/Need to collect information	
5	Available/Need to collect information	
6	Available/Need to collect information	
7	Available/Need to collect information	
8	Available/Need to collect information	

WORKSHEET 16: ALLOCATING MANAGEMENT RESPONSIBILITY

Having decided on one or more strategic actions, the organization needs to assign responsibility for successful implementation of the action. The managers may be in an operational role and the action may be implemented through operational planning. Alternatively the implementation of strategic actions may be organized through project management and then a project manager may be given responsibility for their delivery. It is also possible to identify to whom progress is to be reported and by when.

Strategic action or programme (brief title)	Manager responsible for implementation	Progress Reporting: (a) to whom	(b) how often
1			
2			
3			
4			
5			
6			
7			
8			

WORKSHEET 17: DEVELOPING A CALENDAR FOR INTEGRATION OF CORPORATE PLAN PROCESSES WITH BUDGETARY AND OTHER PROCESSES

There is evidence that corporate plans (and strategic plans generally) need to be integrated with other management systems to ensure their effectiveness. Most critical among these other management systems are budget processes and performance measurement and management systems.

One measure for improving integration (tight linkages) is to produce a calendar showing the linkages between the corporate planning and other processes.

This worksheet is therefore a matrix that can be used to produce the first draft of a calendar to suit the specific needs of your organization.

Processes	Month											
	Jan	Feb	Mar	Apr	May	Jun	Jul	Aug	Sep	Oct	Nov	Dec
Political processes												
Corporate planning processes												
Budgetary processes												
Performance management processes												
HR processes												

Appendix 2

Self Assessment Development Tool for Strategic Leaders in Public Services

INSTRUCTIONS FOR WORKSHEET A

Please complete Worksheet A using the following steps:

First, consider each item listed and rate yourself using the following scoring:

1 = 'I am very good at this'
2 = 'I am satisfactory'
3 = 'I need development'

Please choose the score that most closely matches you (in your judgement). Please write this score in the column headed self-rating. Your own self rating can be checked against the ratings of others; these other ratings can be recorded in the appropriate columns.

Second, consider the demands and challenges of your current job. You may wish to think about demands and challenges at the present time, but also think about them in two or three years time if you think your job will evolve. Again, consider each listed item and make a judgement about the importance of this personal ability or personal quality for the job (and for a future job you might do in the next two or three years). Score the importance using the following ratings:

1 = 'Not important'
2 = 'Slightly important'
3 = 'Very important'

Please write the scores in the column headed 'Importance Rating'.

Third, please calculate a developmental score for each item by multiplying your self-rating by your rating of importance. Record this in the column on the far right, which is headed 'Developmental Score'.

Next, please note the eight items that emerge with the highest developmental scores and consider their ranking. Do you think these are important abilities or qualities that you need to develop? Does this set of eight items make sense to you? Do you think that increasing these abilities or qualities would help you make your organization more successful? Are these, in other words, a priority for any developmental programme you undertake?

Worksheet A

Item	Personal Ability or Personal Quality	Rating of me by my line manager	Rating of me by staff who report to me	Self-rating on this ability/ quality (C)	Importance Rating (I)	Developmental Score (= C*I)
1	Clarifying a strategic vision or direction					
2	Ensuring strategic goals and priorities are sufficiently focused					
3	Communicating a strategic vision or direction to my staff					
4	Taking difficult decisions and implementing them					
5	Handling crisis situations effectively					
6	Correcting or changing the strategic vision and plan as circumstances change					

7   Setting a good example to others in terms of commitment to the goals contained in the strategic plan

8   Ensuring that the vision promotes equalities and diversity

9   Being personally energetic and resilient

10 Inspiring staff to work hard and enthusiastically

11 Contributing to the effectiveness of the management team to which I belong

12 Considering and influencing plans of partners as well as other parts of own organization

13 Good internal and external networker

14 Drawing a great deal on customers' perspectives when setting direction

15 Demonstrating a high degree of personal commitment to service improvement and service innovation goals

16 Sponsoring and championing improvement and innovation initiatives and projects

17 Challenging established ways of doing things

18 Change management skills

19 Conflict management skills

20 Problem solving skills

21 Personal honesty and integrity

22 Willingness to instigate improvements and innovation that take my staff outside of their usual comfort zones

23 Feeding back up the management line bad news as well as good news

24 Recognizing and rewarding staff who do a very good job

25 Effectively managing poor performance among my own staff

26 Taking a personal interest in the careers and development of individuals whom I line manage

27 Supporting the career development of individuals whom I line manage

28 Effectively supporting elected politicians in developing new policies

29 Effective working with elected politicians in developing strategies to deliver policies

30 Effective co-operation with representatives of partner organizations

31 Understanding the details of organizational systems and activities

32 Understanding the preferences and views of the public and service users in relation to services we provide

33 Deciding on risk-reward trade-offs when selecting from strategic options

34 Competence in assessing the feasibility of proposed strategic actions

35 Managing the linkages between strategies, budgets, and performance management

36 Motivating staff to deliver strategic plans

37 Ensuring partnership strategies are proactive and add value

38 Good at translating strategies into operational plans or delivery plans

39 Good at delivering efficiency as well as managing strategies and innovation

40 Understanding of current business model to deliver good public services

41 Skilled at designing and implementing better business models

42 Effective in allocating roles and responsibilities

43 Effective in managing within accountability and performance reporting systems

44 Good at developing management information systems

45 Good at using
    performance
    information to
    plan and deliver
    improvements

46 Skilled in
    developing a
    customer-centric
    organization

47 Effective in
    budgetary
    management and
    control

48 Good role model
    for own staff in
    terms of learning
    and self
    development

49 Skilled in
    developing a
    learning
    organization

50 Do as well as talk

51 Keep my promises

52 Good at
    stakeholder
    analysis

53 Good at
    stakeholder
    management

54 I respect the
    different needs of
    diverse customers

55 I use feedback
    from customers
    effectively to
    make service
    improvements

INSTRUCTIONS FOR WORKSHEET B

Please complete this worksheet using the following steps:

First, write three top priority development needs in the spaces provided in the left hand column and place them in rank order. Second, consider the various methods for addressing the developmental needs and indicate your first and second preferences by ticking the appropriate row in the two columns on the right of the worksheet. You can add two more methods in each case if you have preferences for a method that are not shown.

Worksheet B

Top 3 Developmental Needs	Method of developmental intervention	First Preference (Tick one)	Second Preference (Tick one)
Top Developmental Need (write here)	360 degree feedback		
	MPA – Masters of Public Administration		
	MBA – Masters of Business Administration		
	Secondment – internally		
	Secondment – to other organization		
	Innovation or improvement project		
	Coaching		
	Mentoring		
	Short course		
	Structured training programme		
	Other (please specify)		
	Other (please specify)		
2nd Top Developmental Need (write here)	360 degree feedback		
	MPA – Masters of Public Administration		
	MBA – Master of Business Administration		
	Secondment – internally		
	Secondment – to other organization		

	Innovation or improvement project
	Coaching
	Mentoring
	Short course
	Structured training programme
	Other (please specify)
	Other (please specify)
3rd Top Developmental Need (write here)	360 degree feedback
	MPA – Master of Public Administration
	MBA – Master of Business Administration
	Secondment – internally
	Secondment – to other organization
	Innovation or improvement project
	Coaching
	Mentoring
	Short course
	Structured training programme
	Other (please specify)
	Other (please specify)

Bibliography

Alban-Metcalfe, R. J. and Alimo-Metcalfe, B. (2000) 'The transformational leadership questionnaire (TLQ-LGV): a convergent and discriminant validation study', *Leadership & Organisation Development Journal*, 21, 6: 280–96.

Aldridge, S. (2007) Oral Evidence, in House of Commons Public Administration Select Committee, *Governing the Future*, Second Report of Session 2006–07, Volume II, HC123-II. London: The Stationery Office Limited.

Alimo-Metcalfe, B. (2003) 'Stamp of greatness', *Health Service Journal*, 26 June 2003: 28–32.

Alimo-Metcalfe, B. and Alban-Metcalfe, R. J. (2001) 'The development of a new transformational leadership questionnaire', *Journal of Occupational and Organisational Psychology*, 74: 1–27.

Alimo-Metcalfe, B. and Alban-Metcalfe, R. J. (2002) 'The great and the good', *People Management*, 8, 1: 32–34.

Alimo-Metcalfe, B. and Alban-Metcalfe, J. (2003) 'Under the influence', *People Management*, 16 March 2003: 32–5.

Argyris, C. (1990) *Overcoming Organizational Defenses: Facilitating Organizational Learning*. Boston: Allyn and Bacon.

Ball, I. (1994) 'Reinventing Government: Lessons Learned from the New Zealand Treasury', *The Government Accountants Journal*, Fall: 19–28.

Barber, M. (2007) *Instruction to Deliver*. London: Politico's.

Bass, B. M. (1998) *Current developments in transformational leadership: Research and applications*, Invited address to the American psychological Association, San Francisco, August 1998.

Bass, B. M. and Avolio, B. J. (1994) *Improving Organizational Effectiveness through Transformational Leadership*. Thousand Oaks CA: Sage Publications.

Baudrillard, J. (1975) *The Mirror of Production*. St. Louis: Telos Press.

Baudrillard, J. (1981) *For a Critique of the Political Economy of the Sign*. St. Louis: Telos Press.

Beckhard, R. and Harris, R. T. (1987) *Organizational Transitions*. Reading, Massachusetts: Addison-Wesley.

Bennis, W. and Nanus, B. (1985) *Leaders: the Strategies for Taking Charge*. New York: Harper and Row.

Berry, F. S. (2000) 'Innovation in public management: the adoption of strategic planning', *Public Administration Review*, 54, 4: 322–30.

Berry, F. S. and Wechsler, B. (1995) 'State agencies' experience with strategic planning: findings from a national survey', *Public Administration Review*, 55: 159–68.

Bichard, M. (2000) 'Creativity, Leadership and Change', *Public Money and Management*, April–June: 41–6.

Bichard, M. (2007) Oral Evidence, in House of Commons Public Administration Select Committee, *Governing the Future*, Second Report of Session 2006–07, Volume II, HC123-II. London: The Stationery Office Limited.

Birt, Lord (2007) Oral Evidence, in House of Commons Public Administration Select Committee, *Governing the Future*, Second Report of Session 2006–07, Volume II, HC123-II. London: The Stationery Office Limited.

Blair, A. (2007) Speech on modernisation of the Civil Service (24/02/2004) http://www.number10.gov.uk/output/Page5399.asp; (accessed on 4 December 2007)

Blair, T. (1996) *New Britain: My Vision of a Young Country*. London, Fourth Estate.

Borins, S. (1998) *Innovating with Integrity; How Local Heroes are Transforming American Government*. Washington DC: Georgetown University Press.

Boyatzis, R. E. (1982) *The Competent Manager*. Chichester: Wiley.

Boyle, R. (no date) *Developing an Integrated Performance Measurement Framework for the Irish Civil Service*, Committee for Public Management Research, Research Paper 3. Dublin.

Boyle, R. (1989) 'Partnership in Practice', *Local Government Studies*, 15, 2: 17–27.

Boyle, R. (1995a) *Developing Management Skills*. Dublin: Institute of Public Administration.

Boyle, R. (1995b) *Towards a New Public Service*. Dublin: Institute of Public Administration.

Boyle, R. (1996) *Measuring civil service performance*. Dublin: Institute of Public Administration.

Brown, G. (2008) Speech on the National Health Service (7 January 2008) http://www.number-10.gov.uk/output/Page14171.asp; (accessed 25 January 2008).

Bryson, J. M. (1988) *Strategic Planning for Public and Nonprofit Organizations*, 1st edition. San Francisco: Jossey-Bass.

Bryson, J. M. (1995) *Strategic Planning for Public and Nonprofit Organizations*, 2nd edition. San Francisco: Jossey-Bass.

Bryson, J. M. (2004) *Strategic Planning for Public and Nonprofit Organizations: A Guide to Strengthening and Sustaining Organizational Achievement, 3rd Edition*. San Francisco: Jossey-Bass.

Bryson, J. M. and Anderson, S. R. (2000) 'Applying Large-Group Interaction Methods in the Planning and Implementation of Major Change Efforts', *Public Administration Review*, March/April, 60, 2: 143–62.

Burns, T. (1966) 'On the plurality of social systems', in T. Burns (ed.) *Industrial Man*. Harmondsworth: Penguin Books.

Burns, T. and Stalker, G. H. (1961) *The Management of Innovation*. London: Tavistock.

Byrne, D., Walter, K., Rogers, S., Tuohy, B., Dully, J., Mulherin, T., Ryna, O., Tutty, M., Gravey, D., O'Hanlon, G. and Treacy, C. (1994) *Strategic Management in the Irish Civil Service: A Review Drawing on Experience in New Zealand and Australia*, M.Sc. Dissertation, Trinity College Dublin.

Cameron D. (2011) Prime Minister's Speech on Modern Public Service (17 January 2011) http://www.number10.gov.uk/news/speeches-and-transcripts/2011/01/prime-ministers-speech-on-modern-public-service-58858; (accessed 3 February 2011)

Campbell, A. and Stott, R. (eds) (2007) *The Blair Years: Extracts from the Alistair Campbell Diaries*. London: Hutchinson.

Capability Reviews Team (2007) *Capability Reviews Tranche 3: Findings and Common Themes. Civil Service – Strengths and Challenges*. London: Cabinet Office. Crown copyright. (Ref: 279915/0307/D2.4)

Chalmers, A. (1997) *Strategic Management in Eleven National Libraries: a Research Report*. Wellington: National Library of New Zealand.

Charlesworth, K., Cook P. and Crozier G. (2003) *Leading Change in the Public Sector: Making the Difference*. London: Chartered Management Institute.

Cobb, R. W. and Elder, C. D. (1972) *Participants in American Politics: The Dynamics of Agenda Building*. Newton, Mass.: Allyn & Bacon.

Collier, N., Fishwick, F. and Johnson, G. (2001) 'The processes of strategy development in the public sector', in G. Johnson and K. Scholes (eds) *Exploring Public Sector Strategy*. Harlow: Pearson Education.

Collins, N. (2007) 'NPM: a new orthodoxy', in N. Collins, T. Cradden, and P. Butler, *Modernising Irish Government: The Politics of Administrative Reform*. Dublin: Gill and Macmillan.

Common, R., Flynn, N. and Mellon, E. (1992) *Managing Public Services: Competition and Decentralization*. Oxford: Butterworth-Heinemann.

Commonwealth Secretariat (2002) *Current Good Practices and New Developments in Public Sector Service Management*. London: Commonwealth Secretariat.

Comptroller and Auditor General (2008) *Department for Work and Pensions: The Roll-out of the Jobcentre Plus Office Network*, HC 346 Session 2007–08. London: The Stationery Office.

Corrigan, P., Joyce, P., McNulty, T. and Rose, A. (1999) 'Towards a model of user-led innovation in local government', *The Third International Research Symposium on Public Management*, at Aston University, Birmingham, UK. (Conference Paper)

Crozier, M. (1964) *The Bureaucratic Phenomenon*. Chicago: The University of Chicago Press.

Davies, A., Joyce, P., Beaver, G. and Woods, A. (2002) 'Leadership boards of directors', *Strategic Change*, 11: 225–33.

Davies, P. (2004) *Policy Evaluation in the United Kingdom*, [UK Cabinet Office] Paper presented at the KDI International Policy Evaluation Forum, Seoul, Korea, 19–21 May 2004.

DCLG (2006) *Strong and Prosperous Communities: The Local Government White Paper*, Cm 6939-1. London: Department for Communities and Local Government.

Department for Work and Pensions (2005) *Five Year Strategy: Opportunity and Security Throughout Life*, Cm 6447. Norwich: TSO.

DETR (1998a) *Modernising Local Government: Local Democracy and Community Leadership*. London: Department of the Environment, Transport and the Regions.

DETR (1998b) *Modern Local Government: In Touch with the People*, Cm 4014. London: Department of the Environment, Transport and the Regions.

Drumaux, A. and Goethals, C. (2007) Strategic Management: A Tool for Public Management? An overview of the Belgian federal experience, *International Journal of Public Sector Management*, Volume 20, No 7, pp. 638–54.

Drumaux, A. and Goethals, C. (2007b) De l'intention à la mise en œuvre stratégique dans l'administration fédérale belge, *Revue Politique et Management Public,* Paris, Volume 25, No 4, pp. 21–44.

Duncan, W. J., Ginter, P. M. and Kreidel, W. K. (1994) 'A Sense of Direction in Public Organizations: An Analysis of Mission Statements in State Health Departments', *Administration and Society*, 26, 1: 11–27.

Duncan, W. J., Ginter, P. M. and Swayne, L. E. (1995) *Strategic Management of Health Care Organisations*. Oxford: Blackwell Business.

Dunoon, D. (2002) 'Rethinking leadership for the public sector', *Australian Journal of Public Administration*, 61, 3: 3–18.

Dyson, R. G. (1990) *Strategic Planning: Models and Analytical Techniques*. Chichester: Wiley.

Eadie, D. C. (1983) 'Putting a powerful tool to practical use: the application of strategic planning in the public sector', *Public Administration Review*, 43: 447–52.

Eadie, D. C. (2000) 'Change in Chewable Bites: Managing the Strategic Change Portfolio', in J. Rabin, G. J. Miller, and W. B. Hildreth (eds) *Handbook of Strategic Management* (Second Edition). New York: Marcel Dekker, Inc.

Flynn, N. and Talbot, C. (1996) 'Strategy and strategists in UK local government', *Journal of Management Development*, 15: 24–37.

330

Follett, M. P. (1941) 'Some discrepancies in leadership theory and practice', in H. C. Metcalfe and L. Urwick (eds) *Dynamic Administration: The Collected Papers of Mary Parker Follett*. Bath: Management Publications Trust.

Frost-Kumpf, L., Wechsler, B., Ishiyama, H. J. and Backoff, R. W. (1993) 'Strategic action and transformational change: the Ohio Department of Mental Health', in B. Bozeman (ed.) *Public Management*. San Francisco: Jossey-Bass.

Gabris, G. T., Golembiewski, R. T. and Ihrke, D. M. (2000) 'Leadership credibility, board relations, and administrative innovation at the local government level', *Journal of Public Administration Research and Theory*, 11, 1: 89–108.

Gabris, G. T., Grenell, K., Ihrke, D. and Kaatz, J. (1999) 'Managerial Innovation as affected by Administrative Leadership and Policy Boards', *Public Administration Quarterly*, 23, 2: 223–50.

Gellis, Z. D. (2001) 'Social work perceptions of transformational and transactional leadership in health care', *Social Work Research*, Volume 25, No 1, pp. 17–25.

Goodwin, D. R. and Kloot, L. (1996) 'Strategic communication, budgetary role ambiguity, and budgetary response attitude in local government', *Financial Accountability and Management*, 12: 191–205.

Gordon, G. (2005) 'From Vision to Implementation: The Changing State of Strategic Planning', *Public Management*, 87, 8: 26–8.

Greer, J. (2001) *Partnership Governance in Northern Ireland: Improving Performance*. Aldershot: Ashgate.

Hamel, G. (2002) *Leading the Revolution*. Boston: Harvard Business School Press.

Hamel, G. and C. K. Prahalad (1994) *Competing for the Future*. Boston, Massachusetts: Harvard Business School Press.

Hartley, K. and Huby, M. (1985) 'Contracting Out in Health and Local Authorities: Prospects and Pitfalls', *Public Money*: 23–6.

Harvey-Jones, J. (1988) *Making it Happen*. London: Fontana.

Heath, R. L. (1997) *Strategic Issues Management*. London: Sage.

Heifetz, R. A. (1994) *Leadership Without Easy Answers*. Cambridge, Massachusetts: The Belknap Press of Harvard University Press.

Heifetz, R. A. and Linsky, M. (2002) *Leadership on the Line*. Boston, Massachusetts: Harvard Business School Press.

Heifetz, R. A., Grashow, A. and Linsky, M. (2009a) *The practices of adaptive leadership*. Boston, Massachusetts: Harvard Business School Press.

Heifetz, R. A., Grashow, A. and Linsky, M. (2009b) 'Leadership in a (Permanent) Crisis', *Harvard Business Review*, July–August 2009, pp. 62–9.

Heslin, J. A. (1966) *A Field Test of the Likert Theory of Management in an ADP Environment*. Master's thesis, The American University.

Heymann, P. B. (1987) *The Politics of Public Management*. London: Yale University Press.

Hibbs, D. A. (1976) 'Industrial conflict in advanced industrial societies', *The American Political Science Review*, 70, 4: 1033–58.

331

Hibbs, D. A. (1978) 'On the political economy of long-run trends in strike activity', *British Journal of Political Science*, 8, 2: 153–75.

HM Government (2009) *Working Together: Public Services on Your Side*. Norwich: TSO.

House of Commons Public Administration Select Committee (2007) *Governing the Future*, Second Report of Session 2006–07.

Hussey, D. (1999) *Strategy and Planning: A Manager's Guide*. Chichester: John Wiley and Sons.

Huxham, C. and Vangen, S. (1996) 'Working Together: Key Themes in the Management of Relationships between Public and Non-Profit Organisations', *The International Journal of Public Sector Management*, 9, 7: 5–18.

Jantsch, E. (1975) *Design for Evolution: Self-Organizing and Planning in the Life of Systems*. New York: Braziller.

Johnson, G. and Scholes, K. (1989) *Exploring Corporate Strategy: Text and Cases*. London: Prentice Hall.

Joyce, P. (1999a) *User-Led Innovation in Local Government, 1996–1998*, ESRC Research Project. Award Reference Number L125251044. Principal researcher: Professor Paul Joyce.

Joyce, P. (1999b) *Strategic Management for the Public Services*. Milton Keynes: Open University Press.

Joyce, P. (2000) *Strategy in the Public Sector: A Guide to Effective Change Management*. Chichester: Wiley.

Joyce, P. (2004) 'The role of leadership in the turnaround of a local authority', *Public Money and Management*, August 2004, Volume 24, Issue 4, pp. 235–42.

Joyce, P. (2007) 'The Integration of Performance Management into the Management of the London Borough of Lewisham', in F. Longo and D. Crisofoli (eds) *Strategic Change Management in the Public Sector: An EFMD European Case Book*. Chichester: Wiley.

Joyce, P. (2008) 'The Strategic, Enabling State: A Case Study of the UK, 1997–2007', *The International Journal of Leadership in Public Services*, 4, 3: 24–36.

Kaletsky, A. (2010) *Capitalism 4.0*. London: Bloomsbury.

Kaplan, R. S. and Norton, D. P. (1992) 'The Balanced Scorecard – Measures that Drive Performance', *Harvard Business Review*, January–February: 71–9.

Karp, T. and Helgo, T. (2008) 'From Change Management to Change Leadership: Embracing Chaotic Change in Public Service Organizations', *Journal of Change Management*, 8, 1: 85–96.

Kay, J. (1993) *Foundations of Corporate Success*. Oxford: Oxford University Press.

Kearney, A. T. (2000) 'Change Management – An Inside Job', *The Economist*, July 15, 2000, p. 87

Kerr, C., Dunlop, J. T., Harbison, F. and Myers, C. A. (1973) *Industrialism and Industrial Man*. Harmondsworth: Penguin.

Kettl, D. (1996) *Testimony: Statement Before a Joint Hearing: Committee on Government Reform and Oversight, U.S. House of Representatives, and Committee on Governmental Affairs, U.S. Senate. March 6, 1996*. Online, available http://www.brook.edu/default.htm, Accessed September 1997.

Klein, J. A. and Hiscocks, P. G. (1994) 'Competence-based Competition: A Practical Toolkit', in G. Hamel and A. Heine (eds) *Competence-Based Competition*. Chichester: Wiley.

Kooiman, J. and van Vliet, M. (1993) 'Governance and Public Management', in K. A. Eliassen and J. Kooiman (eds) *Managing Public Organizations*. London: Sage.

Korpi, W. and Shalev, M. (1979) 'Industrial relations and class conflict in Capitalist Societies', *The British Journal of Sociology*, 30, 2: 164–87.

Kotter, J. (1990) 'What Leaders Really Do', *Harvard Business Review*, 79, 11: 85–96.

Kotter, J. P. (1990) 'What Leaders Really Do', *Harvard Business Review*, May–June: 103–11.

Kotter, J. P. (2007) 'Leading Change: Why Transformation Efforts Fail', *Harvard Business Review*, January: 96–103.

Kouzes, J. M. and Posner, B. Z. (2007) *The Leadership Challenge*. San Francisco: John Wiley and Sons.

Lefebvre, R. (2009) La démocratie locale, in M. Bonnard (ed.), *Les Collectivités Territoriales*, Paris, La Documentation Française, pp. 121–29.

Lewin, K. (1952) *Field Theory in Social Science*. London: Tavistock Publications Ltd.

Lewis, M. A. and Gregory, M. J. (1996) 'Developing and Applying a Process Approach to Competence Analysis', in R. Sanchez, A. Heene, and H. Thomas (eds) *Dynamics of Competence-Based Competition: Theory and Practice in the New Strategic Management*. Kidlington/Oxford: Pergamon.

LGC Warwick University, CRC West of England University, Office for Public Management and EIUA Liverpool John Moores University (2003) *Evaluation of Local Strategic Partnerships: Report of a survey of all English LSP*, Office of the Deputy Prime Minister and Department for Transport.

Likert, R. (1977) *Past and Future Perspectives on System 4*. Ann Arbor: Rensis Likert Associates.

Likert, R. (1981) 'System 4: A Resource for Improving Public Administration', *Public Administration Review*, Volume 41, No. 6, pp. 674–78.

Likert, R. and Araki, C. T. (1979) *Improving the Performance of a Governmental Agency, in Proposition 13 and its Consequences for Public Management*. Cambridge: Council for Applied Social Research: 141–49.

Lindquist, E. A. (2000) 'Reconceiving the Centre: Leadership, Strategic Review and Coherence in Public Sector Reform', in OECD, *Government of the Future*. Paris: Organisation for Economic Co-operation and Development.

Lonti, Z. and Gregory, R. (2004) 'Accountability or Countability? Trends in performance measurement in the New Zealand public service, 1992–2002', in Jenei, G., McLaughlin, K., Mike, K. and Osborne, S. P. (eds) *Challenges of Public Management*

Reforms: Theoretical Perspectives and Recommendation. Selected papers from the Eighth International Research Symposium on Public Management hosted by Budapest University of Economic Sciences and Public Administration.

Lyotard, J. (1984) *The Postmodern Condition: A Report on Knowledge*. Manchester: Manchester University Press.

Martin, J. (1999) 'Leadership in Local Government Reform: Strategic Direction v Administrative Compliance', *Australian Journal of Public Administration*, 58, 2: 24–37.

Mason, R. (1969) A Dialectic Approach to Strategic Planning, *Management Science*, 15 (8), B403–B414.

Mason, R. O. and Mitroff, I. I. (1981) *Challenging Strategic Planning Assumptions*. New York: Wiley-Interscience.

Mattessich, P. and Monsey, B. (1992) *Collaboration: What Makes it Work*. Minnesota, St. Paul : Amherest, H. Wilder H. Foundation.

Mayo, E. (1949) *The Social Problems of an Industrial Civilisation*. London: Routledge and Keegan Paul.

Melchor, O. H. (2008) *Managing Change in OECD Governments: An Introductory Framework, OECD Working Papers on Public Governance*, No. 12, OECD Publishing.

Meny, Y. (2008) France: The Institutionalisation of Leadership, in J. M. Colomer, *Comparative European Politics*. Abingdon: Routledge.

Metcalfe, L. and Richards, S. (1990) *Improving Public Management*. London: Sage.

Methe, D. T., Wilson, D. and Perry, J. L. (2000) 'A review of research on incremental approaches to strategy', in J. Rabin, G. J. Miller and W. B. Hildreth (eds) *Handbook of Strategic Management* (Second edition). New York: Marcel Dekker.

Miles, R. E. and Snow, C. C. (1978) *Organizational Strategy, Structure, and Process*. London: McGraw-Hill.

Milner, E. and Joyce, P. (2005) *Lessons in Leadership: Meeting the Challenges of Public Services Management*. London: Routledge.

Ministry of the Economy, Finance and Industry (no date) *Budget Reform and State Modernisation in France*. Paris: MINEFI.

Mintzberg, H. (1978) Patterns in strategy formulation, *Management Science*, Volume 24, pp. 934–48.

Mintzberg, H. and Waters, J. A. (1985) 'Of strategies, deliberate and emergent', *Strategic Management Journal*, 6: 257–72.

Mitroff, I. I. and Emshoff, J. R. (1979) 'On Strategic Assumption-Making: A Dialectical Approach to Policy and Planning', *Academy of Management Review*, 4, 1: 1–12.

Moore, M. (1995) *Creating Public Value: Strategic Management in Government*. London: Harvard University Press.

Mulgan, G. (2007) Oral Evidence, in House of Commons Public Administration Select Committee, *Governing the Future*, Second Report of Session 2006–07, Volume II, HC123-II. London: The Stationery Office Limited.

Mulgan, G. (2009) *The Art of Public Strategy*. Oxford: Oxford University Press.

Norman, R. (2004) 'Recovering from a Tidal Wave: New Directions for Performance Management in New Zealand's Public Sector', *Public Finance and Management*, 4, 3: 429–47.

Nutt, P. (1999) 'Surprising but true: Half the decisions in organizations fail', *Academy of Management Executive*, 13, 4: 75–90.

Nutt, P. (2008) 'Investigating the success of decision making processes', *Journal of Management Studies*, 45, 2: 425–55.

Nutt, P. C. and Backoff, R. W. (1992) *Strategic Management of Public and Third Sector Organizations*. San Francisco: Jossey-Bass.

Nutt, P. C. and Backoff, R. W. (1993) 'Transforming public organizations with strategic management and strategic leadership', *Journal of Management*, 19: 299–347.

Nutt, P. C. and Backoff, R. W. (1995) 'Strategy for public and third-sector organizations', *Journal of Public Administration Research and Theory*, 5: 189–211.

O'Dowd, J. (1995) 'Strategic management: an alternative view on personnel', *Administration*, 43, 4, 51–6.

OECD (1999) *Synthesis of Reform Experiences in Nine OECD Countries: Government Roles and Functions, and Public Management*, PUMA/SGF(99)1. Paris: OECD.

OECD (2000) *Government of the Future*. Paris: OECD.

OECD (2005) *Modernising Government: The Way Forward*. Paris: OECD.

OMB (2007) *Program Assessment Rating Tool Guidance No. 2007-02*.

Osborne, D. and Gaebler, T. (1992) *Reinventing Government: How the Entrepreneurial Spirit is Transforming the Public Sector*. Reading, Massachusetts: Addison Wesley publishing company.

Osborne, D. and Plastrik, P. (1997) *Banishing Bureaucracy: The Five Strategies for Reinventing Government*. New York: Plume.

Osborne, S. and Brown, K. (2005) *Managing Change and Innovation in Public Service Organizations*. London: Routledge.

Ostroff, F. (2006) 'Change Management in Government', *Harvard Business Review*, 84, 5: 141–47.

PA Consulting Group (2002) *Evaluation of the Progress of the Strategic Management Initiative/Delivering Better Government Modernisation Programme*. Published by PA Consulting Group, Embassy House, Herbert Park Lane, Ballsbridge, Dublin 4, Ireland.

Patrizi, P. A. and Patton, M. Q. (2011) (eds) *Evaluating Strategy*. San Francisco, Jossey-Bass.

Patton, M. Q. (2002) *Qualitative Research and Evaluation Methods*, Third Edition. Thousand Oaks: Sage.

335

Perrott, B. E. (1996) 'Managing Strategic Issues in the Public Service', *Long Range Planning*, 29, 3: 337–45.

Peters, T. J. and Waterman, R. H. (1982) *In Search of Excellence*. New York: Harper Collins.

Pettigrew, A., Ferlie, E. and McKee, L. (1992) *Shaping Strategic Change*. London: Sage.

Pettigrew, A. and Whipp, R. (1991) *Managing Change for Competitive Success*. Oxford: Basil Blackwell.

Pettigrew, A. M. (1977) 'Strategy formation as a political process', *International Studies on Management and Organization*, 7: 78–87.

Poister, T. H. and Streib, G. D. (1999) Strategic Management in the Public Sector: Concepts, Models and Processes, *Public Productivity & Management Review*, Volume 22, No 3, pp. 308–325.

Poister, T. H. and Streib, G. D. (2005) 'Elements of Strategic Planning and Management in Municipal Government: Status after Two Decades', *Public Administration Review*, January/February 2005, 65, 1: 45–56.

Poister, T. H. (2010) 'The Future of Strategic Planning in the Public Sector: Linking Strategic Management and Performance', *Public Administration Review*, December, pp. S246–S254.

Pollitt, C. and Bouckaert, G. (2004) *Public Management Reform: A Comparative Analysis*. Oxford: Oxford University Press.

Prime Minister's Delivery Unit, Cabinet Office (2006) *Capability Reviews: the findings of the first four reviews*. London: Delivery Unit.

Prime Minister's Strategy Unit, Cabinet Office (2003) *Strategy Survival Guide*. London: Strategy Unit.

Prime Minister's Strategy Unit, Cabinet Office (2005) *Strategic Audit: Progress and Challenges for the UK* (Discussion Document). London: Strategy Unit.

Prime Minister's Strategy Unit, Cabinet Office (2006) *The UK Government's Approach to Public Service Reform*. Crown Copyright.

Prime Minister's Strategy Unit, Cabinet Office (2007a) *Building on Progress: Public Services*. London (March 2007).

Prime Minister's Strategy Unit, Cabinet Office (2007b) *Building on Progress: The Role of the State*. London (May 2007).

Prince, L. and Puffitt, R. (2001) 'The Maslin Multi-Dimensional Matrix: a new tool to aid strategic decision making in the public sector', in G. Johnson and K. Scholes (eds) *Exploring Public Sector Strategy*. Harlow: Financial Times Prentice Hall.

Revill, J. (1999) Anger at new Dobson hospital 'death scores', *Evening Standard*, Wednesday 16 June, pp. 1–2.

Ring, P. S. and Perry, J. L. (1985) Strategic Management in Public and Private Organizations: Implications of Distinctive Contexts and Constraints, *The Academy of Management Review*, Volume 10, No 2, pp. 276–86.

336

Robinson, M. and Brumby, J. (2005) *Does Performance Budgeting Work? An Analytical Review of the Literature*, IMF Working Paper WP/05/210. (International Monetary Fund.)

Rutter, J. (2007) Oral Evidence, in House of Commons Public Administration Select Committee, *Governing the Future*, Second Report of Session 2006–07, Volume II, HC123-II. London: The Stationery Office Limited.

Schick, A. (2001) *Reflections on the New Zealand Model*. Lecture at the New Zealand Treasury.

Seldon, A., with Snowdon, P. and Collings, D. (2007) *Blair Unbound*. London: Simon and Schuster.

Slywotzky, A. J. (1996) *Value Migration: How to Think Several Moves Ahead of the Competition*. Boston, Massachusetts: Harvard business School Press.

Smith, R. J. (1994) *Strategic Management and Planning in the Public Sector*. Harlow: Longman.

Sorkin, D. L., Ferris, N. B. and Hudak, J. (1985) *Strategies for Cities and Counties, A Strategic Planning Guide*. Washington DC: Public Technology.

Stonich, P. J. (1982) *Implementing Strategy: Making Strategy Happen*. Cambridge, Massachusetts: Ballinger Publishing Company.

Sussman, L. and Herden, R. P. (1985) 'Dialectical Problem Solving', *Business Horizons*, Fall.

Thomas, J. C. and Poister, T. H. (2009) 'Thinking about stakeholders of public agencies: The Georgia Department of Transportation Stakeholder Audit', *Public Organisational Review*, 9: 67–82.

Thurley, K. and Wirdenius, H. (1989) *Towards European Management*. Pitman Publishing, London.

Toft, G. S. (2000) 'Synoptic (One Best Way) Approaches of Strategic Management', in J. Rabin, G. J. Miller and W. B. Hildreth (eds) *Handbook of Strategic Management* (Second edition). New York: Marcel Dekker.

Trosa, S. (2009) Les reformes vues d'en bas, *Revue Pyramides*, 17: 1.

Tuohy, B. (1996) 'Strategic management choices and imperatives', in R. Boyle and T. McNamara (eds) *From Intent to Action: The Management of Strategic Issues in the Public Sector*. Dublin: Institute of Public Administration.

US General Accounting Office (1996) *Executive Guide: Effectively Implementing the Government Performance and Results Act*, GAO/GGD-96-118, Washington, DC.

US General Accounting Office (1997) *Performance Budgeting: Past Initiative Offer Insights for GPRA Implementation*, GAO/AOMD-97-46, Washington, DC.

US General Accounting Office (2004a) *Performance Budgeting: Observations on the Use of OMB's Program Assessment Rating Tool for the Fiscal Year 2004 Budget*, GAO-04-174, Washington DC.

US General Accounting Office (2004b) *Results-Oriented Government: GPRA Has Established a Solid Foundation for Achieving Greater Results*, GAO-04-38, Washington, DC.

337

Vinzant, D. H. and Vinzant, J. (1996) 'Strategy and organizational capacity: finding a fit', *Public Productivity and Management Review*, 20, 2: 139–57.

Walsh, K. (1991) *Competitive Tendering for Local Authority Services: Initial Experiences*. London: HMSO.

Walsh, K. (1995) *Public Services and Market Mechanisms*. London: Macmillan.

Wechsler, B. and Backoff, R. W. (1986) 'Policy making and administration in state agencies: strategic management approaches', *Public Administration Review*, 46: 321–27.

Wechsler, B. and Backoff, R. W. (1987) 'The dynamics of strategy in public organizations', *The Journal of the American Planning Association*, 53: 34–43.

Wilson, A. and Charlton, K. (1997) *Making Partnerships Work. A Practical Guide for the Public, Private, Voluntary and Community Sectors*. The Joseph Rowntree Foundation, York Publishing Services Limited.

York, R. O. (1982) *Human Service Planning: Concepts, Tools, and Methods*. Chapel Hill: The University of North Carolina Press.

Zanetti, L. A. and Cunningham, R. B. (2000) 'Perspectives on Public-Sector Strategic Management', in J. Rabin, G. J. Miller and W. B. Hildreth (eds) *Handbook of Strategic Management* (Second Edition). New York: Marcel Dekker, Inc.

Index

339